The

Great Philadelphia

Fan Book

The
Great Philadelphia
Fan Book

Glen Macnow
Anthony L. Gargano

Middle Atlantic Press

Manufactured in the United States

4 5   07 06 05 04 03

Library of Congress Cataloging-in-Publication Data

Macnow, Glen.
  The great Philadelphia fan book / Glen Macnow, Anthony L. Gargano.—
1st American pbk. ed.
    p. cm.
  ISBN 0-9705804-4-4 (Trade Paperback)
  1. Sports spectators—Pennsylvania--Philadelphia—Anecdotes. 2.
Sports—Pennsylvania—Philadelphia—History. I. Gargano, Anthony L.,
1968- II. Title.
  GV715.M33 2003
  796'.09748'11—dc22
                          2003021603

Material from *The Art of Criticism* by Glen Macnow
Copyright © 1992, *The Philadelphia Inquirer*, Philadelphia Newspapers, Inc.
Used with permission of *The Philadelphia Inquirer*

The Old Timers by Anthony L. Gargano
Copyright © 1999, *The Philadelphia Inquirer*, Philadelphia Newspapers, Inc.
Used with permission of *The Philadelphia Inquirer*

Cover Design: Vicki Manucci and Terence Doherty
Interior Design and Composition: Vicki Manucci

For information write:
Middle Atlantic Press
10 Twosome Drive
Moorestown, NJ 08057

To Florence Gargano who caught my first foul ball, with her angelic fingers, off the Cubs' Steve Ontiveros; and to Anthony R. Gargano, whom I respect everything about, except the fact that he is "arggghhh" a Dallas Cowboys fan. And to all the People from South Philadelphia who helped stoke my passion for sports.

—A.L.G.

To my three mentors: Marvin Macnow, Professor Timothy Cohane, and Hilary Hayes. Thanks for the guidance.

And to Judy. Now, more than ever.

—G.M.

ACKNOWLEDGMENTS

A bevy of experts on Philadelphia sports and its fans helped put this book together. Special thanks go to Jayson Stark, Ray Didinger, Stan Hochman and Bill Conlin, a veritable Mount Rushmore of sports writers who provided expert guidance with specific chapters.

In some cases, the text relies on accounts of the *Philadelphia Daily News*, *Philadelphia Inquirer* and *Philadelphia Evening* and *Sunday Bulletin*. Other texts used for background information include "Full Spectrum," by Jay Greenberg;" "The Pro Football Chronicle," by Dan Daly and Bob O'Donnell; "Worst to First: The Story of the 1993 Phillies," by the *Philadelphia Inquirer* staff (most notably Frank Fitzpatrick); and "It's Gooooood!," by Merrill Reese and Mark Eckel.

Help also came from public relations officials of the local teams, including Ron Howard and Derek Boyko of the Eagles, Zack Hill of the Flyers, Karen Frascona of the Sixers, and John Brazer and Larry Shenk of the Phillies.

Some major Philadelphia sports figures opened up doors and memory banks for us, including Larry Bowa, Tom Brookshier, Anthony "Butchy" Buchanico, Harold Carmichael, Bob Clarke, Dave Coskey, Dallas Green, Ron Jaworski, Keith Jones, Bob Kelly, Billy King, Jeffrey Lurie, David Montgomery, John Nash, Andy Reid, Gov. Ed Rendell, Ed Snider, John Spagnola, Stan Walters and Joe Watson.

Our gratitude is also extended to an informal panel of sports fans who contributed their passion and insight: Harry Blaker, Joe Sharp, Kevin Johnson, Deborah "Bo" Sullivan, Eric J. Miller, Adam Levin, Steve Lapin, Stephen Sisson, Bob Schofield and Rick Cutler.

Bob Koen gave the go-ahead to publish this book and—despite his affinity for soccer— Terry Doherty, "The British Gentleman," showed a great touch in shepherding this project from start to finish.

Thanks and love to friends and family, including Jimmy Head, Joey Tomasetti, Joan Macnow, Paul McGovern, the Sunday Night Poker Club and our WIP colleagues Angelo Cataldi, Al Morganti and Joseph A. Weachter, Jr. And thanks to WIP Program Director Tom Bigby for giving us the daily format to listen to Philadelphia sports fans.

And finally, our appreciation to Michael Wilbon of the *Washington Post*, T.J. Simers of the *Los Angeles Times* and other pompous windbags who have made their bones ripping Philadelphia from afar. You helped inspire our impassioned defense of the best fans in America.

1974 Stanley Cup Champions.

CONTENTS

FOREWORD

I was born and bred in Philadelphia and, naturally, grew up a Philadelphia sports fan. There was never an alternative! Cut me and I would proudly bleed Philly colors, regardless of their ugly shades over the years.

I suffered through the Phillies' collapse of 1964, danced down Broad Street when the Flyers won their consecutive titles in 1974 and 1975, and enthusiastically climbed the grated wall of Veterans Stadium to sneak into Eagles games in my youth.

Upon graduation from boyhood to manhood, the Philly spirit remained in my soul, but luckily my college degree helped channel the energy from my crazy sports escapades into the business of sports medicine. My joy as a fan was magnified when I was able to use my new-found knowledge to treat and train Philly's finest, Michael Jack Schmidt, Julius Erving, Bobby Clarke, Bobby Jones, Charles Barkley, Eric Lindros, Garry Maddox, Tim Kerr, Davey Poulin, and later transform them into friends.

The journey of this Philly sports fan only got better when I conceived and helped consummate a mega-deal to purchase the Philadelphia 76ers in 1996. For the next five years, on a thrilling ride from worst to first, the fans were finally in charge! They hooted and hollered and gave suggestions and recommendations and poured their souls and senses into the resurrection of a Philly franchise.

Their franchise.

I still get chills thinking about the night we beat the Milwaukee Bucks, in Philadelphia, in the deciding Game Seven to clinch the Eastern Conference title in 2001. I considered myself a representative of the fans when I stood at center court with my wife at my side and surrounded by our city's team, hoisting the silver trophy with 20,000 of my closest friends in attendance. It was a special moment in time because I was living every Philly fan's dream and representing them with pride and passion.

Speaking of passion, Anthony Gargano and Glen Macnow have been covering our sports triumphs and tragedies professionally for two decades, first as newspaper reporters, then as talk-show hosts, and now as authors. But Bonz and Mac are fans first. They understand the heart and psyche of the Philadelphia sports fan, because deep down they bleed our teams' colors too. And like all of us Philly fanatics, they always believe that this year will be our year!

The Great Philadelphia Fan Book will treat you to a roller-coaster ride that has been our Philly sports scene. It's packed full of all the high-fiving, chest-bumping, head-banging, food-throwing, and finger-tossing moments that put a smile on your face or an object through your TV set, a stream of joyous tears on your cheeks or a scream of merciless boos in your throat.

Yes, the Philadelphia sports fans are a special breed. Passion oozes from their pores. Prayers leave their lips for heaven before every game. And the gospel of sports is lived every day, especially NFL Sundays.

And now, without further adieu, here is a new bible for Philly sports fans to cherish. And, on rare occasions, to throw at the TV.

—Pat Croce

This story begins with the end. Because that's the part everyone around here knows by heart. It's as predictable as sunset, devoid of the beauty, of course, unless you are one of us: a Philadelphia Sports Fan. Here, suffering is familiar and familiar is nice because familiar is comforting. We know the way home to disappointment, displeasure, distress, disenchantment, discontentment and plain ol' dissed, and all of that, by the way, is our shroud in sports life. Don't you see? This is our calling.

We are the tragic figures of the arena, the gargoyles of glum, pock-marked descendants of Shakespeare's muse.

Forget that counterfeit curse in boo-hoo Boston or the stupid Cubs or any of these poser towns or cities that profess pain from sport. If winning and losing are the two forces in the universe of sport, their essence is housed in two polar places: New York and Philadelphia. Guess which goes where.

Everything else is in between, as banal as the landscape along the Jersey Turnpike. And if we're the anti-Elysium, the Hades of hockey and hoops and baseball and beloved football, home of the boorish bottom-dwellers, well, at least that's an identity. Say what you want, we the sports fan damned, care more than a damn. We care-care, dammit.

So here we are at the end of a story that is the reason for this book, Rhonde Barber already in the end zone and the Buccaneers whooping it up on the sidelines, strutting peacocks on enemy sidelines, waving their pirate flags in conquest, only hooting "dawg" instead of "matey,"and there is a deafening silence of the lambs, their faces drawn and colorless as they exit the stadium. The Vet is entirely flat, anesthetized by a sure thing gone poof in a January cold, the super celebration cancelled at the last minute. So they shuffle into the night with stilted strides, heads bobbing with the rhythm of shock and loss. They do not mourn or boo or curse. Zombies, I swear.

The scene is creepy. Police in their shimmering black leather jackets, looking like Storm Troopers, looking to preserve the field in the last football game ever at Veterans Stadium, encircle the field on their horses and motorcycles. The week before, the Saturday night of the Atlanta playoff game, this same police production seemed rather cool, spooking the opponent. It seemed a display of Eagle might. Of course, everything seemed different a week ago . . . hell, three hours ago, when the fighter jets whooshed over the stadium and Brian Mitchell returned the opening kickoff deep in Tampa territory and Duce Staley galloped into the end zone and for once a Philadelphia Story seemed to include a storybook ending.

My God, could it be any more perfect? The last game at the Vet is the NFC Championship against a team the Eagles had beaten three times in three meaningful games, a team that fares worse in the cold than chicken noodle soup. My God, the synergy felt as strong as Philadelphia cynicism. After all, the Eagles had made it to the conference championship game the year before, playing the Rams to the final possession in St. Louis, the perfect playoff lesson. And these Eagles had taken a step further each year under coach Andy Reid, climbing the ladder of success a perfect, concise one step at a time. The rung that read Super Bowl begged to be reached, so much so that Donovan McNabb talked about being shooed from that St. Louis dome so the Rams could celebrate and taking that feeling of slight into this game against the Buccaneers.

The stars were so aligned they spelled out San Diego. The Eagles emitted an aura all season long, like on that Monday night in another California city. His mangled arm in a sling, the last man ambled into the old baseball dressing room and wafted toward to the masses and the masses parted on impulse, gently guiding him to his spot to the right of the coach. The hero's spot. Oh, how proud the masses were. They loved this man the way we love a scruffy dog, because a scruffy dog is personable and loyal and always grateful. This man is a grunt's grunt, as nondescript as cardboard, as the double-sided human adhesive that bonds the masses tighter than tight, abnormally so considering the profession, fraught with jealousy and egotism and racial rift. And on that breezy night by San Francisco Bay, against a pedigreed foe, the man proved gallant, rescuing their purpose.

So the masses exhaled exhilaration and grew silent with smiles when the coach thrust a football into the air with his chunky right hand. "This," the coach boomed, "is for Koy Detmer!"

The masses burst into an ovation that could be sipped in Wine Country. "Speech," chortled the tight end.

Koy Detmer didn't say a word. He just stood there sporting that goofy aw-shucks grin, whacked on elation and pain medication. An hour ago, his right elbow had twisted and harrumphed from its socket, and Detmer writhed on his back in the middle of the field, his legs gyrating like a grasshopper's, from the blast of pain. Now, though, the coach squished an Eagles baseball cap over Detmer's greasy, mangy hair.

"Hey, listen, guys," the coach said. "Great, great job tonight. I've never been more proud. You deserve to bask in this one."

The masses nodded dutifully and the coach commanded, "Okay, let's pray." The masses, sixty or so men, reeking of rank flesh, in various stage of undress, dropped to one knee and clasped the taped paws of the men on either side, and recited the words humbly, in complete unison:

"Our Father, Who art in heaven

Hallowed be Thy Name;

Thy kingdom come,

Thy will be done, on earth as it is in heaven . . ."

It always feels better to pray in appreciation, as opposed to the other way, bogged by begging and beseeching, born unto the battle cry: "Why have You forsaken me?" And so I listen to these men, these football players, recite the Lord's Prayer with a monotone honesty while holding hands in a cramped locker room with peeling walls, and I feel what the masses feel: empowered.

On that night, still November 24th in the west, the Eagles won their biggest game of the regular season, in effect setting the stage for this January night. They did so in romantic fashion, beating the storied Niners, on national television, without their franchise quarterback, who was back in Cherry Hill in front of a giant plasma screen with two Italian hoagies, his broken ankle propped on a pillow. In fact, Donovan McNabb called a while ago, right after Detmer went down and the ref put a hand on him as if he might writhe away and waved frantically for the medical staff. "Call me immediately," he said. "Let me know how Koy is," was McNabb worried message on trainer Rick Burkholder's cell phone.

I'll never forget that euphoric red-eye ride on the Northwest 747, nothing harder than soda pop and juice on the flight home. Mormon coach Andy Reid disavows alcohol, so the celebration consisted of hunks of burgers and chicken, a stark difference to, say, the Ray Rhodes' era, when a fog of Jack Daniels would fill the cabin upon touchdown and mini whiskey bottles would roll empty down the aisle like marbles. Koy Detmer eased down the aisle, careful not to ding his elbow, and the Philadelphia fatalists screamed, "Oh, Lord, not again! Two quarterbacks lost in two weeks, it's over."

Of course, it wasn't. That's the way it is in the National Football League, especially for good teams like the Eagles. The season is a string of manic moments, of endless obstacles that make for relentless ardor.

I can recall another moment, on another Monday night, before the Giants game. We shared a moment. Sixty or so men stared in silence. The eyes were transfixed, hypnotized by the thought, leaving their expression blank—not stupid blank, but preoccupied blank. Because it is now, during the final moments before kickoff, that a football player prepares to play football.

Outside these walls, organized chaos governed. The flock juggled their beers and jostled for their seats and jiggled their pom-poms and hawked their merchandise and hollered for the night to commence. All for these sixty or so men, who were alone with their thoughts in the company of men.

The digital clock read 8:51. The silence was such that I could almost hear the red lights morph into 52 . . . 53 . . . 54 . . . the angular numbers twisting, bleeding into one another. Jon Runyan, the big, nasty offensive tackle with the square head, sat plopped in front of his locker stall hugging a prison guard's stare. Our eyes locked for a moment. Nothing. I don't exist or I am suddenly inanimate. Surely it was nothing personal but I turned away just the same.

Jon Runyan was born to make men feel uncomfortable, the classic Midwest behemoth, six-foot-seven, 330 pounds, as cuddly as a coffin. At least that's so on the field, where he is dirty and dastardly, picking up league fines like they're parking tickets. At home, he will tell you he is a yes-dear bloke, dutifully following the commands of his teeny wife, five-foot-tall Mexican spitfire Loretta, a former street cop in Houston. "I'm completely approachable," Runyan insists.

That's so with offensive linemen. Position often dictates demeanor. For example, cornerbacks are usually elegant, cats prancing with their noses skyward, like Bobby Taylor, the part-time male model who prefers fitted berets, and Troy Vincent, the polished veteran who carries a briefcase on the road and dons perfectly contoured suits by Ermenegildo Zegna. Meanwhile, other tackle Tra Thomas, another mountain of man at six-seven, 349 pounds, prefers sweatsuits and makes no bones that his biggest goal in life is to "slide on through."

Glory averts the offensive linemen, the protectors of the field, and this thankless lot makes them appear so very Joe Normal, only super-sized. Like portly center Hank Fraley, a godsend from the leftover pile whose pudding tummy pouts over his pants, causing Andy Reid to say, "Everyone in those bars in South Philly, yeah, they love Hank Fraley, Mr. Budweiser Belly, Mr. Everyone." Thanks to everyman analyst John Madden, Fraley's belly has become the NFL's answer to J.Lo's rear. "Really bad body, really good player," Madden says, and Fraley eats it up. You can tell as he waddles to the shower, resisting vanity. Suck it in? Hell, no.

"I'd like to get a deal with Tastykake," he offers. "You know my nickname is Honeybun."

Tastykake actually sent Fraley a case of their Honeybuns. "He eats six of 'em a day. They're his diet," guard John Welbourn reports.

Meanwhile, Brian Dawkins sat hunched in the back of the locker room with the rest of the defense, imbibing emotion. He was still but something seethed inside, his expression washed with wince, face pocked with tics, eyes vacant. The Transformation of Brian Dawkins that began with a twitch when he pressed the Breathe Right strips over his nostrils and slipped on his beanie cap was nearly complete. Football players need to kindle their emotions in the same way cops need to be armed, so on the surface Dawkins' conversion into creature—or whom he called "Idiotman"—might seem a bit contrived. But there was something organic about his transformation.

Lost in a state, Dawkins explained: "There's this click. It's like something hit me in the head. That's when the man starts peeking out. I find the transformation. I cross that door."

The digital clock read 8:57. Sixty or so men and there was nothing but this whirling energy. The closest thing to noise was the faint screech coming out of Tra Thomas' headphones.

Finally . . . SOUND.

The doors slammed open and swung closed behind Butch Jr.—son of Eagles security chief Butch Buchanico, the former decorated Philly cop, dubbed "Mr. Wolf" after Harvey Keitel's character in "Pulp Fiction" because of his cool in crisis. So Butch Jr., a sergeant on the force, burst into the middle of the room and boomed a warming signal that would have made Paul Revere's a whisper.

"Two minutes! Two minutes! Let's go! TWO MINUTES!"

There was an instant stir, the kind on the floor of the stock exchange just before the opening bell, followed by instant chatter, mostly inaudible idle chatter, mixed with players fumbling for their helmets and fixing their pads. They gathered in a circle, and Reid emerged from his nearby office. "All right men, you know what you have to do," the coach said.

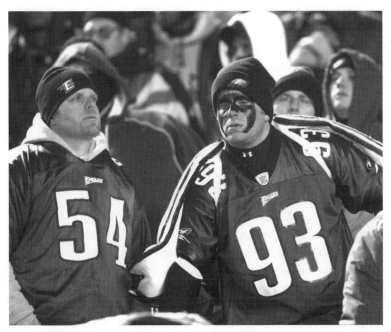

The pain is registered on the faces of two despondent Eagle fans.

While Hugh Douglas gathered his team in the circle, ordering hands atop hands atop hands, Andy Reid bustled out the door, past the security guards and positions along the cold, crusted iron railing facing the locker-room entrance. The players exited, one, two at a time, helmets on and cleats clomping against the cement ramp in rhythmic patter, upright with their protruding shoulder pads, looking incredibly Roman. As they trumpeted by, Reid bumped his fist with theirs, slapped their hands, their shoulder pads, offering each a slingshot of final words.

"C'mon, big boy!"

Further into the tunnel, at the edge of the spout, the defense gathers. The players jumped in place, led by Douglas, helmet cradled to his side. His hair in locks, spraying out like Medusa's snakes, he didn't stop talking. "Let's do it for the big girls!"

"I'm turnin' green! Like the Hulk," he continued without transition.

From inside the pack, someone yelled, "The whole world's watching."

I followed the sound of football players—the hoots, the deep and engorged breathing, spiked by adrenaline, the flatulence ("Cuz, football is primal," return man Brian Mitchell explained)—from the smelly, dank tunnel to the giant inflatable football helmet on the field, a sort of pre-game weigh station from which each player springs when his name is boomed to an adoring crowd, a house that hot-air hype built. What has become abundantly clear in the new millennium is that sport is show, all show, particularly the NFL, where the off-gridiron frill is orchestrated as fully as a smash Broadway musical. Everything was in place, including the fog machine.

The image through the fake fog paced wildly, a glob of human froth lost in our animal extraction, arms dangling dementia-style, hands balled into a fist, while the head bobbed and emitted a muffled wail from out of the wilderness. The raging Brian Dawkins said to himself, "Calm down, dawg. It's all right, dawg. You good. You real good." His name was the last to be announced to the crowd and he shot through the opening of the giant inflatable football helmet bellying the worm between a row of cheerleaders and fireworks crackled.

They played well and won that night, and Andy Reid said at 1:30 in the morning, "I'm going to celebrate with a cheeseburger" and disappeared into his office to watch the game film.

Things have a way of changing suddenly in the NFL, and so the first boos of the season wafted through the stadium in the fifth home game of the season, a reminder of how bad it once was here. The Vet had an ornery feel that day against the Colts. The 6-2 Eagles entered the game on course for the Super Bowl run and a nine-point favorite over supposedly inferior Indianapolis, and here they were losing terribly at halftime. The banner by Sign Man that draped across the 400 Level partition seemed ominously prophetic: CHAMPIONS DON'T LET DOWN.

The team played with the spark of soggy matches, while Colts quarterback Peyton Manning found a portal and emerged as Johnny Unitas. Manning seemed to anticipate every defensive call—Move Old Coyote, Fargo Pinch, Freeze—altering his counter-strategy at the line of scrimmage, frantically pointing, shrieking code.

Reid's round face reddened during his final address at halftime. "I need all kinds of energy from you," he barked. "This is not how we play!" He huffed and harrumphed out of the locker room, the team filing behind him. In the tunnel, Hugh Douglas declared, "It's not gut-check time, it's nut-check time."

The game ended without mercy, with Reid, accompanied by Butch Sr., being accosted at the tunnel by the green monsters that appear after losses like this one. "You fat slob," a man of ample flab spewed. "You stink." Reid refused to acknowledge him, though later Butch Sr. would return to the scene and shoot back, "Come back next week. We'll make you happy. You should lose some weight yourself."

Shame overcame the man. "I'm sorry," he said.

Butch Sr., upon Reid's order, directed his security staff that only team members are permitted in the locker room. "No kids. No friends. Nobody. Lock it up."

A silence filled the room, the kind that comes with calamity, broken only by sigh or Brian Mitchell slamming his helmet. The bulldog veteran—who once invited an irate caller to our radio show because the caller told him he couldn't return government cheese—hated to lose, especially this way, because he assumed a personal stake in the team's mental state.

"Bring it in," ordered Reid as he stepped into the center. "Let's go." A few stragglers dawdle and Reid's voice flared, wielding an uncharacteristic edge. "Let's go! Let's go! Get over here!"

The masses condensed, and Reid declared, "We've got seven games (left). SEVEN GAMES! It's time to do it. We can't play three good games then let down. We need seven straight. It's time! We can do it. There are a lot of veterans in this room. It's time to be leaders. It's time to reach down! I'm talking to everyone. The players, the coaches, everyone. We lost this game. It wasn't the offense. It wasn't the defense. It was us. Everyone in this room. It's time to dig deeper!"

Reid's verbal flogging of his team is conspicuously PG. His voice spiked in a manner of menace, but the words stream sanitized, in tribute to his faith. Andy Reid flexed his message through his enormous girth, posturing his point.

"All right," Reid said, his voice still peppered with disgust. "Let's pray."

The masses recited the Lord's Prayer. Their tone was drab, beaten hollow. Then silence. That bad silence.

"Let the media in in 12 minutes," Butch Sr. finally said.

Amid a soft gentle mist the following week a more important loss transpired, the quarterback messiah crumbling under a heap of bones and flesh, his ankle buckling forward in the wrong direction, splintering, seemingly, like season. That was our first reaction, scarred as we were from before, from 1991, the year Randall broke his leg in the opener, and from all those other phony raptures. A condemned city, forced to repeat heartbreak the way a Top 40 station does the hits, thank you kindly, football gods.

It's hard to look at Five's fracture in a historic vein, though someday someone will repeat the story in a fake Facenda voice, right after the one where Ronnie Lott cut off the tip of his finger to get back on the field: How the brave Donovan McNabb broke his ankle on the game's first series against Arizona, fixed it with tape and spit and threw four touchdown passes. (Insert theme from "Gladiator", opening battle scene.)

McNabb couldn't make it on the jumbo jet that departed with 180 people from the old International Terminal. The movie was "Men in Black II" and dinner was either a filet or baked pasta. The destination was officially San Francisco, but no one really knew . . . . Way up there, in the clouds, it seemed right that the Eagles could go into Candlestick Park and beat the 49ers on Monday night football without McNabb and then beat the Rams on a short Thanksgiving week, then the Seahawks out there, the Redskins, the Cowboys in Dallas and come within a last-second chip shot field goal from automatic David Akers of toppling the

Giants at the Meadowlands in the season finale, the latter five games quarterbacked by a former college backup named A.J. Feeley.

Way up there, in the clouds, they all subscribed to that same belief, the kind born in your bones. The last time I encountered such conviction was in Evander Holyfield's hotel room in the MGM Grand before his first fight with Mike Tyson. Holyfield opened as a 25-1 underdog and he implored me to write that all poor people bet the rent on him. "God don't like no gambling, but this one time it's okay," he said. Later, after he finished Tyson impressively, I asked him how he knew. "My soul told me," he said.

Sean Landeta, the mystic punter, leaned in the kitchen area next to the basket of Snickers bars and said with that same, knowing look, "You watch, Koy will be fine." So of course I sought out Koy, who was engrossed in Booray, a Louisiana card game, and appeared completely unfazed. He wore a short-sleeved print shirt, Old Navy khakis and a ratty green baseball cap. "What?" cracked Burkholder. "You thought maybe he'd bring a suit because he's on national TV and will have to do an interview after the game? Uh . . . no." The joke about Koy was that he's a dirtball, that all he brought on a road trip was his toothbrush and playbook. That he borrowed toothpaste, sometimes deodorant, and ignored his unruly neck hair. That he washed his underwear while wearing them in the hotel pool or hot tub.

They believed in Koy, and there was Douglas, before the game, in the old baseball dressing room at Candlestick Park, babbling: "I believe. I believe. I believe." He said it fifty times, mushing the words together to make them sound like "Ah-be-lee."

Douglas said everything fifty times. He talked like God was about to take his tongue. Like exhaust from a car, words just slipped out of him. Quotes. Barbs. Songs. Gibberish. When he entered the locker room, he always made a proclamation. Before the playoff game against the Falcons and much-hyped quarterback Michael Vick, he busted through the door in his heavy jogging suit and cackled, "Michael who? Michael who? Who dat?"

He continued, "You can run, Michael Vick, but you can't hide. I'm comin' to git ya, Michael Vick."

Like a streetcorner prophet, he blathered without direction or destination to a preoccupied audience of the masses moving by him without a stir or a raised eyebrow.

In San Francisco, Reid addressed the team: "Let your personality show. Let's have fun. But remember who you are. You earned the right to have three Monday Night Football games. You did! This is your time! Hugh? Where's Hugh?"

Replied Douglas: "Ah-be-leee! Ah-be-leee! Ah-be-leee!"

Laughter ensued, led by Reid.

"We crazy!" shouted Douglas. "We craaaazee."

Reid left the room for the field and Douglas gathered his team in a circle. "Okay, y'all," he said. "We supposed to lose, right? We supposedly lost. That's what everybody say. Right, then. We ain't got nothin' to lose. Just play our way. Balls out. On three. One. Two. Three . . . ."

"Balls out," they barked in unison."

We shared a moment. Sixty or so men sprinted through the tunnel, mushrooming onto the field. The coaches and staff made a right toward the visitors' sidelines, while the players continued straight to the center of the field. Tight end Chad Lewis had asked Reid if the players could go out as a team rather than in units of offense and defense.

See why I speak of synergy? Teams that go to Super Bowls do things like that, and it becomes good fodder for the video that gets sold to commemorate the season. Teams that go to the Super Bowl beat up a team like the 49ers on the road on national television and survive a popped elbow by its three-quarter backup hero. Detmer kicked his feet against the soft, damp grass to ease the agony of the elbow, turned inside out, and when he released his pain-pried eyes he saw his teammates surrounding him. "I just thought I needed to be near him," linebacker Levon Kirkland said. "Next thing I know everybody's near me doing the same thing."

Players on teams that go to the Super Bowl say things like that, and do things like they did on the flight home, sidling up to Detmer, one by one, before takeoff, asking how he feels. Just like they did when he came back on the field for the end of the game and he held court, pie-eyed from the pain medication, reenacting what transpired. "Good job," he gosh-darned them all, and the masses felt chummy, inordinately chummy, before the plane's engines began to bray and they lay their heads gently back in a darkened cabin, perfect to savor the feeling. Trips like that one become a blood oath, and a point of conversation while sipping champagne to celebrate going to the Super Bowl.

Believe me, they all believed they'd win, beat Tampa and Gruden, down to the last man and equipment boy. They believed the way we believed, so strangely strong, like we were all reading the boxscore in the next day's paper. Hugh Douglas entered the locker room that day in another sweatsuit and boomed, "Who's packed? Who's comin' wit' me to San Diego? C'mon now, who's packed? Jump on my back. I'm packed. I'm goin'."

The players smiled, a healthy, confident but not overconfident smile, a knowing smile. All the while, outside on the field, the sun beginning to dip, Ron Jaworski and Wilbert Montgomery play-acted the play that signified the last and only Eagles' trip to the Super Bowl, 22 years and an entire generation before. I sat under a green army blanket that itched, next to my father, for that game and stood on the Eagles sidelines for this one, and my God, I felt good karma like the cold on my nose. I thought of what so many people had told me in the days leading up to this game, "I just want to see the Eagles win one Super Bowl before I die."

This is the year, I thought.

I thought that even when Tampa took the lead in the second quarter and the Eagles' offense began to sprout snow shoes and Donovan McNabb looked like a quarterback recovering from a broken ankle and Andy Reid sternly spoke to his players at halftime, imploring them in a quick address to do what got them here. Halftime was more about the business of adjustments than a shock a jock call to arms. For though they appeared somewhat confused at the notion that this was a football game, let alone one they were losing, they weren't panicked.

The players gathered in a circle before heading out for the second half, hands atop of hands, and screamed in unison following a 1-2-3, "San Diego."

This is the year, I thought.

The rest of the story leading up to the ending was a blur. I remember the clock racing, time melting into memory. Gradually, gravity grew on the sidelines spreading like poison ivy from man to man. I remember catching eye contact with linebacker Ike Reese. His eyes widened in non-blink mode and he pursed his lips in prayer, as if to say, "I don't know what the hell's goin' on but we better get it right, right quick." I concurred in a nod to him.

This is the year . . .

But now Rhonde Barber is running and he is not stopping and my heart is sinking and reality is biting hard once again. Soon the silence of disbelief will turn into sobs and grief. Everyone feels the same thing. In here, a locker room chocked up. Out there. Across the bridges. Up and down 95. Out 76. Throughout this entire region, now snarled with same ol', same ol'.

A man later said he told his crestfallen teenage son as they slipped into their car for the disappointing ride home, "Well, kiddo, you made your bones."

For us, synergy is heresy. Because, whether it's the 76ers or Phillies or Eagles or Flyers, the story always ends the same way. And you know what? It doesn't matter because until death do us part and because, like we always say, next year is definitely the year.

ANATOMY OF THE FANATIC

We are four hours from kick-off, and the half-naked man named Tuna is anxious. The green body paint he so carefully picked out for this special game is freezing up in the 17- degree mid-January chill. Beyond that, he has miscalculated—one small jar isn't going to cover his 260-pound girth.

"You got another problem, Dude," offers Tuna's pal, Jimmy J, who's applying the paint. "The stuff keeps getting caught in your back hair."

This is very important. Tuna's beloved Eagles are about to face the Atlanta Falcons in the 2002 NFL playoffs. He knows this is the penultimate game at Veterans Stadium (although he has no concept of *that* word), and he must be fully prepared. In his mind—addled as it may be by a steady afternoon diet of Miller Genuine Drafts—the fans' performance tonight is as critical to the Eagles' success tonight as Andy Reid's game plan. He is not here to be entertained; he is here to participate, to have a direct impact on his team's success.

He is a Philadelphia fan.

This only works, however, if Tuna can fully enter his persona. The body paint, applied over his bare torso, is supposed to resemble an Eagles jersey. It is no less crucial than any suit of armor worn by any real player.

But he erred by bringing just one jar of paint. And now that is freezing into slush.

"Spread it thin, man," he orders his make-up artist.

"Dude, you weigh like 500 pounds. I can only spread it so much."

Jimmy J does his best. Tuna's Buddha belly stays pretty much pink and his faux jersey takes on a sleeveless look. But as Jimmy applies the finishing touch—painting "TUNA" in black, high on the back to resemble a player's nameplate—our hero enters into character, right here in the parking lot of the South Philadelphia Holiday Inn.

"E-A-G-L-E-S—EAGLES!"

By "G," a few dozen nearby tailgaters instinctively join the chorus, like barking walruses echoing the raspy leader of their pod. Soon, we will all crowd into the Vet, that rat hole of a stadium—66,000 "Twelfth Men" giving their team the best home field advantage in football.

There is nothing quite like the Philadelphia sports fan. No town supports its home teams more, bad season after bad season; yet no town challenges our national reputation for surliness. No city hosts as impressive a championship parade (trust us if your memory doesn't go back that far); yet no city derides its own players as mercilessly, even if they are future Hall of Famers.

Give us a flicker of hope and we will embrace it, nurture it, cherish the moment. Maybe even get a little carried away. Consider 2001, when the 76ers made an improbable run for the NBA title. Every car in town seemed to boast a Sixers flag. Normally sane people got the team's swirling logo tattooed on their biceps. The team may have fallen apart soon after that season, but the art work is forever.

Can you imagine *très chic* Los Angeles fans defiling their Beamers with a team flag? Or proper Bostonians lining up to sacrifice their skin as a sign of team loyalty?

"Greatest fans in the world," says former Sixers President Pat Croce, who started as one of us and grew up to run the team. "There's no other city in America where the people care so much about sports—win or lose. There is a passion to our sports fans. Sometimes it comes out as a negative, sometimes we look like lunatics to outsiders. But I'll sure take those highs and lows over apathy."

From week to week, game to game, Philadelphia is an ever-changing black-and-white world of heroes and bums. Today's toast of the town is tomorrow's stale crust. "When are they gonna fire that idiot football coach?" an apoplectic caller shouted on a WIP call-in show after Andy Reid's team lost to the Indianapolis Colts in November 2002. At the time, the Eagles had won six games and lost just three.

Reid shouldn't take it personally. Few have escaped unscathed—not Eric Lindros, not Allen Iverson, not Randall Cunningham. Bobby Clarke's honeymoon with fans ended the moment he skated off the Spectrum ice toward the front office. Perhaps the ultimate tribute to Julius Erving is that no one recalls his ever being booed during his 11 seasons in Philadelphia.

The Eagles-Falcons playoff game is about to begin. As each Falcon is announced, his name is greeted by a chorus of "Sucks!" Meanwhile, the Eagles are introduced as a single unit—no individuals on this team—and the Vet becomes one huge echo chamber, reverberating with sound.

Patti LaBelle, a local, shrieks through a painfully slow National Anthem, turning the words "red glare" into a 23-syllable throat exercise. Up in Section 712, we frozen faithful can take it no more. Jeff, a computer analyst and apparent captain of our section, bellows out, "Foooottball!!" Immediately he is joined by hundreds of other fans who may be as patriotic as the next guy, but know we are here to see Falcons carnage, not to hear an aging singer impress herself.

The cacophony grows to a din as the Falcons get the ball for their first drive. Imagine a rock concert on an airport landing strip, toss in a few hundred jackhammers, and you begin to approximate the decibel level. Michael Vick, Atlanta's talented young quarterback, can't hear —or think—above the noise and burns an early time out. Clearly, he is frustrated.

"We own him now," screams Jeff, who is wearing his lucky green fleece pullover. A few hundred yards below, safety Brian Dawkins raises his arms to the crowd, exhorting us to crank the volume up yet another notch.

On Atlanta's next series, Vick throws an out pattern along the sideline. Bobby Taylor, the Eagles Pro Bowl cornerback, swipes the ball in full stride and lopes 39 yards into the end zone. The Eagles lead, 7-0. There is no doubt up in Section 712 that we have all played our part well.

"It's our time," says Jeff, his voice already cracking from the frigid air and the excitement. Then quietly, perhaps to himself, he mumbles, "Of course, I've been thinking it's our time for the past 20 years. Don't break my heart now, boys."

The Philadelphia fan believes in predetermination. The boys up in the cheap seats may put their hopes in earsplitting shouts and body paint (one even carries a Michael Vick voodoo doll), but at the pit of their souls there is a tiny nagging voice reminding them that, in the end, they will be crushed again.

We have seen this before. Every January hot streak the Flyers go on brings fresh hope of a Stanley Cup—only to see our skaters collapse in the first round of the playoffs. Every Sixers draft pick comes in billed as the next Big Thing, only to see him become the next Kenny Payne. Walk up to any Phillies fan in his fifties and whisper the year 1964. You'll see the shudder of realization that our teams, to be sure, were put here to provide us with pain.

In fact, this 2002 Eagles dream will die a painful death one week after the Atlanta game. Football's farewell to the Vet—a 27-10 loss to the Tampa Bay Buccaneers—left these same fans numb and shell-shocked. How could we not have seen it coming? How could we have missed the set-up?

"To follow sports in this town is to suffer," said longtime city councilman Thacher Longstreth.

Which begs the question: Why don't we all just give it up? Sports, after all, is supposed to be a diversion, not an aggravation that induces a Rolaids-popping habit.

"Well, I think it's in the blood," says Pennsylvania Governor Ed Rendell, who moved here from New York to attend the University of Pennsylvania and never left. "You can't just tell a fan not to feel passionately about something he lives for. People here look at the sports teams as part of their extended families. The players aren't here to entertain them, the players are part of their lives."

Rendell, a passionate sports fan, doesn't argue against the notion of Philadelphia fatalism. But, perhaps as part of his liberal roots, he sees an opposing current of emotion running beneath all the layers of pain and suffering. It is perpetual hope.

That is why, the governor says, the fictional film "Rocky" was so well placed in Philadelphia. The underdog who perseveres, who comes out of nowhere to become world champion—"that's what the city is all about. We may lose for 20 years, but we still have dreams of winning."

It is a jumble of emotions. And, to be sure, we are a schizophrenic fan base. We cheer and we boo. Sometimes the same player. Sometimes on the same day. Our national image, stoked mostly by shallow out-of-town media, is that we are the criminal element of sports fans.

But, as Rendell offers, "For every time the fans embarrass themselves, there are 50 times when they bring glory to themselves and the teams."

Against the Falcons tonight, we are here to bring glory—if not civility. The Eagles have taken a 13-0 lead, and the great unwashed in the 700 Level are shouting full volume every time Atlanta has the ball. Down the row, two middle-aged brothers dressed in the old Kelly green Eagles jerseys have worked out a system. On alternate plays, one screams and the other takes a nip from the little tin flask with the Eagles logo on it. Then they switch jobs.

We are abusive and impolitic and more than a little obscene. A good third of the folks in the section would probably flunk a Breathalyzer test. We are 90 percent men, and any woman venturing into the section (at least one between the ages of 18 and 40) has to be prepared for cries of, "Show us your tits!" None takes up the offer but, on the other hand, none appears too insulted by the request. Beyond that, their own boyfriends appear more intent on the game than on chivalry.

In front of Section 360, John Rodio, AKA "Sign Man," has hung his weekly message. Rodio, a landscaper from Hammonton, N.J., paints three-foot letters on 33 feet of industrial wrapping paper and unfurls his epopee at each Eagles game. Invariably, his sign captures the essence and gravity of the event.

"You're Not in Lambeau Anymore!"

Beautiful. The week prior, the Falcons went up to Lambeau Field in Green Bay and upset the heavily favored Packers. Lambeau may be a tough place to visit and Wisconsin's Cheeseheads may be knowledgeable fans, but that was nothing like venturing into the seventh ring of Hell that is the Vet.

One Falcon, and then another, collapses to the Vet turf with a serious injury. There is none of the indecent cheering that enveloped Michael Irvin when he lay stretched on the field in 1999, unable to move and awaiting an ambulance. Nor, however, is there much respect.

"Get him off and let's get going," yells a guy in a Jerome Brown jersey. "I'm freezing my ass off here."

By the game's third quarter, momentum has shifted a bit. The Falcons claw back with two field goals and are threatening to tie up the game. Here we are, 20 minutes from the NFC Championship Game, riding the wave of a 12-4 season, and up in Section 712, patience is running low.

"Dammit, Andy, blitz that son of a bitch!"

"Call a time out and get your f——in' act together, you idiot!"

"I didn't come here to watch you a——holes lose again!"

What is it that makes us so quick to scream for their scalps? So venomous in our critiques? So ready to heckle?

"Some of these people," Pete Rose once offered, "would boo the crack in the Liberty Bell."

"You know what they do when the game's rained out?" cracked former Phils catcher Bob Uecker. "They go to the airport and boo the landings."

Funny stuff, but is it a fair perception?

Temple University basketball coach John Chaney consistently calls Philadelphia sports fans, "the worst in the world."

In February 2000, Reid was courting free agent tackle Jon Runyan and his wife at Ruth's Chris Steakhouse on Broad Street when Chaney charged their table to offer his opinion.

"Remember, you're coming here for these coaches," snarled Chaney. "Don't come here for these fans. Because I hate these fans. I've been here all my life and I hate them all."

In subsequent interviews, Chaney said part of the problem is that we feel the obligation to live up to our reputation as the country's most churlish fans. That, plus our legacy.

"Their granddaddies booed, their daddies booed, so they feel they have to boo," he said.

Former Sixers general manager John Nash takes a more positive view.

"The image of booing is as tied to Philadelphia as cheesesteaks and soft pretzels," says Nash, who grew up in Drexel Hill. "But you can get those foods in other cities. And people in other cities boo, as well. I think the Philadelphia fan is more sophisticated than fans in other places. He's more knowledgeable about the games and less likely to swallow the pabulum fed to him by the teams. I don't see that as a bad thing."

Okay, we're smarter. More discriminating. No argument here. Through the years, however, local jocks who view the role of the fans differently than Nash have complained of being unappreciated. In 1985, Mike Schmidt characterized the locals as "beyond help" in a Montreal newspaper and carped that, had he played in Los Angeles or Chicago ("someplace where they were just grateful to have me around"), his career numbers would have been better. A decade later, Phils manager Jim Fregosi called the fan base "a bunch of guys from South Philly who sleep with their sisters." Randall Cunningham once treasonously suggested that Eagles fans should take loyalty lessons from Washington Redskins fans. "They root for their team," he said. "They don't boo them or anything. When you play here you have to fight against the boos *and* the other team. This is a tough place to play."

We'd rather listen to Larry Bowa here. The Phils manager spent 12 seasons in a (mostly dirty) Phillies uniform. Initially, he found the fans to be overly demanding. Over time, however, their passion forced him to improve his game, rather than face their abuse.

"I would not have been as good a player as I became if I had not played in Philadelphia," he says. "They built my character. If you can understand the fans here, you become better for it."

We are now in the fourth quarter. On the field, the Eagles had taken control. In the courtroom under the Vet stands, Judge Seamus McCaffery has done the same. There are just 23 arrests on this night—or about one for every 3,000 fans. Not bad. Most are gate crashers trying to sneak in without tickets, or entrepreneurs selling counterfeit Eagles merchandise. Not much violence. The most outrageous escapade is a fan in a Donovan McNabb jersey who somehow finds his way down to the Eagles bench and tries to chat up the players.

A 20-year-old who got caught trying to crawl into the stadium under a fence faces the judge.

"How do you plead?" asks McCaffery.

"Judge," the kid says, "I plead stupid."

"I can't do that. Is it aggravated stupid or simple stupid?"

"Whichever is the lesser of the offenses."

Turns out the kid is a Temple University student majoring in criminal justice. "Tonight," he tells the judge, "I was majoring in dumb-ass."

A pass from McNabb to receiver James Thrash gives the Eagles a 20-6 lead with minutes to play. When Vick comes back on the field, those of us in Section 712 break into the familiar sing-song mocking his name, "Miiii-chael, Miii-chael."

With two minutes to go, a sudden display of police power takes over. Cops on horses, on bikes, on fat choppers surround the field. If anyone had considered rushing forward to pat a player on the back or abscond with a stadium souvenir, that's now out of the question.

"Wait until next week," says a section mate, anticipating the final game at the Vet. "They'll need twice as many cops."

Another Falcon is injured and carted off. That makes three.

"Six more and we equal the Body Bag game," crows the guy down the row wearing a bright orange jump suit and Elmer Fudd hunting cap. He is referring, of course, to the Monday Night game against Washington in which the Eagles defense was so fierce that nine Redskins had to be scraped off the Vet floor and driven away. If there is one thing that Philadelphia fans like better than beating their opponents, it is beating them up.

If Philadelphia is a tough place to play, it is a tougher place to visit. Our Animal House reputation has been exaggerated a bit, so that an occasional snowball or D-cell battery tossed from the seats is made to sound like the Rape of Nanking. But it's come to this: if visiting players, coaches and fans choose to be frightened by our lack of couth, we'll let it work in our favor. Go ahead and be intimidated, we won't talk you out of it.

Before this playoff game, Falcons owner Arthur Blank was so scared of Eagles fans that he requested special police protection at the Vet. You would think no Philadelphian would even recognize Blank—who's about as noticeable and colorful as his last name—but they caught him coming out of his limo and gave him an earful. He scurried up to hide in a luxury box.

"Philadelphia is the only place where you pull up on the bus and you've got the grandfather, the grandmother, the grandkids, the kids, everybody flicking you off," said New York Giants defensive end Michael Strahan. "The other stadiums, they kind of wave at you and give you the thumbs-down. Here, they give you the middle finger."

Michael Irvin, whose career ended here, has this advice for any visiting player coming to Philadelphia for the first time: "I hope he's okay with Jesus, because he's about to come as close to seeing his maker as you can get without passing away. The fans will bring the kitchen sink and all the silverware at him."

Irvin insists he was never unsettled by us, but the numbers tell a different story. In 10 games here, he averaged fewer than three catches and 48 yards per game—far below his career numbers. He scored just three touchdowns at the Vet. Perhaps Bobby Taylor had a bit to do with that, but we'll take some credit, as well.

"I was the guy who would come into their town, their stadium, every year and wreck their team," he says, perhaps still feeling the delusional effects of that final hit. "It was them versus.

the Cowboys, America's Team, and I did it with flair. So I can understand that when I was down they were thinking, 'Hey, no more abuse from you.'

"So I didn't take it bad. Believe me, every city that has a football team wants fans like the nutsos in Philadelphia."

Some local players realize that, even if the Scott Rolens and Rich Kotites never understood. Soon after the Eagles dispatch the Falcons—final score, 20–6—defensive end Hugh Douglas thanks the populace for heckling Atlanta players at the Philadelphia International Airport, and, generally, giving them no peace as they toured our fair city. Douglas urges fans to treat Tampa Bay Bucs players the same way when they arrive for the upcoming NFC Championship game.

"Go to their hotel, whatever you did before," he tells the folks. "This is a tough atmosphere for any team. At this point, as a player, you feed off the crowd's energy. I'm chasing Michael Vick around and my back's tightening up, my legs are sore. But I hear the people screaming and it gets me through it. They inspire me to keep moving."

Thank you, Hugh. Man, do we miss you.

We are at Nick's Roast Beef at 20th and Jackson, a South Philly institution, following the Eagles win over Atlanta. We have toasted McNabb's return from injury, Reid's game plan, Taylor's brilliant interception, kicker David Akers's leg and any other football triviality that seemed a good excuse to hoist a Yuengling lager.

Closing in on 2 a.m., folks keep streaming into the bar. Some are known to the regulars, some are newcomers. It doesn't matter. Everyone hugs and high-fives. Women kiss total strangers, not in a sexual way, but more as a celebration, like Times Square on V-J Day. We break into a sloppy round of the Birds' fight song, "Fly, Eagles, Fly," for about the 20th time in the last two hours.

"I love Andy Reid," shouts Joey Chag, a South Philly native who has relocated to Havertown. "I love Todd Pinkston. I love Jeremiah Trotter."

Reminded that Trotter left the team a year ago, Joey blusters, "That's okay. I still love him." Pointing around the bar, he adds, "I love you, and you, and you, and all of you."

Maybe it's the beer talking (Joey prefers his with ice cubes), but there is an unbridled joy tonight. As many people as can squeeze into this place at 19th and Jackson are here to share in a beautiful moment. They may not necessarily have a lot else in common but tonight they are wearing so much Eagles garb that you could go green-blind.

Sports, at its best, brings people together. Diverse populations—city and suburban, black and white, rich and poor—can bond over a ball club like nothing else. In the Delaware Valley, where we are more passionate and opinionated about sports than any city in the nation, it is the single best unifying institution we have.

And that's why we are fans.

THREE

BIRTH OF THE BOOS

The Great Philadelphia Boobird was born in the 1920s in the shadows of Shibe Park. He gained national fame during the Great Depression, added snowballs and airplane banners to his repertoire in the 1960s and migrated to South Philly in the 1970s.

He survives today in good health.

The Boobird has heckled presidents and first-round picks, Hall of Famers and washouts. He has been chastised, celebrated, imitated and even banned from the NFL draft. He has seen his share of misery—69 last-place finishes by our major-league teams since 1920. And he has seen too little joy—just 11 world titles.

"To be a Philadelphia sports fan is to be an eternal pessimist," says Dave Coskey, President of Marketing for the 76ers and Flyers. "You go through life expecting the worst because, all too often, bad things happen."

So, if your heroes always break your heart, why not just walk away from the affair?

"Because it's in your blood," says Coskey, who grew up in South Jersey and shudders when recalling the 9-73 Sixers season of 1972-73. "In a sense, fans in Philadelphia view the teams as their own children. You want them to do better on their report cards. You want them to behave better in public. They don't always meet your demanding expectations. But you love them just the same.

"Philadelphia is a tough city, the fans are very tough," he adds. "When we're in the middle of a win streak, I don't hear a thing. But as soon as we lose, I get 35 e-mails—the coach stinks, get rid of Allen Iverson. The positive of that is we can never rest. If ever there is an opportunity to sit back and push cruise control, the fans here will kick us in the butt."

They may needle the Sox in Boston. Or belittle the Giants in New York. But in terms of bad image, no one challenges the residents of Philly's unfriendly confines.

Nary an Eagles game goes by that television viewers aren't reminded that 30 drunken fans ventured up to New York in 1999 and booed the selection of Donovan McNabb. Never mind that in New Orleans, Saints fans cheered as their own quarterback lay prone with a head injury. Or that in Cleveland, residents of the Dog Pound reduced their young quarterback to tears. We're the great unwashed.

"Philly fans are so mean," jokes former Phillies catcher Bob Uecker, "that one Easter Sunday, when the players staged an Easter egg hunt for their children, the fans booed the kids who didn't find any eggs."

Actually, there is no evidence to support Uecker's charge. It just sounds good in a stand-up comedy routine. But it captures the image of Philadelphia fans.

The Eagles may be on a four-game win streak. But let them start a Sunday afternoon with a few three-and-outs and you'll hear the throaty voice of the discontented:

"Boooooooo."

"My first time?" ponders former Eagles quarterback Ron Jaworski. "It was against the Cowboys in 1977, my first season here. I was getting pounded by their defense. I remember coming onto the field after we got the ball, and I hear this noise coming from the stands: 'Oooooh.' Very deep, very loud.

"I didn't understand what it was at first. I asked my tackle, Stan Walters, what was going on. He looked down at me and says, 'Big guy, they're booing the quarterback.' Booing me? I got angry. Didn't they know I was trying my best? Hell, we all were. I took it very personally.

"It took me a few years to understand that they booed me because they cared so much. Hey, maybe they even liked me. It's just the nature of this city to boo. Always has been. Who even knows how it even got started?"

Actually, the Birth of the Boos can be traced all the way back to our founding fathers. While the Quakers who first settled Philadelphia never shook an angry fist from the cheap seats, they provided the blueprint for future denizens of the 700 Level.

"Cheering against the home team is a time-honored tradition in Philadelphia," wrote E. Digby Baltzell, the noted University of Pennsylvania sociologist who spent a lifetime studying the local psyche.

Indeed, the first recorded rip on our fans came in 1910. In an era when immigrants were being blamed for most of America's ills, *The Sporting News* defended America's newest residents by pointing the finger at us. "Do not blame unruly baseball behavior on foreigners," the paper noted, "since it is long commonplace in Philadelphia."

In his book, *Puritan Boston and Quaker Philadelphia,* Baltzell (who died in 1994) argued that self-deprecation "is deeply rooted in the Philadelphia mores, at all levels of society.

Ricky Watters never would have made it as a Quaker.

If the Quakers started the routine, a pair of Jewish fruit vendors from North Philly were the first to put some bite into it. Most likely, you've never heard of the Kessler Brothers. Their first names are long forgotten. But their contribution to local sports history rivals that of Wilt Chamberlain, Bob Clarke or Pat Croce.

The Kesslers, according to legend, converted heckling from a small-time display to a full-fledged theatrical production. During the 1920s, they owned a fruit stand a block away from Shibe Park (fittingly, it was across the street from the Philadelphia Hospital for Contagious Diseases). On afternoons, they closed the stand in mid-afternoon and headed to the ballpark to abuse Connie Mack's Athletics.

The brothers sat on opposite ends of the tiny park—one behind first base, the other behind third. They spent nine innings organizing chants deriding the home team.

Al Horvitz, a longtime baseball writer for the defunct *Philadelphia Ledger*, recalled the Kesslers in Jerome Holtzman's 1973 book, *No Cheering in the Press Box*: "These guys were needlers. They never let up. They knew all the ballplayers' habits, where they were drinking, and the girls they were with. And they would go out and yell the names . . . The needling and booing caught on with the other fans and became a big thing."

The Kesslers' favorite target was Bill Lamar, the A's talented left-fielder whose good looks and late-night carousing had earned him the nickname "Goodtime Bill."

"The Kesslers got on him," said Horvitz. "The guy was dropping fly balls in the outfield. They really had him intimidated."

Lamar batted .345 his first two seasons in Philadelphia. After the abuse began, his average dropped to .290 the following two years. He retired from baseball at the age of thirty, the first recorded example of local fans chasing a player out of town.

Connie Mack, who owned the A's, went to court, seeking to stop the brothers and their devotees. He lost, as the judge explained the First Amendment to a perplexed Mr. Mack. Then Mack offered the Kesslers a free season's pass if they would just lay off his players. But, said Horvitz, the caustic fruit sellers "said they'd prefer paying and having a chance to yell."

Good Philadelphia fans cannot be bought off.

Through the 1920s, booing remained our little secret. There were no outside reporters of the Michael Wilbon ilk to label us America's nastiest fans. But that all ended when the A's hosted the St. Louis Cardinals for Game 2 of the World Series on October 2, 1930.

Among the 32,000 fans on hand that sunny afternoon was President Herbert Hoover, looking for a few hours of escape from the gloomy economic news of the time. In those days—despite the Depression and Prohibition—heckling a president was unheard of. But as Hoover's limousine drove onto the field near third base, the murmurs began. And when Hoover stepped onto the field and tipped his top-hat, the crowd let loose.

"From everywhere in the park the boos came," said Horvitz. "I never heard such booing in my life. Then they started yelling, 'We want beer.' It reverberated over the whole park."

Consider the guy who sneaks a flask into the ballpark nowadays. Chances are he is the great-grandson of one of those leather-lunged critics who offered Hoover his opinion on liquor laws seven decades ago.

The fans' behavior that day was bigger news than the A's 6-1 win over the Cards. It made national headlines—"An Embarrassment to Liberty!" screamed the *St. Louis Globe-Democrat*. Whether Liberty felt threatened or not, the president certainly did. Hoover vowed never to return to Philadelphia.

The behavior of our forefathers is understandable in this context: The teams they paid good money to see by and large stunk up the joint. Most of our old-time owners were so cheap as to make Bill Giles look like Regis Philbin. So for every Norm Van Brocklin, there were a dozen "Dynamite" Dave Smuklers; for every Robin Roberts, there were a dozen "Losing

Pitcher" Mulcahys—so titled because his name in the box score was always followed by the words, "losing pitcher."

"The problem was that Mack and (Phillies owner Gerald) Nugent continuously sold their stars to other clubs for the money," longtime Philadelphia city councilman Thatcher Longstreth told author Glen Macnow for a 1991 *Philadelphia Inquirer* article. "Jimmy Foxx, for example, was adored by the local fans, but Mack sent him to Boston at their height of his powers. It left the local fans feeling cynical, where we'd rather boo than cheer. That way, when they sold the star, at least it didn't break our heart."

The Phillies never finished higher than fourth place between 1918 and 1945. They wound up in last place five seasons in a row (1938-42), averaging about 2,500 fans a game at the Baker Bowl. High up the rightfield fence at that park was a sign proclaiming, "The Phillies Use Lifebuoy" deodorant soap. Underneath those words, a clever fan with brush and paint scrawled, "Because they Stink!"

Even when they improved—winning a National League pennant in 1950—it didn't calm the crowd.

The most-heckled man of that era was leftfielder Del Ennis, who hit .311 with 31 homers in the year of the "Whiz Kids." Ennis grew up in Olney, and rationalized that the fans who razzed him every game during his 11 years with the Phils were South Philly locals, envious that a North Philly kid had made it. Or, he figured, they were mostly gamblers who massed in the left-field bleachers and took out the sting of their losses on the nearest player.

Regardless, he eventually had enough. On Fan Appreciation Day in 1950, a particularly grating fan stayed on his case all afternoon. So after the game, as the club was giving away a car, Ennis showered, dressed and then ventured into the Shibe Park seats to slug it out with his tormentor.

"I really snapped," he recalled years later. "I grabbed the guy around the collar and was about to punch him out when I thought, 'Del, what the heck are you doing here?' From that moment on, I never let the fools get to me."

The Phils set a record in 1961 by losing 23 straight. In 1964, they led the National League by 6-½ games with two weeks to go, only to collapse and forever leave us pessimists. There are grown men in this town who still wake up screaming in the night from another nightmare of Chico Ruiz stealing home.

The Phillies' first—and only—world championship came in 1980, their 98th season.

The Eagles didn't fare much better. In their first 45 years they managed all of 14 winning seasons and just two NFL titles. Occasional bright moments would be followed by sustained darkness. Consider that after the Birds won their last NFL title in 1960, they celebrated by going 50-84-6 over the next decade.

The nadir came in the mid '60s under the buffoonish Jerry Wolman. As owner, Wolman accomplished several firsts: He was the first man to go broke owning an NFL franchise, and the first to offer a coach a "lifetime" contract, which he awarded to the inept Joe Kuharich in 1964.

By 1968, Philadelphia fans accomplished their own "first." They leased a prop plane that flew over Franklin Field during an Eagles game toting a sign reading "Joe Must Go." Kuharich never twitched, and insisted afterward he hadn't seen the message from above.

Eight years later, another Eagles coach would hear the hoarse voice of the crowd—and this one would react. Dick Vermeil, in his first season here (and before he lifted the Eagles to the Super Bowl), was jogging toward the locker-room after a disappointing loss to the Cowboys. An angry fan screamed out, like thousand before him and thousands after, "Hey, Coach, you son of a bitch, why don't you go back where you came from?" Unlike most coaches, Vermeil couldn't ignore it.

"Criminy, I just snapped," he recalled. "I jumped into the stands after the guy."

Luckily for Vermeil (or perhaps the fan), Eagles assistant coach Chuck Bednarik, a former all-pro linebacker, caught up with the incensed coach and tackled him. Bednarik sat on Vermeil until he calmed down.

"He saved me from making a total fool of myself," Vermeil said. "I still remember the pain from Chuck sitting on me."

Vermeil, you may recall, is the guy for whom the phrase "coach's burnout" was invented. He was compulsive and tightly wound, so much so that, for years, he had a cramp in the back of his neck that prevented him from turning his head sideways. So it should not be startling that one badgering fan could drive him over the edge. What is surprising is his retrospective view of Philadelphia fans.

"Oh, they're tough and judgmental and pretty darn vocal," he says. "But they're unbelievably loyal. The local clubs are part of their family.

"Sports isn't a social event in Philadelphia, it's religion. People go to games to vent their emotions. They go prepared to do battle. And if a coach doesn't do the job, they vent their emotions on him."

Vermeil left the Eagles in 1982 but never left town. He returned to coaching 14 years later, leading the St. Louis Rams to a Super Bowl win before moving on to the Kansas City Chiefs.

"I've coached a lot of places," he said, "but nowhere else are fans so deeply immersed in every play of every game. They live from Sunday to Sunday, and the outcome of each game affects their lives all the way up until the next Sunday. Criminy, they boo because they care so darn much."

"No one says no to Santa Claus—unless you live in Philadelphia, where they throw snowballs at him." —*Washington Business Journal, 2001*

"Philadelphia is a tough, nasty city where fans have been known to throw snowballs at Santa." —*Ottawa Sun, 2002*

No event has been used to tar-and-feather Philadelphia fans as much as the day we chucked a few at Santa down at Franklin Field.

And no event has been as exaggerated, misconstrued and inaccurately recalled. Snowballs-at-Santa has become pure mythology, our Greek tragedy.

Yeah, it happened. But somehow a minor laugh-it-off incident evolved into Christmas Armageddon. To hear our critics (chief culprit: Howard Cosell) tell it, poor St. Nick was virtually killed under an avalanche of angry, icy projectiles.

And now, let's hear from Santa himself: "I thought it was funny."

More from the jolly one in a moment. First, let's set the record straight. We'll begin by setting the scene.

The date was December 15, 1968. It was the last game in the last season of the Joe Kuharich Era (soon to be followed by the equally dismal Jerry Williams Era). The Eagles record stood at 2-11. Actually, they had been 0-11 before beating the Detroit Lions and New Orleans Saints. Those late-season victories might be cause for consolation in other years, but all they did in 1968 was take the team out of the running for the nation's top collegian, future Hall of Famer O.J. Simpson.

The Eagles were playing the Minnesota Vikings on a miserable Sunday afternoon. It had snowed steadily since the night before. By game time, the temperature had dropped to 22 degrees and gusting winds approached 30 miles per hour. Fans arriving at Franklin Field found their wooden seats covered with a three-inch layer of slush.

That 54,535 would show up in a snowstorm to see a last-place team is a testament to the loyalty of Philadelphia fans. That angle, however, rarely gets mentioned.

Anyway, on this day, the Birds got off to a surprising lead. Early in the second quarter, split end Gary Ballman took a swing pass from quarterback Norm Snead and bulled his way five yards into the end zone for a touchdown. For a brief moment, Eagles fans considered the notion that, even if the team was out of the O.J. sweepstakes, finishing the season with three straight wins might be something to build on.

That feeling didn't last long. Minutes before halftime, Snead threw an interception into the hands of safety Paul Krause. A few plays later, Vikings quarterback Joe Kapp threw a deep pass to fullback Bill Brown at the Eagles' 20-yard line. Brown knocked over two would-be tacklers, eluded another and rumbled in for a 57-yard touchdown.

And so, as the half arrived, the cold, wet fans considered the lot of their team.

They considered how owner Jerry Wolman, who bought the club in 1963, dismantled a strong, proud franchise. The Eagles began the 1960s as NFL champions. They were ending the decade as a laughingstock.

They considered how Wolman signed Joe Kuharich (official nickname: "The Dumbest Coach in Notre Dame History") to a fifteen-year contract extension during the 1964 season. Kuharich could not hide his glee over the $900,000 deal ("Now I know how Sutter felt when he found all that gold," he publicly crowed), and went on to go 22-34-1 after signing it. By 1968 planes flew over Franklin Field towing signs reading, "Joe Must Go."

They considered how Kuharich—serving as coach and general manager—traded Hall of Fame quarterback Sonny Jurgensen to Washington for journeyman Snead. The swashbuckling Jurgensen was adored by Eagles fans, but the prudish Kuharich chafed at Sonny's playboy ways. Kuharich tried to explain the unexplainable by calling the quarterback-for-quarterback deal, "rare but not unusual."

Jurgensen went on to throw more touchdowns than any other NFL quarterback in the 1960s. Snead led the decade in another category: interceptions.

So, as the half ended, the fans sat there—frozen, frustrated, their galoshes soaking in snow that no one had shoveled away. Some sucked warmth out of flasks. Others huddled under mounds of heavy clothes. Kuharich trotted to the locker room in a short-sleeve shirt and sports jacket, looking, according to the *Philadelphia Daily News*, "as if he were strolling down the boardwalk in Atlantic City."

Could you really fault the fans for what was about to happen?

The Christmas Pageant was about to begin. Eagles cheerleaders—then known as "Eagle-ettes"—were decked out in elf costumes, modest by today's standards but considered risqué at the time. A 50-piece band, "The Sound of Brass," was cued up to play carols. Bill "Moon" Mullen, the Eagles entertainment director, figured that the fans may not see good football but, dammit, they were going to see a good halftime show.

Except there were a few problems. Fifteen hours of snowfall and thirty minutes of football had reduced the field to muck. Zaberer's Restaurant, a Jersey Shore institution back then, had built a Christmas float to parade Santa around the joint. The float was huge, carrying an ornate sleigh dragged by eight life-size fiberglass reindeer. Indeed, it was so huge that it got stuck in the mud before it ever got onto the field. Santa would have to hoof it.

That was, if they could locate Santa. According to most reports, the regular St. Nick hadn't made it through the storm. The Eagles needed a stand-in. Mullen, now in his eighties, does not recall seeking a replacement Kris Kringle, but concedes, "It may have happened that way."

They apparently found one in the end zone. Sitting in the seats with his family was 20-year-old Frank Olivo of South Philadelphia. Olivo had worn his red corduroy Santa suit and fake beard to the game, hoping the TV cameras might find him.

Olivo—who stands all of five-foot-six and weighed 170 pounds those days—says Mullen approached him in a panic and begged him to stand in for the AWOL Rent-a-Santa.

"I figured, what the heck, this could be fun," recalls Olivo, who now lives in Ocean City, N.J. "Little did I know what was about to happen."

Mullen gave his faux Santa a big toy bag and stationed him under a gate in the end zone. The dancing Eaglettes formed two 100-yard columns down the field. When the brass band struck up "Here Comes Santa Claus," little Frank Olivo was cued to jog between the cheerleaders and wave to the crowd.

"That's when the booing started," Olivo recalls. "At first, I was scared because it was so loud. But then I figured, hey, it was just good-natured teasing. I'm a Philadelphia fan, I knew what was what. I thought it was funny."

There remains debate on how much of the fans' ire came from Santa's less-than-rotund physique and ragged red suit. Olivo describes himself as "a terrific Santa. That was a $100 suit back in the Sixties. I looked really good."

Others aren't so sure. "He was the worst-looking Santa I'd ever seen," recalls Jim Gallagher, who was the Eagles public relations director at the time. "Bad suit, scraggly beard. I'm not sure whether he was drunk, but he appeared to be."

Regardless, when Olivo finished his run down Santa Claus Lane, he got into range. A fan in the upper deck threw the first snowball. As Santa hit the south end zone, one turned into ten, then into 100.

"Oh, I got pelted," Olivo says. He remembers being hit by several dozen snowballs, which suggests that many of the upper-deck denizens were more accurate passers than Snead. "I didn't mind," he says. "I started kibitzing with some of the people throwing the snowballs."

Olivo also rationalizes that no one was *really* unloading on Father Christmas. He was merely a surrogate for Wolman, Kuharich and Snead.

Still, he had his limits. "When I finished, Mr. Mullen asked if I wanted to do it again the next year," Olivo says. "I told him, 'No way. If it doesn't snow, they'll probably throw beer bottles.'"

One of the strong-armed fans that afternoon went on to become a perennial Pro Bowl player in the NFL. Matt Millen grew up an hour west of Franklin Field and still proudly describes himself as "a Philly rowdy through and through."

"It was a miserable day and a miserable team," recalls Millen, who was 11 years old at the time. "That was the only fun part of the game, and everybody joined in—fathers, sons, even the old ladies. That guy had it coming. I still remember the song, 'Here Comes Santa Claus' —BOOM! Got 'im! Hey, it was just the thing to do at the time. No big deal."

Millen is now president of the Detroit Lions. How would he feel if fans threw snowballs at his stadium? "Well, we play in a dome," he says. "So I guess they'd have to smuggle them in.

"But it was different in that era," he adds. "Very passionate. Franklin Field was a crazy place. People took their football seriously. Hell, they'd run on the field to get at the players and coaches."

Indeed, during the second quarter that day, one fan sprinted to the Eagles bench to debate Kuharich's coaching methods. The man's point of view was muffled by a forearm from huge offensive tackle Bob Brown. Another fan danced to the 50-yard line dragging an effigy of Wolman. Yet another hung a green-and-white sign on a flagpole above the north-end stands reading simply, "Kuharich Stinks." Appropriately, it was hung upside down, the international signal of distress.

Years later, these men's offspring would come to be known as "The 700 Level."

Anyway, the second half began and, to no one's surprise, the Eagles finished the season with a 24-17 defeat. Driving home afterward, few people thought much of the snowball incident. Most focused their thoughts on how the Eagles would bollix their next first-round draft pick (which they did by taking Purdue running back Leroy Keyes and promptly turning him into a defensive back).

The local papers made scant mention of the St. Nick affair. *Inquirer* columnist Frank Dolson worked it into the eighth paragraph of his story, saying that Santa "made his tour of the stadium, waving cheerfully in the best holiday tradition. The fans responded, pelting him with snowballs, in the worst Philadelphia tradition."

The *Bulletin's* Ray Kelly spent most of his column describing a gruesome eye injury that Eagles fullback Tom Woodeshick sustained in the game. In his eleventh paragraph, Kelly wrote, "The fans even threw snowballs at Santa when he paraded around the field at halftime."

And that was that. The entire incident might have been forgotten if late Sunday night the local news had not been followed by the "ABC Weekend Report," a national news show featuring Howard Cosell on sports. Two years before his Monday Night Football gig, Cosell contributed a weekly package of NFL highlights to the show. When the whip-around got to Franklin Field, Cosell showed no football. Instead, he aired the pelting of Santa, accompanied with his polysyllabic verbiage shaming the Philadelphia faithful.

And so, our infamy began.

"The Cardinals are off to Philadelphia, about to encounter fans that once threw snow-balls at Santa Claus." —Dan Bickley, *Arizona Republic,* 2002

"Philadelphia sports fans are notoriously hard to please and irascible. Some are just plain crazy. This is, after all, where fans once booed and hurled snowballs at Santa Claus." —Eric Westervelt, *National Public Radio,* 2001

Not long after the season ended, Wolman fell into deep financial trouble. A bankruptcy referee in Baltimore oversaw the team's sale to trucking magnate Leonard Tose, who would later have his own money problems. One of Tose's first acts as owner made him an instant hero. He fired Kuharich, even though he had to pay the bumbling coach another 11 years' salary.

It would take another ten years before the team produced a winning season under Tose and head coach Dick Vermeil. Still, the Snowballs-at-Santa afternoon at Franklin Field put the punctuation mark on one bad era. Things could only get better from there.

Problem is, long after the scale and circumstances of a minor incident recede from memory, the label of hooligan remains the albatross slung around our collective necks. The fact that Eagles fans turned out year after year to support a bad football team becomes irrelevant. That a few folks had some laughs and let out frustrations by pasting a sad-sack Santa becomes permanent fodder for anyone looking to bash our town. Hey, Richard Nixon and Patty Hearst got pardoned. Why not us?

"Everybody was laughing when the thing happened," says Jim Gallagher, the former PR man. "Who knew it would endure for all these years?"

"It wasn't a big deal at the time," echoes Bill Mullen, the entertainment director. "But it grew and grew and over the years it became huge. Every time some one needs to say something negative about Philadelphia, they pull out the Santa episode."

On the other hand, maybe it's better that our critics regard us as the great unwashed. If visiting players think we're rabid enough to go after the symbol of Christmas cheer, perhaps they'll look over their shoulder a bit when they come to town.

"They throw snowballs at Santa Claus in Philly . . . That's why there's a jail under the stands." —Elfin and Snider, *Washington Times,* 1999

"Philly, the city that throws snowballs at Santa Claus and the Easter Bunny, has embraced the Sixers as a team with a very hot future." —John Shivers, *San Francisco Express Metro,* 1999

Nobody ever gets this right. Hell, the Vet Stadium jail came nearly 30 years after the Franklin Field Santa. And we never threw anything at the Easter Bunny. Didn't even boo him. That urban legend derives from a joke by former Phillies catcher and stand-up comedian Bob Uecker, who always cracked his oft told Easter Sunday joke about fans booing children who couldn't find any eggs in the Easter egg hunt.

Again, not true.

We did, however, host a second Snow Bowl. If there was ever any chance of escaping our Animal House reputation, it ended in 1989 when we aimed a few hard-packed grenades at the impeccably perfectly coiffed hair of Dallas Cowboys coach Jimmy Johnson.

Eagles fans welcome Jimmy Johnson to Philadelphia.

What a season that was. The Birds were headed to the playoffs under Buddy Ryan. The Cowboys would finish 1-15 and, in our glee, we hadn't yet realized that Johnson was building the nucleus that would win three Super Bowls.

In the Thanksgiving Day game earlier that year, Eagles linebacker Jesse Smalls knocked Cowboys kicker Luis Zendejas woozy with a cheap shot. Zendejas later learned from Eagles special teams coach Al Roberts (the rat!) that Ryan had placed a $200 bounty on his head. The diminutive kicker hired *four* lawyers to sue Ryan and whined for weeks to anyone who would listen. That only served to whip up Philadelphia fans headed into the mid-December rematch.

Snow fell for several days in the city, but none of the folks who managed Veterans Stadium thought to shovel it away. Once again, customers arrived at the game to find their seats blanketed under several inches.

Everyone expected an ugly affair. NFL Commissioner Paul Tagliabue came to oversee the players' behavior (if not the fans') and brought along 25 league security officials. Jimmy Johnson was flanked by two Philadelphia policemen everywhere he went—starting the night before the game. Zendejas wore a mouthpiece for the only time in his career and taped shut the ear holes on his helmet. Still, he ran down the field with his head on a swivel.

The precautions didn't really matter. As players scuffled on the field, fans started hurling the snow that accumulated around their seats. Initially they aimed at a section of Cowboys fans (the lone star logos made easy targets) cowering in the 100 Level at the Vet's southwest corner. Eventually, they expanded their range to include Cowboys players, Eagles cheerleaders, quivering referees and woozy police officers. They bombarded the open-aired CBS broadcast booth with such fury that Verne Lundquist compared our town to Beirut.

The mood at the Vet grew so intoxicating that it swept in a career politician, who goaded a section-mate with the challenge, "Betcha $20 you can't reach the field." The missile landed at the feet of a referee, and Ed Rendell—typical Philly fan—went on to become mayor and governor. It was never recorded whether he paid off his wager but, like most of us, he had a good laugh that day.

The fun was followed by a scolding. The network news shows broadcast the bombardment, again and again, comparing us to British soccer hooligans. Eagles owner Norman Braman (who made Wolman seem lovable) called us "a disgrace." Specifically citing the 700 Level, he said, "If they can't come here and behave in a normal, decent manner, than we don't want them here."

That from a man who sat in a heated luxury box eating catered food. Nobody saw Norman Braman pushing snow off his seat with a frozen mitten that afternoon.

The quotes that really counted came from enemies other than Braman. Cowboys linebacker Eugene Lockhart called Eagles fans "classless animals." And Jimmy Johnson termed us "thugs," adding that he'd rather not ever play here again.

And that, in many ways, was the point. The Eagles won the game, 20-10, and we, as fans, felt we deserved at least a game ball for our well-aimed contributions.

"Eagles fans are really booing their punter. Remember, these are the same fans who once booed Santa Claus."   —*Fox Network* announcer Sam Rosen, 2002

"(Jim) Thome can stay in a city that adores him or he can go to a place where they throw snowballs at Santa Claus. Is there really any decision to make?" —*Cleveland Plain Dealer*, 2002

In Cleveland, they only throw beer bottles at replay officials, and cheer when *their own* injured quarterback is lying motionless on the field. In New York, Giants fans had their own Snow Bowl, sending a San Diego Chargers assistant to the hospital with a concussion. In Denver, they hit their own defensive back in the eye with a size E battery, putting him on the injured list.

But we're the bad guys. Because decades ago, our dads tossed a few at a laughing, undersized Santa.

Hey world—get over it.

Snowballs at Santa isn't the only historical event that has been mis-colored in order to smudge the image of the Philadelphia faithful. Here are a few others:

We chased away our best players. The press gets blamed for this more than the fans, but either way, it's blatant nonsense.

"The media ran Scotty Rolen out of town," insists Charles Barkley, who had his own issues with the local sports press. "Scotty was a good guy, but when he turned down the money, they turned on him. They ran Eric Lindros out of town, and they ran Randall Cunningham out of town. I'm the only one they didn't run out of town."

"They're good fans, but what happens is that when the press turns against you, they kind of roll with the punches. Once they turn on you, you've got no chance."

Barkley isn't alone in spewing this nonsense. So let's set the record straight here.

1). Scott Rolen left Philadelphia for the St. Louis Cardinals because (a) he wasn't an East Coast kind of guy and (b) he became convinced that the Phillies ownership had neither the will nor the desire to build a winning franchise.

2). Eric Lindros's war was with Flyers President Bob Clarke—not the media or the fans. In fact, Lindros always had a cordial relationship with local reporters and analysts. And, even as he was banished to New York, he went out of his way to thank Flyers fans for standing by him.

3). Randall Cunningham? Hey, the guy played 11 seasons with the Eagles. If we were all trying to chase him away, he must have been even more elusive than he was billed. Truth is, Randall left Philadelphia because after all those years of being under-coached, he didn't have it in him to learn John Gruden's West Coast Offense.

Hmm, let's see. I suppose we did run Lance Parrish and Andy Ashby out of town. Maybe Rich Kotite as well. Crucify us for that if you wish, Charles. I think we were doing the city a service.

We buried J.D. Drew under a barrage of batteries. Drew, you may recall, was a can't-miss prospect who warned the Phillies not to draft him with the No. 1 pick in 1998. He refused to sign with the club on what he called "principle"—which apparently meant that he wanted John Kruk's weight in gold bullion. Drew held out a full year, re-entered the draft and finally signed with St. Louis.

He showed up at the Vet in a Cardinals uniform in August 1999. Although idiot Phillies manager Terry Francona proclaimed, "I don't have any ill will toward this kid," more than 45,000 fans came the first night to express a different opinion. In their minds, Drew hadn't rejected the *organization*, he had rejected *them*. Even the Phanatic got into the act by tying three sacks with dollar signs to a make-believe detonator outside the Cardinals' dugout and trying to lure Drew with the money.

Drew, typically, wouldn't play along. In fact, he sat out the game with a bruised thumb.

The next night, he deigned to play. Another 48,000 folks heckled, chanted and hurled invective at the young centerfielder. Some brought hand-painted signs, including one reading, "Greed D. Drew." Mostly, they just booed. It wasn't exactly good-natured, but neither was it out of line.

During a St. Louis pitching change in the eighth inning, one fan threw a D-cell battery Drew's way. Then another. Cardinals' manager Tony La Russa started to pull his team off the field. Umpire Ed Montague threatened the Phillies with a forfeit. PA announcer Dan Baker warned the fans to stop.

Which they did. And that was the end of it. To hear the story years later, you would think Drew faced a volley similar to the first ten minutes of "Saving Private Ryan." In truth, it was two batteries.

Let's see—48,000 fans, two batteries. That equals one nitwit per every 24,000 fans. We'll live with that ratio.

We heckled native son Kobe Bryant at the 2002 NBA All-Star Game. You bet we did. But, hell, he started it.

It's not like we hold a grudge against every local kid who goes on to star elsewhere. Mike Piazza, Rasheed Wallace and Mike Richter never had a problem with Philadelphia fans.

But Kobe was different. For one, he went Hollywood after signing with the Lakers. And cool doesn't play in Philadelphia. We like our superstars more gritty than polished.

Second, Kobe loaded up the truck and moved to Beverly—Hills, that is—so quickly that he let us know that Philly (or Lower Merion) was never anything more to him than a weigh station. "As far as going home, it's really nothing to me," he said right before the 2001 NBA Finals against the Sixers. "To me, it's just basketball."

And this: Asked during the Finals if he would arrange tickets for his former high school teammates, he said "I'm not getting them anything, because they're all just Sixers fans anyway."

And this: Jawing with Sixers fans before Game 3 of the Finals, he said, "We're going to cut your hearts out."

It's one thing to see the local kid take off for the bright lights of L.A. It's another to hear him hold such animosity toward the town that nurtured him.

So when Bryant scored 31 points and was named MVP of the 2002 All-Star Game at the First Union Center, the fans (at least the 3,000 locals sprinkled among the 21,000 corporate honchos at the game) gave him back some of his attitude. You start something with us, you're going to see it returned ten-fold.

"Hey, my kids booed Kobe," says 76ers and Flyers marketing president Dave Coskey. "Anyone who abandons his hometown probably deserves it."

Except the national reporters covering the event didn't grasp the historical context. So, led by *Washington Post* blowhard Michael Wilbon, they trotted out the tired clichés: "*City of Brotherly Shove*," and all that. It may have been the biggest overreaction to a non-story in boobird history.

Some guys just never get it.

SIX

GREAT MOMENTS 1: BATTLING THE BLUES

The Flyers developed their reputation as the toughest, brawlingest franchise in NHL history midway through the 1970s.

Their fans got there a few years earlier.

Several seasons before the Flyers had the nerve to fight back against the St. Louis Blues, their patrons did so on a cold January night in 1972. First-level customers and Philadelphia cops fought side-by-side against an invasion of Blues into the Spectrum stands. When it was over, the St. Louis coach had a ten-stitch gash in his head and four members of the team were hauled off to the police station for a night in the holding cell.

"This community will not tolerate hooliganism," Mayor Frank Rizzo said afterward, referring to the Blues, not the fans. Looking back, he said, "We probably didn't need our police officers in that situation. I believe our residents could have taken care of the matter on their own."

All in all, a fine night down in South Philadelphia.

The incident started at the end of the second period, with the Flyers leading, 2-0. Blues coach Al Arbour was furious over how a puck had been dropped for a faceoff that led to a Flyers goal. Arbour chased referee John Ashley across the ice and then, when he was hit with a two-minute penalty for unsportsmanlike conduct, started to go after Ashley down the Zamboni runway leading to the refs' dressing room.

In those days, there were no canopies over the exit runways. As Arbour confronted the referee, his near-hysterical face getting redder and redder, one helpful Flyers fan decided to help him cool down with an ice-cold beer. Unfortunately, the beer was poured over the coach's head.

The Blues charged into the tunnel to protect their coach and then, led by tough-guy defenseman Bob Plager, started scaling the railings to go into the stands.

"Fans started cursing the Blues and throwing things," recalls Flyers founder Ed Snider. "Then Arbour reached over into the seats and some cop hit him over the head with a billy club. Well, that was it. It became instant mayhem."

Snider, who was seated near the area, ran down from his seat to intervene. When he got there, "I saw the glazed eyes of their players and got scared for myself."

The Flyers players had already skated to their own dressing room. So it became the fans and a handful of cops against the marauding Blues. Several players climbed into the stands. Blues center Garry Unger swung his stick wildly, nearly decapitating several innocent onlookers. More intrepid fans moved in to fight back.

Real Brawl Game for Blues

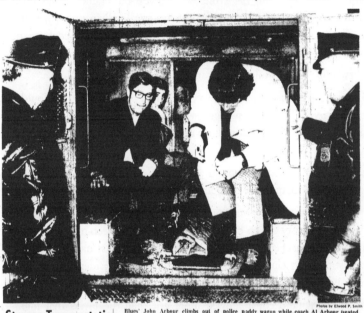

Photos by Elwood P. Smith

Owner to Sue Police

By CHARLES MONTGOMERY and ZACHARY STALBERG

Four members of the St. Louis Blues hockey team were freed on $500 bail each at 6 A. M. today after being arrested last night for assaulting police in a brief but wild brawl at the Spectrum last night in which two of the four players, four spectators and two policemen were injured.

Police said the fight, which erupted at the end of the second period in the game against the Flyers, began after fans poured beer on Blues coach Al Arbour and threw debris at the visiting players. The players charged into the stands after the spectators and later attacked police who tried to get the Blues into their dressing room, according to police.

Blues owner Sidney Salomon, Jr., said he will file suit against the city, the Philadelphia Police Department and "possibly the Flyers."

"That was the worst case of police brutality I've ever seen or heard about," said Salomon, who joined his team in Philadelphia last night after a business trip in New York. "It was worse than the riot in Chicago at the (1968 Democratic) convention."

Salomon claimed a policeman used his billy club on a player and another officer beat a player with a hockey stick.

CHARGED WITH assault and battery on police officers, disorderly conduct and conspiracy were coach Al Arbour, 39; right wing Phil Roberto, 23; defenseman John Arbour, 26, and left wing Floyd Thomson, 22. Thomson was also charged with aggravated assault and battery.

The four were arraigned on the charges during a preliminary hearing at 6 A. M. today before municipal court judge John J. Poserina who set a hearing date for 9 A. M. on Feb. 7 in City Hall court room 796.

John Arbour, who joined the team yesterday afternoon after being called up from the Minor league Denver Spurs of the Western Hockey League, claimed he was struck with a hockey stick by police. He received 40 stitches in his head. He is no relation to the coach.

Al Arbour said he was lying on the floor when he was hit by a police "billy club." He received 12 stitches in his head. Both were treated in the Blues' dressing room.

THE INJURED spectators, all of whom were treated by

Continued on Page 61

Strange Transportation—Blues' John Arbour climbs out of police paddy wagon while coach Al Arbour (seated, left), and two other St. Louis players—Phil Roberto and Floyd Thomson—await booking at police headquarters. They were arrested on a variety of charges following last night's brawl with spectators and police at the Spectrum. The Blues' owner says he will sue the Philadelphia Police Department for brutality.

Snider's Birthday Not Very Happy

By BILL FLEISCHMAN

Life begins at 40 for most people with a nice quiet party. For Flyers' owner Ed Snider, his 40th year began with a near-riot and perhaps the most dismaying loss of his National Hockey League club's five year history.

"I'm sick," Snider said in his Spectrum office last night

as friends and office workers celebrated his birthday in an atmosphere more suited to a wake.

"This was a very important game and our guys blew it," said the owner. "It's time they wake up and find out if they belong in this league. They have the ability — they need the dedication to do it. If they don't, they'll wind up no where."

"NOWHERE" may be out of the Stanley Cup playoffs. A victory over the disorganized St. Louis Blues last night would have lifted the Flyers into fourth place in the West Division. Instead, they lost 3-2 and dropped to sixth place.

The Flyers managed to lose with everything going for them — a two-goal lead, home

Continued on Page 37

Blues vs. Fans

Page 37

Blues hold sticks as battle during brawl with fans.

"Philadelphia Daily News" headline Friday, January 7, 1972.

As fate would have it, the Flyers hosted a giveaway promotion that night—free replica hockey sticks. They may have been just 18 inches long (compared to the Blues' five-foot sticks), but any weapon works in a battle. Soon enough, south end seats at the Spectrum began to resemble a scene out of "Braveheart."

The handful of cops stationed at the Spectrum found themselves outnumbered by the Blues. Sensing that the battle was going the wrong way, 16-year-old Frank Nolan ran from his seat in Section 36 to a payphone, and placed a near-hysterical call to police headquarters. Today, Nolan proudly displays the letter of commendation he later received from the city police department.

Within minutes, a bus full of Philly's finest arrived—well-armed and angry.

"It was the Blues' sticks against our batons," recalls retired patrolman Dave Moulder, who was among the first to arrive. "They were swinging wildly, and caught a couple of people pretty good. Our advantage was that they couldn't keep their balance on the concrete floor on their skates."

The cops wrestled the Blues to the ground and put a few in handcuffs. But a deal was struck with the referees to let them finish the game.

Several fans were hit in the melee, but none was seriously injured. The Blues didn't fare as well. Coach Arbour had a nasty cut on his head and his shirt had been torn off. He coached the third period in his sports jacket and sleeveless undershirt. Defenseman John Arbour (no relation) needed 40 stitches to close a gash in his head. Blues President Sidney Salomon blamed the violence on cops, calling it "the worst example of police brutality I've ever seen."

Unfortunately, the fans (and cops) showed more grit than the Flyers that night. The stirred-up Blues pushed the Flyers around in the third period and popped three shots by goalie Doug Favell to win the game. Bob Plager flashed several hand gestures to the fans as the Blues skated off the ice, thinking their tough night was over.

But it wasn't. Rizzo ordered a paddy wagon driven right into the arena runway and, as the Blues exited the ice, three of them, plus coach Arbour, were plucked and taken to the police station at 24th and Wolf Streets. They were charged with disorderly conduct and assaulting police officers. They cooled down until 6 a.m. before Snider came by to reluctantly put down $2,000 to bail them out.

"I was angry," Snider recalls, "not about the fight, so much as the game. Blowing a two-goal lead made me sick."

Soon after that, the team began replacing its pacifists with the core that became the Broad Street Bullies. You can say that the fans showed the way.

SEVEN

AMERICA'S SHOWPLACE

I wore gray polyester pants that itched in the crotch, a crisp white dress shirt with a clip-on tie and a blue blazer that looked eerily similar to my parochial elementary school uniform. I wiped down the seats with a dirty rag and numbered the rows of my section with chalk. I played the first-goal pool each hockey game and sang along with Lou Nolan as he boomed, "Flyers goal scored by number 22 . . . Rick Tocchet." I once escorted Charles Barkley to his car and fell asleep guarding Guns and Roses' instruments overnight. I hung out at the press box, walking down the cramped stairwell to the pressroom, where the Sixers used to give the reporters little bags of corn chips and Cokes. I thought it was as cool as the Zink's rolling "Errrrving and three for two."

I made $17.50 per night, and I loved every second of it. I worked as an usher at the Spectrum, America's Showplace, an arena that looked like a tuna can from the outside and smelled of cigarettes on the inside. Funny, what we remember. The smoke was as thick as morning fog in the concourse between periods. People would cram themselves along the stairways that led to the second level, puffing away a cold winter's night, and then they would return to a seat that provided a most enviable view. No, there wasn't a bad seat in the house, even way up on the skinny, six-row third level, where the hockey organ played the tune of "Let's Go Fly-ers, dent, dent, de-de-dent."

Older than the Vet, the intimate Spectrum never felt as diseased, merely outliving its usefulness to the Sixers and Flyers as the need for luxury boxes surfaced with the boom of winter sports. Oddly, the move from the Spectrum to the First Union Center affected the teams differently. The Sixers played to sparse crowds at the Spectrum, despite some of the most exciting times in the history of the franchise. Even during the championship season of 1983, the Sixers barely played to packed houses. In fact, the only sure sellouts during the regular season were against the rival Lakers or Celtics.

How strange it seems now to look back and see a team that went to the NBA Finals four times in a seven-year span struggle for attendance. I recall the Easter Sunday playoff game with barely 5,000 people in the joint and my mother buying tickets the day of Game 5 against the Nets in 1984, before which Doc said, "Mail in the stats," and the Sixers inexplicably lost. The place grew even more barren for basketball in the following years, despite Barkley and sans the yearly four or five appearances by Michael Jordan, who scored more points in the Spectrum than in any other opposing arena.

Conversely, the magic never fully followed the Flyers across Pattison Avenue. Soaring ticket prices, a less cozy building and a thawing of tradition left many pining for the old place. Somehow the new digs sanitized the Flyers, their home ice left lukewarm compared to the raucous setting of the Spectrum.

Perhaps because the Flyers first won a championship there, they staked their claim to the building. Black and orange banners hung first from the rafters; thus, Spectrum lore always began with the hockey team, literally, too, like during the Flyers' first season in 1967-68, when high winds blew part of the roof off the brand new building. The first hole appeared before an Ice Capades performance, an estimated 150 feet by 50 feet at the west end of the roof. Repairs were made but two weeks later the roof shifted again and the Flyers were forced to play their final 14 regular season games on the road. The Spectrum reopened for the playoffs but the West Division champion Flyers lost in the first round to St. Louis.

The Blues later played a part in one of the most infamous brawls in league history. At the end of the second period of a game on Jan. 6, 1972, a fan doused coach Al Arbour with beer as he argued a Flyers goal with referee John Ashley. Some 14 Blues entered the stands and a melee erupted between the players and fans, security guards and police. Over 150 nightstick-wielding police officers were dispatched to the Spectrum that night, and one officer allegedly grabbed a stick from player John Arbour and hit him with it, opening a wound that needed 40 stitches to close. Another officer was hit in the mouth with a hockey stick.

In the end, Al Arbour, John Arbour and two other players (Floyd Thomson and Phil Roberto) were arrested on charges of disorderly conduct and assault and battery on policemen, and the men weren't arraigned until 5:15 in the morning. The charges were later dropped.

However, the Spectrum could hardly go toe to toe when it comes to black-eyed incident, sans the concerts, of course. In the end, we remember the Spectrum for Kate Smith and Sign Man and the old guy who used to dance at Sixers games and the bronzed statue of Bobby Clarke scoring the winning goal and the chants, "Berr-nie . . . Berr-nie . . . Berr-nie."

We remember what transpired on the ice or the court deep into the playoff springs. Maybe that's why there's no ill will from the masses like there is regarding the Vet. Indeed, the success of sport still resides in the soul of the building, even now in its past due days as the step-child-venue home of the Phantoms and some college hoops and "B" concerts. The good times of Philly sports can be traced to the place. Think about it. The Spectrum housed three champions and seven other teams that went to the Finals. It housed Clarke and Doc and Bernie and Pelle and Hexy and Toney and Barkley and Cheeks and Moses. It housed the day the fabled USSR team walked off the ice and the night Magic Johnson jumped center for the injured Kareem Abdul-Jabbar in Game 6 of the NBA Finals.

Funny what we remember. I worked the night of Game 6 against Edmonton, perhaps the greatest hockey game ever played in Philadelphia. It was a Friday night in 1987 and the building shook, the Flyers forcing a seventh game with the Great Gretzky and the mighty Oilers. I remember the tears of Julius when he scored his 20,000th NBA point and the commemorative postcards fluttered down from the rafters and the night that he retired in 1987. Similar, the fortunes of Bob Clarke, when he scored his 1,000th career point and more postcards drifted down and later hung up his skates to an adoring, teary crowd.

In hindsight, another difference between the Spectrum and the Vet was that the arena had personality. While the Vet paled next to places like Wrigley and Fenway and Yankee Stadium, the Spectrum, though not as old and storied, could be compared to Boston Garden and Chicago Stadium and Madison Square Garden without mocking snickers.

Funny what we remember. I walked Gene Hart up to his radio perch one night and he smiled that hearty, bearded smile. I couldn't wait to tell my friends. Therein lies the true difference between the venues for us: The Vet was vast and open-air, a playground open for fun in the school-free days of the summer, while the Spectrum had the connotation of dress-up and grown-up. My friends once stole a keg of beer on the 700 Level of the Vet, rolled it noisily down the ramps and out one of the gates. They took a shopping cart from the nearby supermarket on Packer Avenue and wheeled the keg to a hiding spot in an alleyway.

At the Spectrum, we just cheered.

Philadelphia fans turn out to show their appreciation for the Stanley Cup Champions.

They are, today, middle-aged men whose bodies show the effects of too many body checks and late-night beers. The scars and broken noses they earned in their twenties contrast with the receding hairlines and widened bellies that curse them in their fifties.

"We're not very pretty to look at," concedes Bob Kelly, one of the original Broad Street Bullies. "But then, we never were."

Beautiful, no. But these Flyers from the mid-70s remain more adored than any group of athletes who ever passed through Philadelphia. Decades after they all retired, in an age when many fans know them only through scratchy recordings of Gene Hart's famous voice, they are the aging princes of our sports realm. More admired than Schmidt, more applauded than Doc, more adulated than Wilbert.

If ever a team embodied the spirit of a city, it was the Bullies. To call someone a Blue Collar athlete has become cliché, but they were strictly row homes and lunch pails. In a sports town that despises pacifism, they were, literally, a punch in the face. Sure, there were Hall of Famers among them. The most celebrated, however, were the clock-punchers and line workers, the guys who did the dirty work without complaint.

Beyond all that, they won. Two titles in a row, in 1974 and 1975. No local team had accomplished that feat since the 1948-49 Eagles. None has come close since.

The 1974 win over the Boston Bruins broke a seven-year cold spell in Philadelphia. It inspired two million people to head to South Broad Street for the Stanley Cup celebration. There are grown men in this town who can't remember their wife's birthday but can still point out the tree they hung from as the Flyers first parade passed by.

And then they did it all again.

"In the history of sports world-wide, I don't think there was ever a turnout like we got for those two parades," recalls Flyers founder Ed Snider. "The first year, everybody rationalized it as an explosion of fans who had never seen a champion. But the second year's parade was just as big, if not bigger."

Compare that with the first procession ever held for the Flyers. That was in 1967, when the brand-new franchise was welcomed to town with a march down Broad Street. Defenseman Joe Watson, an original member of the team, recalls, "There were more players walking in that parade than people watching it. Folks were screaming from the sidewalks that we'd move to Baltimore within six months."

Mayor William Green was scheduled to greet the Flyers, but failed to show. "He sent about the eighth-in-command," says Watson. "The secretary of agriculture or something."

Hockey was largely a foreign sport to Philadelphia when the Flyers debuted. The Spectrum opener drew 7,800 fans (most expensive ticket: $5.50). Local papers didn't send reporters on the road with the team. And, strangely, for most games, the radio broadcast started with the third-period faceoff. Hart and Stu Nahan often signed on explaining that the Flyers trailed 4-1, but there was plenty of time left to catch up.

Not exactly a great way to grab ratings.

Several factors helped turn that around. Bobby Clarke showed up as a 20-year-old rookie in 1969. Even as a kid, his tenacity and fierce determination put an imprimatur on the club: Losing was worse than dying. Fred "The Fog" Shero came on as coach in 1971 and did something radical for the Flyers—he installed a system. Eventually, goalie Bernie Parent would provide the final, and largest, piece of the puzzle.

Another change helped the Flyers both on the ice and at the gate. It was borne out of their humiliating playoff losses to the St. Louis Blues in 1968 and 1969. The early Flyers were a small team built on defense. The Blues, well, they were built to inflict pain.

Fighting in the NHL was different in those days. There was not the modern code, in which two tough guys agree to square off, and the battle ends when they tumble to the ice. Back then, anything went—two-on-ones, tag teams, beat-up-the-superstar. Professional wrestling had nothing on expansion-era hockey.

The Blues featured a cadre of thugs, and they routinely pounded the locals. One time, St. Louis defenseman Barclay Plager held down Ed Van Impe, while his brother, Bob, broke Van Impe's nose with a left hook. In another episode, Claude Laforge, a pacifist Flyers winger, stood watching a fight between two other players. Blues tough guy Noel Picard skated up behind Laforge and delivered a knockout sucker punch to the head.

Snider watched and fumed from his Spectrum seat.

"The Blues totally manhandled us," he recalls. "They beat us up. Afterward, I went up to (general manager) Keith Allen and said, 'I never want to see the Flyers get pushed around again. It may take a while to find scorers, but make damn sure that we find ourselves some fighters.' "

So, with their mid-round draft picks, the franchise focused on brawn. Dave Schultz and Don Saleski were picked in 1969. Bob Kelly was chosen in 1970. Burly defenseman Andre Dupont was added in a trade in 1972. Coach Shero loved them for their size. The fans loved them for something else entirely. Where outsiders saw thugs, the loyalists saw liberators, here to rescue them from years of victimization.

"The Spectrum would go nuts when we'd start brawling," says Kelly. "And then, we'd feed off the fans' energy and fight some more. Even guys who couldn't fight, like Van Impe and (Gary) Dornhoefer, got into it. Games started at 8 p.m. in those days and they'd take more than three hours because of all the scrapping. It was a real event."

Kelly, who grew up in Ontario farm country, admits he didn't even know where

Philadelphia was when the Flyers drafted him. He quickly learned that this was a city with a huge chip on its shoulder.

"Philly had been knocked as a city of losers for a long time," he says. "So, when we started shoving guys, it was like we were fighting back for the entire town. Hey, we were just young kids going out there doing a job. But the people really took to us. The Spectrum was like a zoo back then."

In this zoo, Kelly was known as "Hound." Saleski, tall and skinny, became "Big Bird," and Dupont was "Moose." (As a sign of how things have changed, Moose—at 6 feet, 200 pounds—was considered burly in his time; today he'd be undersized.) They came from exotic-sounding places like Flin Flon and Vermillion and Moose Jaw. They roamed the ice with gap-toothed grins, flowing hair (no helmets back then), and, in the case of Bill "Cowboy" Flett, a mountain man's beard.

What wasn't there to love?

The sideshow's chief attraction was Dave "The Hammer" Schultz, one of the toughest men in the history of the NHL. Schultz was not without talent—he was a decent defensive player and created enough of a cushion around himself that he scored twenty goals one season. But his main purpose was to be the surliest policeman on the ice. In 1973-74, he broke the NHL's single-season record for penalty minutes. The next season, for good measure, he shattered his own mark.

Schultz had the nastiest glare this side of Mike Tyson. His fighting style was best described as windmill—overhand lefts and rights that battered opponents and, often, unfortunate linesmen trying to pull him away. In an era when intimidation could win you a hockey game, Schultz was Godzilla out there.

The Spectrum crowd couldn't get enough. A group in Section E named itself Schultz's Army and began to wear orange-painted German military helmets. Schultz became so popular that he cut a novelty record of forlorn love, called "Penalty Box." It included the lyrics "Love is like an ice-hockey game. You get me checking and holding and hooking and then you blow the whistle on me."

Rumor has it that the song was later used by the U.S. Army to blast dictator Manuel Noriega from his Panamanian palace.

One mark of Schultz's enduring status with the fans came at the 1996 closing ceremonies for the Spectrum. All of the old heroes were there for one last skate around familiar ice. There were Hall of Famers in the building that night—Clarke, Parent, Bill Barber—but the biggest hand went to The Hammer.

The best nickname of all belonged to the team. It was first mentioned in January 1973 in a game story written by *Philadelphia Bulletin* beat writer Jack Chevalier:

"The image of the fightin' Flyers is spreading gradually around the NHL, and people are dreaming up wild nicknames. They're the Mean Machine, the Bullies of Broad Street and

Freddy's Philistines."

The *Bulletin's* copy editor showed good sense, choosing the middle nickname for that night's headline: "Broad Street Bullies Muscle Atlanta." Somehow, "Freddy's Philistines" just doesn't have that same ring.

Back in the Seventies, it was impossible for any Bully to pay for his own beer in this town. And the boys liked to go out. After games, they would head en masse to Rexy's or Kaminsky's in South Jersey. Once there, they actually mingled with the fans who adored them. Imagine walking up to a professional athlete today, offering to buy the next round, and then swapping stories for the next few hours.

"Times were different then," recalls Clarke. "Players were tighter with each other, so we hung out in a pack. All of us. And because none of us made much money, we related more to the average working man. We lived in regular neighborhoods, drove regular cars. So going out and drinking a beer with the fans after the game, well, that seemed like the most normal thing in the world."

On Shero's directive, the team formed a charity softball team, which barn-stormed in neighborhoods throughout the Delaware Valley. Clarke recalls playing a game at Havertown's Grange Field, and then walking three blocks with a dozen teammates to the home of the game's umpire. As word spread, and half of Havertown showed up with cameras and autograph books, the Flyers hung on a backyard patio for hours, cracking open beers and grilling hamburgers over a portable hibachi.

"That kind of thing never happens today," Clarke says wistfully. "Players make so much money and they're so far removed from the middle class. They don't have a bond with the fans like we did back then."

At home, the Bullies were working-class heroes. On the road, no one was offering beer, unless it was to hurl it at them. One night in Vancouver, the boys had to fight their way out of arena, and ended up being charged with inciting a riot. In Pittsburgh, fans threw so much debris that the Flyers started going into the stands until Shero pulled them back. NHL President Clarence Campbell threatened Ed Snider and Keith Allen with disciplinary action if they couldn't control their players. Snider chortled at the warning.

"The league hated us, but we were the best thing the NHL had going," says Joe Watson. "We sold out every arena on the road. The Los Angeles Kings used to sell 7,000 tickets a game, but when we came, they sold 17,000."

Attendance may have been pushed that night by a newspaper announcing the Flyers arrival in town with the warning: "The Animals are Here!" The column under the headline suggested Angelinos hide their women and children from the marauding army.

And that's how the Bullies began to see themselves, as a pillaging troupe of Visigoths. If purists considered them a scourge, they were going to make the most of it—brawling with players, officials, fans, anyone who got in their way. And the combat didn't always stop with the game's final whistle.

In an on-air interview with Gene Hart back in 1973, Dupont summed up the team's road philosophy: "We beat up their chicken forwards, win the game, drink all their beer and don't go to jail. Good times, eh?"

Loved at home, hated on the road. But the Bullies' notoriety, in a sense, masked their talent. They were more than just the cast of "Slap Shot." Clarke, through will and work ethic, became one of the greatest players in the history of the league. He was a fabulous forechecker and the best passer of his time. His creative passes mostly went to wingers Reggie Leach (possessor of a 100 mile-per-hour slap shot) and Bill Barber (one of the top power-play triggermen ever). The team also featured second-line center Rick MacLeish, a free-style floater who twice led the post-season in scoring. On defense, mainstays Van Impe, Joe Watson and Barry Ashbee routinely were named to the NHL all-star team.

The key to it all was Bernie Parent, the beloved French-Canadian goalie. During the two-year period when the Flyers won back-to-back Stanley Cups, Parent played as well as any goalie in NHL history. In his history book of the Flyers, *Full Spectrum,* Jay Greenberg described Parent's goaltending as "an art . . . economical and fluid. Parent always seemed to know where the puck had the best chance of hitting him and would patiently wait there for it."

Fans knew that if Clarke was the heart of the Bullies and Schultz was the fist, Parent was the backbone. They loved him for that, as well as his engaging Quebecois accent and the malaprops that sprinkled through his interviews. Every other car in town back then had the bumper sticker, "Only God saves more than Bernie."

Parent had been the most popular player as an original Flyer in 1967. A tearful Keith Allen, desperate for scoring, traded him in 1971, getting MacLeish in return. Bernie defected to the World Hockey Association's short-lived Philadelphia Blazers in 1972 and—when that team went belly-up—returned to the Flyers a season later. His return transformed a very good team into a title team.

"We had talent throughout the lineup," recalls Clarke, "but, really, Bernie won all those games for us. We played a low-scoring style with little margin for error. And he never made mistakes."

In the 1974 playoffs, the Flyers upset the New York Rangers and then the Boston Bruins to win Philadelphia's first world championship in seven years. Who doesn't remember Hart's classic countdown call at the end? "Ladies and Gentlemen, the Flyers are going to win the Stanley Cup, the Flyers will win the Stanley Cup, the Flyers have won the Stanley Cup."

They proved they were no fluke by beating the speedy Buffalo Sabres in 1975 to repeat. And in 1976, they went to the Finals for a third straight season, meeting the Montreal Canadiens in what hockey billed as a Good versus Evil showdown. They lost that series without Parent, who was sidelined with an injury. Truth be told, the goalie never regained his great form after neck surgery that season.

"I really believe that if Bernie hadn't been injured we could have won four or five Cups in a row," insists Snider. "The 1975-76 team was the best we ever had, except for goaltending."

During the two Cup years, Parent won 91 regular-season games, plus another 22 in the playoffs. He earned the Conn Smythe Trophy as post-season MVP both seasons.

So it was only fitting that when the city held the first parade to toast its heroes on May 20, 1974, Bernie got to ride in the lead car. As the procession headed up Broad Street that morning, Parent called a time out. He hopped out of his open convertible and, as thousands watched in wonder, sprinted into a random South Philly row home for a few moments.

Bottom line: The Playoff MVP badly needed to pee.

"The way we later heard it," laughs Snider, "the people who lived in that home didn't flush their toilet for a week."

The *Inquirer* that morning read: "Miracle Flyers Take the Cup And City Goes Wild With Joy." If anything, that headline understated the reaction.

There isn't a grown man (or woman) in town these days who won't insist he skipped school that Monday to head for the parade, which started at the Spectrum and headed up Broad Street. Police expected a crowd of several hundred thousand but, by all accounts, more than two million people showed up. The exuberant fans drank beer, carried signs ("Impeach Nixon. Vote Bernie.") and, as one fad of the time dictated, streaked naked along Broad Street. The people pawed at the Flyers riding along in open cars and tore at their clothes like they were battle-scarred Beatles.

The scene grew so frenzied that some players, including Clarke, ducked for cover and never made it to the destination of Independence Park. Those who did, arrived in varying states of sobriety—mostly because fans kept handing them bottle after bottle of champagne during the three-hour trek up Broad Street. In *Full Spectrum*, former *Daily News* beat man Greenberg wrote that checking line center Orest Kindrachuk, "had ridden in the car with the bubbly." According to Greenberg, Kindrachuk arrived at the rally, "acknowledged his introduction, flashed a triumphant peace sign and swooned backwards into his teammates' arms." To this day, Kindrachuk insists that exhaustion—not champagne—led to his woozy collapse.

One of that day's festive spectators was 15-year-old Gene Prince, who showed up for classes that Monday morning at Holy Cross High School in Delran, N.J., and quickly realized he needed to be at the celebration.

"We all just went wild," recalls Prince, who grew up to become steward of the First Union Center press box. "Literally half the school emptied out as we all hooked up rides over the Ben Franklin Bridge. You had to be there, you just had to."

Back at school the next day, Prince and hundreds of weary schoolmates got a tongue-lashing but nothing more. A year later, as the Flyers marched toward their second Stanley Cup, school officials sent a stern letter home to parents.

"The principal warned that any student who skipped school for a parade would be suspended," Prince says. "Seniors wouldn't be allowed to attend graduation. It was a pretty threatening letter. And you know what? That time, even more kids skipped out of school anyway."

The Flyers, like Catholic school officials, were better prepared the second time around. To prevent their stars from being pawed, the team replaced convertibles with flat bed trucks, which slowly rumbled down Broad Street to a rally at JFK Stadium. This time, 2.3 million fans were on hand—300,000 more than the previous May. The highlight came when Coach Shero took the microphone to tell Philadelphians, "This town is beautiful. It doesn't realize how beautiful yet, but maybe it's learning."

Being a Philadelphia fan never got better than that.

And, as sports goes, things never stay the same. Parent was injured the following season, others were swapped or retired and Shero eventually defected to the hated Rangers. Trying to hold a great team together is like trying to hold water in your hand.

But even as the Bullies dispersed, they never really left. Joe Watson was traded to the late Colorado Rockies, broke his leg, and came back to take a job with the organization. He still works for the Flyers. MacLeish was traded to the Hartford Whalers, Schultz to the Los Angeles Kings, Kelly to the Washington Capitols. Each man finished out the string, retired and returned.

Parent won a subsequent fight with alcoholism, and worked as the organization's goalie coach for a while before going into marketing. Barber spent thirty years with the Flyers, rising to head coach in 2000. He served two seasons before being dumped in one of the most sordid moments in franchise history.

And Clarke, well, he stepped off the ice and into the general manager's office in 1984. Through two lengthy terms in that job, he has learned that Bob Clarke the executive will never be beloved like Bobby Clarke the player.

Clarke has executed dozens of trades in his current post. But looking back to his days as a Bully, he says, "In those days, no Flyer ever wanted to be traded. The Canadiens had been like that. They had a saying that once you played in Montreal, you were a Canadien forever. Well, those of us from the 1970s believed that once you played as a Flyer, it was branded on your ass forever."

At last count, 13 members of the two Stanley Cup teams still live in the Delaware Valley. They swap lies and compare surgeries at occasional reunions and golf tournaments.

But if you really want to see them at their best, head for one of the two dozen games played each year by the Flyers Alumni team.

Started by Joe Watson in the late 1980s, the Alumni skate for charity against local police departments or men's league squads in rinks around the area. The boys have been aided by young blood (if you can consider guys like Bob Dailey or Ed Hospodar young blood) and buttressed by new muscle (Frank "The Animal" Bialowas, ex of the Phantoms, is a fan favorite). But the thousands of folks who attend their games come first and foremost to see the Bullies of the 1970s—Kelly and Schultz, Watson and MacLeish.

"Sometimes, we'll go out with a current or recently retired player," says Watson. "But the fans know the old guy, not the current guy."

I've had the pleasure of playing a few games with the Alumni squad as well as one against them—hey, Hound, thanks for that cross check. Clearly there is a magic between the players and this community of fans. It is not unusual to see three generations—a man in his 50s, along with his son and grandson—meekly come forward to ask an exhausted Bully for an autograph.

In the locker room before a game, the old-timers put their tape on a little more slowly and carefully than they did in their prime. Some still wear the old pads from their playing days. They gripe about the condition of the rinks and their own bodies, but, clearly, they love the moment. For a fleeting instant they are young men again, preparing for war surrounded by the allies they love.

The Alumni play it for laughs—to a degree. Every so often, a young gun-slinger tries to show up Schultz with a glove to the face. The younger man laughs, turns away and is jolted seconds later when his head bounces off the glass. Even in his fifties, The Hammer isn't going to play anyone's fool.

Crowd the crease against Joe Watson—as I once did—and you'll feel the butt-end of a stick quickly jabbed into your kidneys. "I'd move if I were you," Watson calmly said, as I doubled over in pain.

The old boys tend to let their amateur opposition stay in the game for a while. Then someone on the bench says, "Let's play now," and they knock in three or four goals to put things in perspective. Game over, they stick around for hot dogs, hand-shakes and a half keg.

Eventually, they move on to a neighborhood tavern. And suddenly it's Rexy's and the '70s all over again. Stories are told and re-told ("Remember the time Kelly and Saleski double-teamed Mike Christie . . ."). Strangers wander over to buy them a round. Hours pass.

Kelly, the Ontario farm kid who once didn't know where Philadelphia was and then never left, muses over a question of why the Broad Street Bullies became the most beloved team in the city's history.

"I think that a lot of things came together," he says. "We were more tough than fancy, which is what Philadelphia is all about. And we helped break a long losing streak for the city. We had a lot of colorful guys. And we connected with the people.

"You know, maybe the next team that wins a championship here will stay in the fans' hearts as much as we have. That would be great. We're a bunch of dinosaurs now. We're waiting for a place to go and die. You guys just aren't giving us that chance."

NINE

GOD BLESS KATE SMITH

The Flyers had many weapons during their glory years. One of the toughest was a linebacker-sized woman whose career had peaked a good 30 years earlier.

Kate Smith served as the team's good luck charm throughout the 1970s. More specifically, her 1938 recording of "God Bless America" became an unbeatable rallying cry for the boys in orange-and-black. The team's record when the song was played at the Spectrum was a phenomenal 65-13-2.

"It got to the point where we believed we had the game won as soon as Kate's voice came on," says Joe Watson. "What made it work is that the other team believed it, too."

Intimidation was not the original intent. Rather, Smith's version of the Irving Berlin standard was first pulled off the shelf to inspire a little patriotism.

Back in 1969, fans barely stirred for the pre-game National Anthem. Few people attempted to sing the "Star-Spangled Banner." Some didn't even bother to stand. At the time, the Vietnam War had split the nation, making many people self-conscious about public gestures of patriotism.

That apathy bothered Flyers vice president Lou Scheinfeld, so he decided to shake things up. Scheinfeld played several patriotic songs in an empty Spectrum to test them out. Then, on December 11, 1969, he unveiled "God Bless America" to a surprised audience before a game against the Toronto Maple Leafs.

The fans' initial reaction was unenthusiastic. Some thought that any substitute for the "Star-Spangled Banner" was sacrilegious. One so-called patriot even sent the club death threats over the issue. Other fans suggested that Kate was, well, yesterday's news.

Flyers owner Snider—who had not been told of the plan—was even more upset.

"Ed came to me when the song ended and cursed me out," recalls Scheinfeld. "His face was red and steam was coming out of his head. Of course, that was not unusual for Ed. At that point I figured, well, it was worth a try. I didn't expect to do it again."

Writers covering the team, however, noticed that the Flyers—who were in a chilling cold spell at the time—actually won a rare game after Kate blessed America. A month later, Scheinfeld played the LP again. This time, the Flyers beat Pittsburgh, 4-0. In fact, they won five of the first six games the song was used.

And so Smith became part of the lineup.

"My goal, really, was to make people miss the National Anthem by taking it away," says Scheinfeld. "But this became something much bigger. Kate Smith became our rabbit's foot."

To avoid overusing their talisman—and wearing down the grooves of their only recording—the Flyers saved "God Bless America" for key games against division rivals or play-off opponents. Fans on their way to the Spectrum would debate whether this was a night to pull Kate out of the closet.

"It was like Elvis was coming to town," recalls Flyers PA announcer Lou Nolan. "People would ask me before games, 'Is tonight the night?' Usually, I didn't even know ahead of time.

"When the moment would come, Lou would pass me the word and I'd say, 'Ladies and gentlemen, please rise and join Kate Smith . . . well, the roar would be so loud that no one heard the rest of what I had to say."

After the game there would be another roar as the center-ice scoreboard displayed the latest results: "Kate's record is now 29-3-1!"

In 1973, Scheinfeld decided to kick it up a notch. He called Kate Smith's agent, hoping to get the 66-year-old singer to perform live at the season opener against Toronto. The agent, Raymond Katz, huffed that Smith, having sung for presidents and queens, was not about to sully herself at a hockey game.

The agent didn't know, however, that Smith had an 88-year-old uncle in West Philadelphia, who regularly sent her news clips of the phenomenon. Admitting she didn't know a hockey puck from a donut, she agreed to sing at the Spectrum for $5,000, one-fifth her normal fee.

Before the opener, a red carpet was unrolled on the ice, right in front of Maple Leafs goalie (and former Flyer) Doug Favell. As Smith walked onto the carpet, Favell later said, "I knew we were in trouble."

No announcement was made. None was needed. The roar from 17,077 as the organist played the first few bars of "God Bless America" was, many agree, among the loudest ever at the old building. Smith, for her part, said, "The cheers went right through me. I've played before larger crowds, but I've never had a bigger ovation."

The Flyers, naturally, won the game, 2-0.

Smith came back to the Spectrum twice. On May 19, 1974 she performed before the Flyers 1-0 Stanley Cup-winning game against the Boston Bruins. Even the organ brought along to accompany her drew a standing ovation when it was rolled onto the ice.

There are members of that Flyers team who later argued that Kate Smith's name deserved to be etched into the Cup as much as theirs.

One year later, the Flyers booked her in advance to open the Finals again. On their way to destiny, however, they blew a three-game-to-none lead over the New York Islanders in the Stanley Cup Semi-Finals. The day before Game Seven, the club placed an emergency call. Smith, who was vacationing in Palm Beach, was happy to oblige.

So, on May 13, 1975, she sang at the Spectrum for a final time. The Islanders, having read that she was coming, tried to disarm the hefty singer. As Smith stepped onto the ice, New

*Kate Smith warbles out
another win.*

York captain Ed Westfall kissed her cheek and handed her a bouquet of flowers. Each Islander skated up to Smith and said, "God bless you." Flyers fans booed lustily.

The ploy didn't work. Smith belted out the song and the Flyers went on to win, 4-1. Afterward, Smith said, "Those Islanders tried to shake me up. But both my feet were on the ground."

Over the coming years, the Flyers scaled back playing "Good Bless America" until it eventually disappeared from the Spectrum. Smith fell into poor health and died in 1986. The Flyers moved into the First Union Center in 1996.

And that was the end of that. Until, at least May 26, 2000, when the two authors of this book hosted a radio debate on whether the song should be dusted off before Game Seven of the Flyers Eastern Conference Finals series against the New Jersey Devils. Anthem singer Lauren Hart heard the debate and decided to go with "God Bless America." Her version was inspirational.

Unfortunately, it was anything but a charm that night. In what would be his final moment as a Flyer, Eric Lindros was clocked by Devils defenseman Scott Stevens in the first period, and ended up on the ice, concussed and lying in the fetal position. The Flyers lost the game in the final moments when Patrick Elias popped a soft goal over goalie Brian Boucher's shoulder.

There have been a few reprises to the song. The most notable was at the 2001-2002 season opener, which came several weeks after the September 11 attacks on the United States. To honor America that night, Hart began singing Philadelphia's favorite song. Five lines in, the giant scoreboard at the First Union Center suddenly flashed an image of Kate Smith's 1973 appearance at the Spectrum. And together, the two women—both great talents—joined for an electronically engineered duet of "God Bless America."

From the fans to the players to the media, there wasn't a person in the building who wasn't stirred by the moment. Three decades later, Scheinfeld had succeeded in his attempt to rouse patriotism before a Flyers game.

TEN

GREAT MOMENTS 2:
THE DAY WE GOT TO BURT HOOTON

They are highly paid professionals, supposedly deaf to the abuse from the cheap seats, impervious to the invective. You can yell at a player all you want. Chances are, he doesn't hear you. If he does, chances are he's snickering inside. You're not getting to him.

But on Oct. 7, 1977, we got to one. On that night, Phillies fans performed a magical feat by making a major league pitcher forget how to grip a baseball. We chased Burt Hooton from the mound as effectively as Mike Schmidt or Greg Luzinski ever had. We turned a steady veteran into a quivering mass of Jell-O.

"Philadelphians did that day what Philadelphians do best," recalls the great local baseball writer Jayson Stark. "They took a nice, normal human being and made him wish he did something else for a living. The fans actually won a post-season game for the team, except that real life eventually entered and this being Philadelphia . . . ."

More about real life in a minute. First, a little background.

The Phils and Los Angeles Dodgers were tied at one game each in the best-of-five National League Championship Series. The playoffs headed for Philadelphia, where 63,719 raucous fans packed Veterans Stadium.

Hooton, winner of 12 games that season, started Game 3 for the Dodgers. He got through the first inning in order, and was helped by two Dodgers runs in the top of the second off Phils starter Larry Christenson.

Then came the bottom of the second. Luzinski singled to left, then Hooton got Richie Hebner on a force to short, and struck out Garry Maddox. Catcher Bob Boone singled to left. Two outs, first and second.

Up came second baseman Ted Sizemore. Hooton threw one a few inches low and then unfurled a high floater that nearly escaped catcher Steve Yeager. The Vet crowd began to sense something. A few catcalls echoed down from the 700 Level as Hooton threw another one inside and then walked Sizemore on four straight.

Still, even with bases loaded, no one expected much with the pitcher, Christenson up next. Hooton got two quick strikes, wasted a pitch and then nearly ended the inning with a fastball that Christenson just fouled back. Then another ball, then another, and suddenly the count was full.

The fans picked it up. As Hooton wound up, the decibel level approached that of an orchestra of power tools. As a borderline pitch was called ball four by umpire Harry Wendelstedt, the Vet went berserk. Hebner trotted home with the first run and the meltdown was on.

"The fans were standing up, waving towels, screaming," recalls former Phils shortstop Larry Bowa. "They knew they were getting to Hooton, so they picked it up even more. You could tell that Hooton was hearing it. You could see the fear in his eyes."

The clatter of noise would start each time Yeager tossed the ball back to the pitcher. It would swell as Hooton went into his stretch. Each missed pitch created a crescendo—cheers, boos, heckles, hoots, insults. Hooton began to visibly twitch.

He walked outfielder Bake McBride on six pitches. Another run. Three straight walks. More noise—think an army of snare drums.

"It was the loudest I ever heard the Vet," says Bowa. "Looking back, I think it affected the umpire as much as Hooton. He threw some borderline pitches that could have gone either way. The crowd got the umpire thinking that the guy couldn't throw a strike."

As Bowa came up next, the Dodgers bullpen was in a frenzy. Hooton kept looking into the dugout, essentially begging Dodgers manager Tommy Lasorda to save him from the barbarians. He walked around the mound, and the fans jeered him for stalling. Two Dodgers infielders came over to calm him down.

"I knew I wasn't going to swing until he had two strikes on me," recalls Bowa. "I mean, he was out of it. His eyes looked misty. In all my years, I've never seen a pitcher lose his concentration and confidence in one inning the way he did that [day].

"The fans had beaten him."

Hooton walked Bowa on five pitches. Four straight walks, three runs in. The meltdown was complete. Lasorda came out to rescue his shaken pitcher. He might as well have brought a straight jacket. Hooton threw his glove against the dugout wall. That, too, was high and outside.

The Phils later added two more runs on Dodgers errors and carried a 5-3 lead into the bottom of the ninth.

And that's where the story should end. Except, as Stark points out, "This is Philadelphia."

When Phils closer Gene Garber retired the first two Dodgers in the inning, the crowd, knowing Steve Carlton would start Game 4, was on its feet and ready to celebrate. No one really much worried when pinch hitter Vic Davalillo then beat out a drag bunt.

But fate—in the form of manager Danny Ozark's stupidity—came to bite us on the butt. Invariably, Ozark made one lineup move in the ninth, inserting defensive replacement Jerry Martin for leftfielder Greg Luzinski. Except on this [day], he didn't. The next hitter, Manny Mota, hit a long fly that bounded off Luzinski's glove. The return throw got away from Sizemore, allowing Davalillo to score and Mota to reach third.

Then Davey Lopes smashed a ground ball that caromed off Schmidt's knee to Bowa's glove. The shortstop's quick throw seemed to nip Lopes, but umpire Bruce Froemming called him safe. Instead of being over, the game was tied.

"I'm telling you now, he was out," Bowa still insists. "The ump anticipated that Lopes was so fast he'd be safe, but I got him."

Garber's wild pickoff throw sent Lopes to second. Every Phillies fan knew what would follow. Sure enough, Bill Russell's single scored Lopes. The Phils lost, 6-5. It was Black Friday.

"I still remember the faces of people filing out of the stadium that day," recalls Stark, "knowing this was all leading to another Philadelphia crash into the iceberg."

Later, Bill Conlin of the *Daily News* would compare the disaster to the 1964 Phillies collapse, "except that this took 10 minutes instead of 10 games."

The Phils eventually lost the series and Ozark was forever vilified as a fool. He didn't do his job that night.

But the fans, they did their job splendidly.

ELEVEN

MY FAVORITE SEASON: THE 2000-2001 SIXERS

Allen Iverson steps over Laker pug Tyron Lue with an emphatic foot in "yo' face," a sort of Reebok requital, and Boo's living room erupts. Hoots and hollers and hoorays in the form of inaudible grunts and goofy faces by grown men who have been friends for a scary long time, now slugging each other in the arm and chest with a ferocity that makes Boo's wife in the other room chastise, "Play nice."

I freeze the moment. There's Tooch, the finance executive prancing like he once did drunk as a toad on Bourbon Street, though he supposedly hates pro basketball. Tooch preaches that all sport stinks now, though his sentiment coincides with the birth of his second daughter and the move into his dream home and his middle thirties and the all-encompassing second gear of fatherhood and adulthood. Tooch's glee now, however, is sober and honest, like Joe Ben's. And Joe Ben is the ultimate fan, who wears the AI jersey and the AI sneakers and prefers idolatry, because if he paid attention to the nonsense that accompanies sport it would sour him forever. Plus, maybe this way, he gets to keep that part of him alive in one facet of his life, you know, when you were 12 and life, and particularly sport, was truly a cup of cherry water ice.

Boo does a jig, and it looks funny, because for starters, he's 6-2 and 250 pounds with wavy white hair and pink skin, depicting the look of a handsome Irish gentleman 10 years older than he really is, and he's wearing tube socks and the socks are parting from his toes, flopping like two white tails. Boo has always been a big Sixers fan, so his kid delight isn't novel, except, I guess, if you snap the entire picture of Boo, who grew up on tiny Colorado Street as the youngest of five boys whose father died tragically young, who became a lawyer, married his college sweetheart, fathered three adorable children, bought the sprawling home in Delaware County and achieved his main goal in life—reaching the bosom of Americana.

Jimmy Head, Boo's brother John's longtime friend whom Boo and the rest of us adopted to play quasi sage and basketball teammate, is over ten years older than everyone else. And doesn't everybody need an older friend who offers perspective on the '64 Phillies? Ultimately, what drew Head to the group is what has always bonded all of us, especially my cousin Joey and I: The moment that plays before us on Boo's high-def, widescreen television.

Joey, my Aunt Cookie's only son, is three and a half years older than me, and has always been my big brother, perfectly filling out the triad of siblings that includes my sister, Christina. Now Joey and I have watched countless games together, shared countless conversations on the fate of the Birds and Sixers and Phils and Flyers, shared countless sports sections, with each of taking a sliver of the paper. "You take Eagles first," he'd say, "I'll take Sixers." It's like the story of many brothers, playing countless games of basketball, remembering the first time I actually

The toughest "little kid" you ever saw.

beat him one on one, concocting indoor sports like football on your knees with the pillow off the couch and full-court Puff basketball with a wire coathanger circled into a rim at the top of facing doorways. I remember when I unwrapped a Steve Carlton baseball card and he cried and I gave it to him, and later, when he gave me his entire collection because I still liked that sort of thing and he had many dates. I remember some years later, when we went through our growing pains of young adulthood, and the winds of life pulled out apart to put us back closer, sport always kept us talking.

So I freeze the moment for a purpose, because I know this scene in Boo's living room plays throughout our village on this night of the Sixers' victory over the Lakers in Game One of the 2000-2001 NBA Finals. Only the characters are different, and if the characters aren't present, they will call, as did the missing members of our crew, Vinny and Bobby and John and Andy. Because being a Philadelphian, particularly a male Philadelphian, means bonding with your people over nights like this one.

The revelry continues deep into this June night. When I arrive back into the city, accompanied by a joyous Rob Charry on WIP and a host of beeping cars with their Sixers flags flapping on either side, people celebrate on Broad Street and South Street, and they are well behaved and happy. My cell phone rings. It's Pat Croce, our tribal leader, our kindred spirit who symbolizes Sports Philadelphia because he is one of us and he is the architect of this night. "We can win this!" Pat says. "Wasn't that game amazing? Life is great, bro!"

Pat is in Los Angeles, celebrating with his wife, Diane, and his kids, Kelly and Michael, and the team and Pat's vast number of cronies. Philadelphia's First Family—I think of them all, out there, trying to bring something special back home. The fact that the Sixers later lost to the mighty Lakers, I believe, meant little because that night of Game One culminated a fascinating and uplifting basketball season that galvanized a city in dire need of galvanization.

Glen Macnow said it best of the 2000-2001 Sixers: "They represent the spirit of Philadelphia like no other team, bringing together people of different race and creed and social standing. They made us one."

I still find it odd how that Sixers team became mainstream, say, when compared with great teams of the past. The Sixers of the '80s were spectacular, featuring Hall of Fame players like Doc and Moses and Toney and Cheeks, and later, Barkley. They were truly great teams, and they played an elegant, riveting style of basketball. Yet, the fervor from this town wasn't close, even during the championship season in '83. During this decade of great hoops, the only sure Spectrum sellouts were against the Celtics or Lakers and several playoff games didn't sell out, while a ticket during the 2000-2001 run at the larger First Union Center was a major score.

It's true that the NBA didn't reach its height in popularity until the '90s and Michael Jordan, especially among young people, but the game reached the dark ages here during that time frame. Maybe fans were hoops starved because of the Shawn Bradleys and Jerry Stackhouses and Doug Moes and they found the Sixers' success refreshing, or maybe the

2000-2001 Sixers simply embodied Philadelphia better than any other team, beginning with Allen Iverson.

Let's face it. We're an underdog town. We've always been, before Balboa and Balboa's statue, which simply engrained the stereotype. It's in the soil. Think about it. While Los Angeles embraces glitz and New York greatness, we do the dog. It's our thing, and so how could we not fall in love with Allen Iverson? From his size to his background to his mangy look, AI barks the little kid who could. Sure he infuriates no end, but from the beginning there has always been something that connects him to us. From the moment we first saw him knife through the NBA's giants, score, boomerang to ground and get up, bruised and bloodied, we were in love.

Plus, I truly believe we don't like easy because easy makes us uncomfortable. We are the type who likes chaos, and nobody does chaos like AI. That year began after a tumultuous off-season that included public awareness of Iverson's terrible timeliness and practice habits and a near trade to the Pistons. The four-team deal that included the Lakers, Hornets and Pistons would have occurred had it not been for a trade kicker in Matt Geiger's contract.

So we gathered on October 2 in the concourse of the First Union Center for Sixers media day, and Iverson delivered a curse-filled, rambling address that would be the start of the healing process. "I don't want to go to the Lakers, I don't want to go to a so-called contender, I want to be here," Iverson professed that day. He also said he was "embarrassed" by all of the trade talk and vowed that it would be different during the coming year.

I remembered the day being messy. Iverson sat like an angry defendant as reporters thundered away at him. He made faces, some defiant, some pitiful, and he wiggled in his chair and he rolled his eyes and he sulked and he cursed out of incredulousness and callousness, and there were still more questions. Why was he late 60 times? Or was it 70? Could he get along with Coach Brown? Did he want to be traded? Would he grow up? Did he deserve to be captain? And what about his rap album that was due out soon? Did he think the off-color lyrics appropriate? What about his teammates? Did he respect his teammates? How could he respect your teammates if he's late 60 times? Or was it 70? Why doesn't he get practice? Did he know he almost got traded?

The faces crowded him. They kept saying his name—over and over, like this was a bad dream and the hot lights baked his brain: "Allen? Allen? Allen? Allen?" You knew he wanted to hold his ears and close his eyes. Kindly Sixers PR Director Karen Frascona finally stopped the press conference and Iverson harrumphed away.

In the end, it was probably good for Iverson. The questions were all valid, mind you, and maybe that's what helped him have his best season ever as a pro. Really, after that nasty, contentious start, it was storybook for Iverson. He played out of his mind, leading the Sixers to a 41-14 start. He stole the show at the All-Star Game back in his stomping ground of D.C., and was named MVP. After being awarded the trophy, he called out for Brown, longing for his coach's presence like a child for a parent after a first good report card. That night under the national spotlight, the sporting world fell in love with Allen Iverson, and we watched in

Philadelphia beaming.

That season, Iverson truly gained his mass popularity. Honestly, it could have gone either way for AI. He could have been discarded, sent wandering through the league by the Sixers, a faded, jaded star eaten up by his own misdoings, labeled a loser Latrell. Lots of guys endured that path, but whether it was Croce's tough love or Brown's badgering or his own "bleep y'all" pride, he enjoyed a year that will always define his career. The trouble around him since then—the "poom-poom" pants and the "practice, we're talkin' 'bout practice" thing and the shot heard in Old City—will never overshadow the image of Iverson with his hand cupping his ear to the crowd. For what transpired that spring was perhaps the greatest post-season individual performance in the history of Philadelphia sports.

Iverson's body broken and beaten, his legs milled like peppercorns, he averaged an incredible 32.9 points, 4.7 rebounds, 6.1 assists and 2.4 steals in the post-season, while playing a staggering 46.2 minutes per game. After the Sixers lost their playoff opener to scary Indiana, he scored 45 in Game 2 to make for a blowout victory and set the stage for three straight wins. He was simply dynamic in the Toronto series, going off for 54 in Game 2 after the Sixers again lost the opener and 52 in Game 5 with the series tied. He hit eight treys in that game, and then came back with 16 assists in the decisive Game 7 against the Raptors.

Vince Carter and Iverson entered that series on similar ground, both rising stars in the league. But while Iverson wowed, Carter whimpered, literally, begging out of Game 5 with a bum leg and missing a potential series-winning shot on a good look in Game 7. Interesting how Carter's career halted thereafter, Vinsanity becoming Inanity, the player haunted by cries of softness and selfishness.

Iverson fell hard on his bony tailbone in that Game 7, and the injury plagued through the Milwaukee series. But when it counted most, with the Sixers coming off an ugly blowout loss in Milwaukee in Game 6, Iverson scored 44 in the decisive Game 7 that Sunday night at First Union Center. He circled the court that night, calling out to the fans, his hand cupped to his ear, and the building sang like no other I've been, including Chicago Stadium after the Bulls won their first title.

We loved him then, and in fairness, he was the same man he's always been—diabolically lost in a world of self, his ego and insecurities running amok, his genius clashing with his old school ways and his fear of success. Say what you want, however, Larry Brown could coach basketball. And while Larry's legacy in Philadelphia ultimately became stained by a traitorous exit, Brown indeed helped resurrect a wounded franchise.

Brown's defense first mantra was performed with a bloodlust by his team of scrappers. Ultimately, the town fell for their true grit, because their grit transformed into transition buckets and quite exhilarating play, even if they were a true bombadier away from seriously threatening the Lakers.

Brown's bungling of his top draft picks and free agent acquisitions didn't really come to fruition until the long term appeared. For the short term, he managed quite well with a hearty bunch that grew together, led by the elbows-first and knee-scraped George Lynch and selfless point guard Eric Snow and homegrown hero Aaron McKie, who at that time in his career could nail the open baseline trey. McKie, and I swear it's a sin, has never been the same player since, his body worn to the bone, selling him out for those courageous one-arm and one-leg performances against the Bucks and Lakers.

McKie, Lynch, Snow, Iverson all played through the creaks and tears and the various breaks without so much as a whine or bellyache, and how could we not respect that? How could we not absolutely adore that? Our fan mantra is that you're playing if you're not hurting, or donating a limb, so this team was alter ego in full bandage.

They hustled and harassed, and they sweated like only Moses used to sweat, that sweat that looks like it emanates from the Trevi Fountain, or a spigot. Philly people like to say spigot, see? We're earthy folk, and spigot is better than faucet, and when our athletes sweat, we want to see them drip. Everything about this team we embraced, including the much-debated trade for Dikembe Mutombo.

Even those who were staunchly against the deal that broke up a 41-14 team, and sent popular Theo Ratliff and Toni Kukoc to Atlanta, for the big African admired the moxie of Brown and GM Billy King. In a town seemingly cursed to finish second or last, the Sixers rolled the dice for a title, hoping a true center would give them a boxer's chance against Shaq and the Lakers. I remember being ecstatic about the news, especially with Ratliff's constant injury struggles, and I was speaking one night in a Center City cigar lounge with King, who proclaimed with a smile that matched the gleam off his finely manicured bald head, "We're going for it!" Truthfully, I admired that mentality. Though Mutombo later equaled the fitful Keith Van Horn, I still contend that the Sixers needed him to beat Toronto and Milwaukee and that he assimilated quite well here, offering some entertaining deep-throated guarantees and finger wags following blocked shots.

And while Brown should have lost the notion of point guard Larry Hughes and listened to King about Dirk Nowitzki or to player personnel director Tony DiLeo about Paul Pierce, and Brown should have listened to the two about subsequent moves thereafter, that was a team that played in his mirror image. They were clockpunchers who epitomized the sum of all parts, and played until they literally dropped.

I end this story where I began, which is on the subject of bonding and the root of why we root. I am on a private jet over, I believe, Ohio, and the beers are flowing, actually chasing shots of black Sambuca. It's a late Saturday afternoon, and the Sixers have closed out Indiana in the first round, and Pat Croce breathes in a moment. He's staring ahead at no one in particular, celebration around him, and he's just grinning. It's one of those he's so happy he can't stop grinning deals. So he's grinning this half-moon smile, and I swear I can read his thoughts. I'm right.

"Isn't this cool, bro?" he says, with the sparkling honesty of youth. "I mean, sometimes I can't believe this is happening. That we're here, in a private plane, after watching our team—the Sixers—win in the playoffs. And I'm President. And everybody's here, my wife and Bator and my friends. I don't want to wake up."

That is why we love Pat Croce, because he still gets wowed by the moment and he wants to share that moment with the people he loves and he really does believe in the triumph of goodness in life. Because he earned the right to be President of the Sixers and sit in that private jet through hard work, and doesn't wish a second of it away with petty thoughts or take any of it for granted. Because if any of us reached that lofty height in life we'd act the same way and invite the neighborhood and the neighborhood's kid to be a part of it somehow. We'd enjoy every millisecond of the journey, too, cherish the memory and offer thanks to our maker for the opportunity.

Recently, I asked Pat his favorite moments from that season. "Winning Game 7 against the Bucks," he said. "I remember standing there at center court with Diane and the trophy and the fans . . . they were wild! I still get chills."

Even after his association with the team ended, sourly to be honest, Croce remembers that season with all good thoughts. He remembers walking the railing outside the suite level to a chanting crowd and climbing the Walt Whitman Bridge, the news helicopters buzzing about as he helped hang the Go Sixers banner across it.

From that season on, I'll argue the power of positive thoughts with anyone. Truly, I admire Pat Croce for how he handles success as much as I admire his path to success. I've been lucky. In the past years, he has let me cheat off his blueprint for life, and I am especially grateful. He has become a mentor and a dear friend and, dare I blush, a hero. But I'll always remember that day and how he grinned with marvel. We later landed at Atlantic Aviation and caravanned to a restaurant in the heart of South Philadelphia named Mangia to see our good friend Angelo Borgese and continue the celebration over good food and wine. Pat left briefly for some air, and walked along Oregon Avenue. Slowly, the neighborhood spilled out and followed him, the goateed pied piper regaling with the recount of the afternoon's game. Fifty people, maybe more, surrounded him, and they felt like they were in Indianapolis. Mostly, they felt included.

Ah, there it is!

What made these Sixers so lovable, besides Allen Iverson's play and the rest of the team's grit, was the notion that we were all a part of it. So many teams play that card, that card I despise, us against the world, including our fans. "After all," they'd say, "there was that time you booed us." But the Sixers were truly inclusive, the city's team, a notion that Croce fostered and everyone else—Brown, King, Iverson, McKie, Dave Coskey, Allen Lumpkin, the marketing staff, the Dance Team, the guards at the First Union Center—believed with all of their hearts.

I know that scene in Boo's living room happened all over the Delaware Valley. I looked at my cousin Joey after AI stomped over Lue, and we smiled. Earlier that year, we sat in Pat's box for a game. It was just the three of us in there, a rare quiet night, and Joey grinned the way Pat grinned in the plane. "Isn't this cool?" he said. "We used to sneak into the Spectrum, now we're sitting in the owner's box."

In the end, isn't that why we watch? Sport is a memory maker and a bond fortifier, and sport makes guys in their thirties act giddy and foolish and remember life when it was simpler, and isn't that the point?

"They got labeled 'America's Team.' Our players didn't much like that. Then, the Cowboys started being televised everywhere, every week. You'd see them on TV with the cheerleaders and that Coach Landry and their smug attitudes. That stuff made us hate them more.

"You know, I've got nephews here in Philadelphia who became Cowboys fans. That's ridiculous. I try not to invite them to my house."

—Harold Carmichael, American hero

The worst year of Harold Carmichael's life? It came in 1984, when he was released after 13 glorious seasons in the green-and-silver. Not quite ready to give up on the game, the four-time Pro Bowl receiver waited for an offer from another NFL team. It finally came—from Dallas.

Carmichael assured himself that, if the Birds didn't want him any more, he might as well play for their enemy. And he was okay, until . . .

". . . until I had to put my head between those stars on that helmet. I looked in the mirror and said, 'Harold, this is too much.' Sure, (Eagles coach) Marion Campbell had cut me, but it still felt disloyal."

Carmichael spent a half-season in Dallas, playing in just two games. When he was released, he says, "I packed up as soon as I could and got out of there. I never looked back."

Sports rivalries may not mean as much as used to (just witness Allen Iverson showing up for a home game in a Boston Celtics jersey!). But, Carmichael came to learn, you spend a few years in Philadelphia and you'll discover that the Cowboys are held in the same esteem as the tax man, the prime minister of Iraq and Beelzebub himself.

No franchise draws venom from the Philadelphia faithful like the Cowboys. Fools may regard them as America's Team—a name treasonously bestowed by a local, NFL Films Vice President Bob Ryan. But in our town, where America really started, they are Hell's Team. They will always be known to us as the Damn Cowboys, the Stinkin' Cowboys, the Bleepin' Cowboys.

Stand by the Delaware River some night and whisper over the water the word, "Dallas."

". . . Sucks," the echo comes back.

Funny because, by all logic, the Eagles' top rival should be the New York Giants. The two teams play at opposite ends of the New Jersey Turnpike. They've been scuffling in the same division since 1933, when the Giants welcomed the Eagles into the league with a 56-0 pasting. They've inspired classic moments—from Chuck Bednarik's forearm shiver on Frank Gifford to Herm Edwards's Miracle at the Meadowlands.

But while the Giants may have sparked a few 700 Level brawls over the years, they never filled Judge Seamus McCaffery's Vet Stadium courtroom like the Dallas Cowboys.

So how did it come to be that way? Why would a team stationed 1,500 miles away become the Big Poison for Eagles fans? Why not the Giants or, for that matter, the team at the other end of the Amtrak Corridor, the Washington Redskins?

To understand our loathing, you have to look at several factors. Start by considering the dreadful years between 1968 and 1978.

Eleven seasons.

Twenty-two match-ups.

Twenty Eagles losses.

Several, by the way, along the lines of a 45-13 pasting in Dallas back in 1968. Eagles coach Joe Kuharich plotted to stop the Cowboys' potent ground game by employing a soft, three-man rush. Tom Landry countered by ordering quarterback Don Meredith to keep passing the ball—even with the Cowboys up 25 points with two minutes to play.

"Well," Kuharich offered afterward, "I forced Landry to change his game plan. I didn't change mine."

Those were hideous years for Birds fans. The team went a decade without a winning record. Meanwhile, the Cowboys appeared in four Super Bowls, winning two. The better the Cowboys played, the worse the Eagles seemed—and the more we all simmered in hatred and frustration.

Most of us, anyway. Eleven years of bad football takes its toll. While faithful Birds fans dreamt of long-term revenge, others just surrendered. The weak of character succumbed to the dark side. Kid brothers and schoolyard wimps declared themselves loyal to the infamous Lone Star helmet. Those who couldn't hang tough instead bought into "Roger Staubach, American icon." Contrarians among us adorned their bedroom walls with posters of those silicon enhanced cheerleaders.

In short, they bailed.

Back then, the Cowboys Broadcast System (also known as CBS) stuck those starred hats in our faces nearly every Sunday at 4 p.m. When the NFL's draconian rules blacked out the Eagles, the hearty of character listened to the game on radio or went outside to rake leaves. The weak-willed genuflected to Bob Lilly.

Even today—an era in which the good guys routinely pound the Boys—the root of the rivalry remains the same: The hatred is less between the cities or the players. It is between Eagles and Cowboys fans here *in the Delaware Valley!* Consider a 2002 poll conducted by ESPN. The survey found the Cowboys to be the most-hated NFL franchise among Metro Philadelphia sports fans. They were also, however, second in popularity, behind only the

Eagles. A full eight percent of football fans in this area said they prefer Dallas.

One in 12. The fungus among us.

"Who knows why?" ponders Tom Brookshier, a hard-hitting cornerback for the Birds in the NFL's prehistoric days. "I've heard it all—the helmets, the cheerleaders, the appeal of guys like Staubach and Meredith and (Bullet Bob) Hayes."

Brookshier parlayed his seven-year NFL career into a longer one as a broadcaster. For years, he was partnered with Pat Summerall at CBS—often announcing Cowboys games. "In that sense," he concedes, "I guess I'm to blame as well."

Actually, Brookshier was there as a player at the beginning of the rivalry. In 1960, the Eagles won the NFL title. The Cowboys, an expansion team, went 0-11-1. But you wouldn't have predicted that watching the season's second game.

"We went down there to play in front of 18,000 fans," Brookshier recalls. "The Cowboys were brand new. Their players didn't even know each other. I swear I saw two of their guys introduce themselves to each other and shake hands.

"They're shuffling in three quarterbacks, a new one every play. We're laughing, thinking we're gonna win huge."

It didn't turn out that way. The Eagles trailed most of the game before a late bomb from Sonny Jurgensen to Tommy McDonald gave them a 27-25 win. The real hero of the game was Eagles safety Bobby Freeman, who blocked two of Dallas kicker Fred Cone's extra point attempts, the second one with his face.

"Broke his nose, blackened his eye, split open his whole face," recalls Brookshier. "Best play he ever made."

It wasn't the last time an Eagle had his face busted up by the Cowboys.

On November 6, 1966, Eagles halfback Timmy Brown broke two kickoff returns for touchdowns against the Cowboys, tying an NFL mark. Cornerback Aaron Martin also returned a punt all the way, as the Birds won, 24-23.

One year later in Dallas, Brown ran out on a pass pattern, turned around and watched Norm Snead's throw sail over his head. As Brown slowed to a stop, Cowboys linebacker Lee Roy Jordan slammed his elbow into Brown's face. The elusive halfback crumpled, his brain concussed, his jaw dislocated, his teeth scattering on the ground. Wrote the *Inquirer's* Frank Dolson, "The elbow cleared out Timmy's teeth the way a bowling ball knocks down a row of pins."

Jordan drew a 15-yard penalty, but no matter. The Eagles had lost their best weapon. The Cowboys won, 38-17.

Heading home that night, the Eagles' chartered plane had mechanical problems and was forced to land in Wichita, Kansas. The players were told to wait at the airport gate, but Brown—confused by the concussion or the pain medication he was given—wandered off. Thinking he was already back in Philadelphia, he hailed a cab.

When it came time to re-board, Brown's teammates realized he was missing and began frantically searching the airport. The cabbie, baffled by Brown's instructions ("Take me to Germantown Pike"), called the cops. As the legend goes, the Wichita police, who had not been told of the Eagles emergency landing, didn't buy Brown's story of being an NFL player. They called local mental institutions to see if a patient had escaped.

A similar Dallas dirty trick occurred 12 years later. The six-foot-eight Carmichael developed into a star for the Eagles and eventually set the NFL record for consecutive games with a pass reception. The streak was at 127 games on Dec. 8, 1979 when Carmichael ran a routine sideline pattern early in a contest against the Cowboys.

"The pass was overthrown," Carmichael recalls, "so I started to slow down. I was about to step out of bounds, looking up at the ball, when Dennis Thurman nailed me. He knocked me on my butt, and I hit a nerve or something. It took me a while to get up. After that, I could run straight, but I couldn't cut."

The Cowboys cornerbacks realized that the big man couldn't move laterally, so they crowded up to play bump-and-run. Carmichael couldn't push past them. His record receiving streak ended. The Eagles lost the game.

Was Thurman's hit a cheap shot? Carmichael defers, calling it "borderline." (He does boast that he "got Thurman back" a few times over the years on cut blocks.) Certainly, Eagles fans saw it for the dirty football that it was. Another brick in the wall of our odium.

Through the years, Dallas coach Tom Landry seemed to particularly enjoy rubbing the Eagles' noses in it. Consider, for example, a 56-7 Eagles loss in 1966. Up by a mere 42 points with two minutes to go, Landry replaced starting quarterback Don Meredith with backup Jerry Rhome, just so that Rhome could get his chance to throw a touchdown pass against Philadelphia's porous defense.

"Landry was such a huge factor in the rivalry," says Brookshier. "Players come and go, but he was there forever (actually 29 years). And Philadelphia fans could never stomach Landry. He was such a dry, close-to-the-vest type. Sort of a plastic man. Definitely not a Philly guy."

While Dallas had its coaching giant through the '60s and '70s, Philadelphia trotted out a quintet of midgets—Nick Skorich, Kuharich, Jerry Williams, Ed Khayat and Mike McCormack. Eagles players would look at their own coaching staff, gaze across the field at Landry, and know they entered the contest trying to crawl out of a hole.

"When I got to Philadelphia, we'd play hard, but we could just never beat them," says Stan Walters, the huge offensive tackle who played for the Eagles from 1975 to 1983. "A fluky play would cost us the game, or Staubach would do something at the end to steal it. The difference was that the Eagles were hoping to win, but the Cowboys expected to win."

The turnaround began in 1976, when Dick Vermeil was hired as Eagles coach. From his first training camp, Vermeil set his sights on Dallas. He told his players that nothing else mattered until they could smite their evil rival.

"We would run wind sprints," Walters recalls, "and then Vermeil said we needed to run an extra half-hour to catch up to the Cowboys. We'd stay another hour at practice, focusing on Dallas. He told us one time, 'Gentlemen, we're going into uncharted space.' We knew what the target was."

Vermeil still lost to Landry the first six times they played. After each loss, he would face his team and ask, "What is it going to take to beat Dallas?" No one seemed to have an answer.

But, by 1979, the worm had turned. On Nov. 11—the evening before a Monday Night Football battle in Texas—Vermeil called his troops together at the team hotel. He started by going back over all the losses. Then he asked the proverbial question: "What's it going to take to beat Dallas?"

He looked around the room. Silence.

"Gentlemen," he said, "it's very simple. Here's what it's going to take to beat Dallas—just 24 more hours."

Vermeil then turned on his heels and left the room.

The players sat in silence for a moment. Then middle linebacker Bill Bergey, the team's vocal defensive leader, echoed his coach.

"Now is the time," Bergey said. "Tomorrow night is the time."

The players joined in, chanting, "It's our time. It's our time." The chorus, Walters recalls, grew so loud that he figured it could be heard at Texas Stadium more than a mile away.

The Birds went out the next night and whipped Dallas, 31-21. Starting quarterback Ron Jaworski got hurt, so backup John Walton came in and hit Charles Smith with a long touchdown. Tony Franklin set a team record with a 59-yard field goal.

Things had changed. It was, indeed, our time.

The Eagles only split their next eight games with Dallas. But they convinced themselves that the mountain was scaleable. No longer were the Cowboys invincible.

The all-time highlight, of course, came on January 11, 1981, in the NFC championship game.

The windchill factor was minus-17 in Philadelphia that afternoon, with gusts up to 30 miles per hour. Television footage of the game shows 70,000 Eagles fans, most wearing green-and-white Santa hats, huddled under blankets, their breath steaming through mufflers and mackinaws. The cold, however, does not chill their manic enthusiasm. Even on the opening kickoff, Brookshier and Summerall have to raise their voices to be heard over the chant: "E-A-G-L-E-S—EAGLES!!!"

"When we came out and heard the unbelievable noise from the fans," Jaworski said years later, "that's when I *knew*—and I really mean knew—we were going to win."

The Cowboys go three-and-out on their opening drive—highlighted by Eagles linebacker John Bunting snuffing Ron Springs for a six-yard loss on a screen pass. Danny White's weak punt lands at the Dallas 42-yard line. Jaworski throws one away on the Eagles first play from scrimmage, and then . . .

". . . I-Right-46-Slant," recalls Walters. "A play designed to go behind me (the left tackle) from the I-formation. It didn't work out that way, though, did it?"

Jaworski hands running back Wilbert Montgomery the ball five yards behind the line of scrimmage. Montgomery starts to his left, toward Walters, but then spots an opening to the right, where tackle Jerry Sizemore has just pancaked Dallas defensive end Ed "Too Tall" Jones.

On television, Summerall, understated as always, calls the play:

"Wilbert Montgomery now as the deep back in the 'I.' And it's Montgomery with the ball. Montgomery, with room to go, and he might go. Wilbert Montgomery, touchdown, Philadelphia."

Just 29 words to describe our greatest moment in the rivalry.

The Cowboys replaced their middle linebacker with a safety on the play, expecting Vermeil to follow through on his pre-game vow to pass on early downs. The call caught Dallas' defenders flat, and you see them flailing backwards as Montgomery sprints by. You see something else: Most of the other Eagles gallop down the field behind Montgomery. They dash right through the end zone, and into a security tunnel, where they are engulfed by cops and joyous Vet Stadium workers.

The Play is indelibly etched into the minds of all Eagles fans who watched it. The other lingering memory from that frigid afternoon?

"Oh, the noise," says Merrill Reese, who has called every Eagles game on radio since 1977. "I haven't heard a crowd like that in all the years to follow. It was a fever pitch from opening kickoff to the final gun. The Cowboys all went home with headaches. But to the Eagles, it probably sounded like beautiful fireworks."

The crowd was so loud that players couldn't hear each other. "It was the only game I can remember when I could see the guys' mouths moving, but I couldn't hear them," says Walters. "Jaws was right next to me in the huddle, but all I could do was read his lips."

The game was far more lopsided than the 20-7 final score suggests. Montgomery ran for 194 yards, and the Eagles defense held Dallas's Tony Dorsett to 41 yards. Yes, our team went on to lose the Super Bowl to the Oakland Raiders. But even that could not detract from the franchise's greatest win in more than two decades—going forward or backward.

Vermeil left after the 1982 season, replaced by the inept Marion Campbell. And the Birds again became the Cowboys' personal plaything.

Until 1986. That's when Providence came to town in two words: Buddy Ryan.

Say what you want about Buddy—a personal favorite of these two authors. He was arrogant, obnoxious and not as crafty a game-day coach as, say, Joe Gibbs. He failed to develop talented quarterback Randall Cunningham and chronically ignored his leaky offensive line.

He did, however, understand one thing: The way to win the hearts of Eagles fans was to beat Dallas. Twice a year. As thoroughly as possible.

When Buddy first came to Philadelphia, he hosted a weekly radio show from the now-defunct Rib-It restaurant in Center City. "My first show at the Rib-It, I saw a young lady wearing a T-shirt," he recalls. "It said, 'I root for two teams: The Eagles and whoever's playing the Cowboys.' I learned right then that this rivalry was a real special thing here."

In his first season, Ryan split with the Cowboys, losing at the Vet and winning in Dallas. The next year, things got very personal between Buddy and Tom Landry. It led to one of the greatest escapades in franchise history.

It all started during the month-long NFL players' strike. In a foolhardy attempt to keep the league going, NFL owners hired scab players—late-round draft washouts and Canadian football refugees—to wear the uniforms of our heroes. Some cities took to the impostors, but Philadelphia would have none of it. The only scab game played at the Vet drew 4,074 fans—the lowest attendance of any game in the league that season.

Ryan, too, wanted no part of this farce. He hardly coached the pretenders who were brought in for him. And while other coaches urged players to cross the picket line, Buddy told his men to stay together.

"Buddy's message to us was to do whatever we felt was right, but do it as a team" says former tight end John Spagnola, the players' union representative during the strike. "I'm sure part of his motivation was to be a burr in [owner] Norman Braman's shorts. Buddy loved annoying Braman. But the result was that it engendered a terrific loyalty from the players to Buddy."

The second scab game was in Dallas, where many star players had crossed the line. While the Eagles boasted the likes of Guido Merkins and Topper Clemons, the Cowboys used Tony Dorsett, Danny White, Too Tall Jones and Randy White. The game was a farce. Dallas rolled up the score, while laughing at the faux-Eagles' ineptitude. Landry even put his regulars back on the field late, just so they could have more fun beating up the frauds in green.

Ryan seethed and vowed revenge.

Fortune had it that the first post-strike game was at the Vet and against the Cowboys. The Eagles played brilliantly with their regulars back, rolling up a 30-20 lead. They got the ball for the last time with a minute to play. Cunningham took the knee twice, Dallas used up its time-outs and the crowd anticipated one more kneel down to end the game.

Except on third down, Randall faked the knee, stepped back and threw a floater toward the end zone for Mike Quick. Dallas's stunned secondary scrambled back, drawing a pass interference call. On the next play, Keith Byars bulled it in from the one. The game ended 37-20. Even under Landry's unfashionable fedora you could see his neck turning red.

Rubbing it in? You bet. Meaningless touchdown? No way. That one was for Timmy Brown. For Harold Carmichael. For every Eagles fan who suffered through every humiliating loss over the years.

In the post-game news conference, Scott Palmer of Channel 6 asked Buddy, "Don't you think you opened a can of worms?"

"I'd say Landry opened it," Buddy drawled. "I just put the lid back on it."

More accurately, the scab game opened a can of karma for the Cowboys. Regardless, Ryan never again lost to the Evil Empire, winning seven in a row. "The Cowboys knew we were going to beat them," he now says. "They just didn't know how." He takes particular pride in never losing a game to Jimmy Johnson.

And those weren't just games in the Buddy versus Jimmy era; they were crusades. The contests earned titles—"The Bounty Bowl" and "The Snowball Game."

Consider 1989. Before the Thanksgiving Day game in Dallas, Buddy reportedly promised a $200 reward to any player who put a licking on Cowboys kicker Luis Zendejas, whom the Eagles had cut a few weeks earlier. Buddy denied the scheme, but during a kickoff, Birds linebacker Jesse Smalls placed a leg-wobbling wipeout shot on the little man.

Zendejas hired four lawyers and threatened for weeks to sue Buddy. He insisted he had a tape recording of Eagles special teams coach Al Roberts warning him of the bounty, but never produced it.

What he did, by squawking endlessly, was whip up Philadelphia fans, so that when the Cowboys came to town in mid-December, the stage was set for ugliness. Zendejas wore a mouth piece for the first time in his career and taped shut the earholes of his helmet. That may have cut down the noise, but it didn't protect him from the snowballs that rained down that day.

They came from the Vet Stadium seats. They were aimed at Cowboys players, frightened officials, outraged CBS announcers ("This is worse than Beirut," blustered Verne Lundquist) and, most especially, the impeccably coiffed hair of Jimmy Johnson. One fan with an impressive arm and sardonic sense of humor even managed to clip Johnson with a roll of Bounty paper towels.

"These people have no class," Cowboys linebacker Eugene Lockhart said afterward. "I never want to come back."

And that was sort of the point. If the Cowboys feared Eagles fans as much as they feared the Eagles, they would never win in this town.

One other moment from the Buddy era deserves mention, although it involves neither Ryan nor his players. Stan Walters had retired as a player and was working as an analyst on Eagles radio broadcasts. During a game at the Vet, Cunningham was nailed four feet out of bounds by two Dallas defenders. Walters, infuriated there was no call, ranted that Cowboys general manager Tex Schramm "has those officials in his pocket." He went on to call Schramm "the commissioner of scab football."

Schramm, a powerful member of the league's competition committee, was told by his spies of Walters's remarks. He rushed to the window of the radio booth, pounded on it and pulled out his pockets to show Stan there was nothing inside. Walters nearly broke through the glass to throttle Schramm.

The rivalry went back and forth through the 1990s. The Cowboys dominated during their Super Bowl seasons, and the Eagles took control late in the decade. Andy Reid versus Dave Campo? That was like Joe Frazier versus Pee Wee Herman. At least Bill Parcells, hired as Cowboys coach in 2003, portends to be a worthy adversary.

Still, there is talk today that the Cowboys have become irrelevant; that the Giants have replaced them as our No. 1 nemesis. Don't believe the hype. The traitors among us may have stored away their Emmitt jerseys, but they'll emerge from the mothballs as soon as the "Boys" luck into another victory. Like the Asian flu or the seven-year cicada, the outbreak of rampant Cowboy stupidity comes back every few years, just to remind us that, really, all men are not created equally.

Don't forget Tim Brown, or Harold Carmichael. Don't forgive Tom Landry, or Tex Schramm. Say a prayer for Buddy Ryan and wish the best for Andy Reid.

For as long as there is evil in this world, the Cowboys will have their fans.

Thirteen

Moments to Savor

There is no question that Wilbert Montgomery's 42-yard touchdown scamper in the 1980 NFC Championship Game was the greatest moment in the history of the Eagles-Cowboys rivalry. Here are five others worth remembering:

1. Fourth-and-one—twice, 1995.

The Eagles and Cowboys were tied, 17-17, late in the fourth quarter at the Vet. Dallas had the ball, fourth-and-inches, at their own 29-yard line.

Logic called for a punt. But logic was never a big part of Dallas coach Barry Switzer's game. Having too much respect for his offensive line, or too little for the Eagles defense, Switzer opted to go for it. He ran Emmitt Smith off left tackle and Smith was stuffed for a loss.

But wait. Nanoseconds before the snap, the refs had whistled the two-minute warning—which had no chance of being heard above the Vet cacophony. Therefore, Dallas got to go all over again. Did Switzer learn his lesson? No way. Maybe it was pride speaking, maybe it was the Jack Daniels, but Switzer called exactly the same play, and . . .

. . . and, well, here's how Merrill Reese described it.

"Here they go, fourth down. The Cowboys go to Smith and—they stop him again! They stop him again! And this time they can't take it away! It's the same play—it's Groundhog Day!"

The Eagles got the ball. Gary Anderson cranked out a 42-yard field goal, and the good guys won, 20-17.

2. Willis to Vincent to victory, 1996.

The Eagles held a 24-13 fourth-quarter lead at Texas Stadium, thanks to a superb afternoon by backup quarterback Ty Detmer. The Cowboys clawed back with a touchdown and two-point conversion to pull the score to 24-21. Then, Dallas got the ball back with two minutes to go.

Quarterback Troy Aikman drove the Cowboys to first-and-goal at the Eagles three. The Cowboys tried running, but Smith was stopped twice—first by cornerback Troy Vincent, then by backup linebacker Sylvester Wright. On third down, Aikman dropped back, rolled slightly to his right, and threw the ball into the end zone—right into the hands of Eagles linebacker James Willis. He lugged it to the 10-yard line, and then tossed it back to Vincent, who outran 11 gassed Cowboys the rest of the way.

"I looked back," Vincent said, "and nobody was there."

The 104-yard play set the franchise record for longest interception return and sealed a great road win. In fact, the Eagles celebrated so heartily that they lost their next three games. The play was, arguably, the last great moment of the Ray Rhodes era in Philadelphia.

3. Onsides kick announces a new era, 2000.

Never mind Andy Reid's 5-11 first season in 1999. His tenure really began on September 3, 2000 in the 109-degree heat of Texas Stadium. Indeed, this was a game where it became clear that two teams headed in opposite directions have suddenly crossed paths and traded roles. One would never look back; the other would never get up again.

The exact moment of crystallization was the season-opening play. Dallas won the toss, and sent Rocket Ismail back to receive the kick. Reid, heretofore known as a stodgy, conservative bore (and we're not just talking personality), ordered up a surprise onsides kick. Dallas's players were so stunned that there was hardly even a scramble for the ball, and Eagles receiver Dameane Douglas came up with it. Quarterback Donovan McNabb led the team 58 yards on eight plays for a touchdown and the slaughter was on.

"People say our coach is predictable, that our team is predictable," said running back Duce Staley, who rushed for 201 yards on the day. "But Andy's got a bit of gunslinger in him. You wait and see."

Eagles players chugged pickle juice to beat the heat, but the bad taste was left in Dallas's mouth, as the Eagles won, 41-14.

4. A backup becomes a Monday night hero, 1979.

Chances are you don't remember John Walton, a second-string quarterback from Elizabeth City State College who completed all of 31 passes during his four seasons with the Eagles. But on Nov. 12, 1979, the 32-year-old backup became an instant hero in Philadelphia.

The Eagles had lost 13 straight in Texas and things looked bleak after Cowboys defensive end Harvey Martin knocked quarterback Ron Jaworski out of the game with a bruised wrist. But Eagles linebacker Frank LeMaster recovered a fumbled punt return at the Dallas 29, and Walton trotted into the game.

On his very first play, he faked a handoff to Montgomery, then spun right and pump-faked a pass to Harold Carmichael. With the Cowboys secondary scrambling in two directions, Walton threaded a pass between two defenders, hitting wide receiver Charlie Smith at the Dallas five-yard line. Smith tight-roped the last few yards along the left sideline, and fell into the end zone.

The Eagles won, 31-21, proving to themselves—and coach Dick Vermeil—that they were ready to move past Dallas as the NFC East's elite team. The following season they did just that.

5. The longest return, 1974.

The afternoon before the September 23 home opener, Eagles coach Mike McCormack took his players to see the film "The Longest Yard." It proved to be an appropriate title.

Dallas had the ball at the Eagles' one-yard line in the third quarter. Leading 7-0, the Cowboys were about ready to break open the Monday Night Football game. Rookie running back Doug Dennison started sweeping around right tackle when—boom!—middle linebacker Bill Bergey (in his first Vet appearance) belted Dennison, who spit up the ball.

It bounced back to the four, where Eagles cornerback Joe Lavender scooped it up and headed down the sideline. Eagles safety Randy Logan cleared out Roger Staubach with a block, and Lavender had a clear path to the end zone.

"The Dallas bench was screaming at me as I ran by," Lavender said afterward. "I guess they were hoping I'd fall down."

He didn't. Instead, he ran 96 yards for the longest fumble return in team history. Despite not scoring an offensive touchdown, the Eagles won, 13-10, on a late 46-yard field goal by Tom Dempsey. The only other exciting moment came when an Eagles fan sent ABC announcers Frank Gifford and Alex Karras scrambling by lobbing a lit cherry bomb into their booth.

"From that moment on, I had a love affair with Philadelphia fans that goes on today," says Bergey, presumably talking about the game, rather than the explosive.

6. And one we'd rather forget: The snap, the hold, the pain, 1997.

Monday Night Football in Dallas. Eagles down, 21-20, with seconds to play. Ty Detmer hits a wide-open Freddie Solomon over the middle at the Dallas 30, and Solomon sprints all the way to the Dallas 4-yard line. The Eagles call timeout with four seconds left, setting up a potential game-winning 20-yard field goal by former Cowboy Chris Boniol.

It was 12:17 a.m. Eastern Time on September 16.

The snap from Morris Unutoa was right into the hands of holder Tommy Hutton. But Hutton bobbled the ball and . . .

. . . we really don't want to talk about it.

FOURTEEN
GUYS! GUYS! GUYS!

Our all-time favorite Philadelphia athletes were Julius Erving and Reggie White. You may have preferred Gizmo Williams. Point is, being a fan gives you the right to admire—or despise—any player for any reason.

So we've put together a few lists of players (and other sports types) whom we love or hate for certain attributes or failings. You may disagree. That's your right as a fan.

TOUGH GUYS

Chuck Bednarik

Bill Bergey

Tim Rossovich (Hell, he ate glass)

Donovan McNabb (Why? You try throwing four touchdown passes on a broken ankle)

Andre Waters and Wes Hopkins

Dave Schultz

Behn Wilson (The only guy Dave Schultz said he was afraid to fight)

Paul Holmgren

Tim Kerr

Mikael Renberg (No one suffered more horrific injuries—the abdominal tear that required injections through his pelvis, the 250-stitch cut to his face when he was sliced by a skate blade, the infection that nearly forced amputation of his hand)

Rick Mahorn

Allen Iverson

Bob Boone

Darren Daulton (Nine knee operations)

Dallas Green

Mike Keenan

CLASSY GUYS

Dick Vermeil

Mike Quick

Troy Vincent

Garry Maddox

Mo Cheeks, Bobby Jones (Really, most of that '82-'83 Sixers squad)

Jim Lonborg

Jim Eisenreich

Rick Tocchet

Bill Barber

Todd McCollough

SOFT GUYS

Alexander Daigle

Derek Sanderson (In his brief stint with the Philadelphia Blazers, he had a clause in his contract requiring a team staffer to wake him for practices and games)

Alex Johnson

Travis Lee

Danny Tartabull (Fouled a ball off his toe and missed an entire season)

Matt Geiger

Theo Ratliff

GENUINE PHILLY-TYPE GUYS

Joe Frazier

Ron Jaworski

Vince Papale

Jerome Brown

Buddy Ryan

Larry Bowa

Pete Rose

Tug McGraw

Lenny Dykstra

Ron Hextall

Ken Linseman

Rick Tocchet

Rod Brind'Amour

Aaron McKie (A true Philly guy from Simon Gratz High)

Pat Croce (A true Philly guy from Lansdowne)

ALL-UGLY GUYS

Manute Bol

Tyrone Hill

Pete Rose (That jutting jaw, that Moe haircut)

Randy Lerch

Johnny Podres

John Chaney (He looks just like the Temple Owl mascot)

Mike Ricci

Sandy McCarthy

FAT GUYS

Greg Luzinski

John Kruk

David West

Sid Fernandez

Buddy Ryan

Andy Reid

Hollis Thomas

William Perry

Pat Falloon (Teammates called him "Fat Balloon")

Ed Van Impe

Benoit Benjamin

SKINNY GUYS

Harold Carmichael

Todd Pinkston

Manute Bol and Shawn Bradley (or "15 feet of nothing")

Dikembe Mutombo

Caldwell Jones

Kent Tekulve

Von Hayes

BEARDED GUYS

Cowboy Bill Flett

Gene Hart

Ron Jaworski

1980 linebackers—Bill Bergey, Frank LeMaster and John Bunting

Koy Detmer (The joke was that his girlfriend gave him a gold chain for Christmas just to tell where his neck ends and his chest begins)

Al Holland

Steve Bedrosian

GUYS WITH GREAT NICKNAMES

Don "Big Bird" Saleski

Bob "Hound" Kelly

Andre "Moose" Dupont

Dave "The Hammer" Schultz

"Concrete Charlie" Bednarik

Ron "Polish Rifle" Jaworski

Izel "Toast" Jenkins

Lonnie "Skates" Smith

Mitch "Wild Thing" Williams

Von "541" Hayes

Joe "Jelly Bean" Bryant

Andrew "The Boston Strangler" Toney

Billy "Kangaroo Kid" Cunningham

Darryl "Chocolate Thunder" Dawkins

Wilt "The Big Dipper" Chamberlain (He hated being called "The Stilt")

Lloyd "World B." Free (So good he legally changed his name to it)

Doc

OPPONENTS WE HATED

Ron Duguay, Jaromir Jagr (and any other hockey pretty boy)

Billy "Battle Ax" Smith

Scott Stevens

Chris Chelios

Dale Hunter

Matthew Barnaby

Hollywood Henderson

Michael Irvin

Deion Sanders

Dave Parker

Pete Rose

J.D. Drew

Red Auerbach

Larry Bird

Kevin McHale

Danny Ainge

Reggie Miller

Jeremy Shockey

BROTHERS WHO PLAYED HERE

Ron and Rich Sutter

Koy and Ty Detmer

Joe and Jim Watson

Dave and Dennis Bennett

WE GOT THE WRONG BROTHER

Juan Bell (not George)

Jeremy Giambi (not Jason)

Ken Brett (not George)

Gilbert Dionne (not Marcel)

Mike Maddux (not Greg)

Chris James (not Craig, who was much better at football than Chris was at baseball)

Frank Torre (not Joe)

Mark Leiter (not Al)

Mike Golic (not Bob)

Tom Van Arsdale (not Dick)

Jean Potvin (not Denis)

WE GOT THE RIGHT BROTHER

Keith Primeau (not Wayne)

Eric Lindros (not Brett)

Caldwell Jones (not Major)

Richie Allen (not Hank or Ron)

ONE-GAME WONDERS

Al Hill (Scored 36 seconds into his 1977 pro debut. Had five points—two goals, three assists—in his first game, an NHL record)

Andy Delmore (Only NHL rookie defenseman with a playoff hat trick)

Bobby Hoying (313 yards, four touchdowns versus Bengals in 1997)

Willie Burton (53 points—a Spectrum record—against Miami in 1994)

BETTER AFTER HE LEFT

Sonny Jurgensen

Charlie Garner

Jimmy Smith

Cris Carter

John Gruden

Ryne Sandberg

Fergie Jenkins

Curt Schilling

Dave Stewart

Jerry Stackhouse

Sean Burke

GONE TOO SOON

Barry Ashbee

Pelle Lindbergh

Yanick Dupre

Dmitri Tertyshny

Jerome Brown

Hank Gathers

Bo Diaz

PLAYERS VS. ORGANIZATION
Brad McCrimmon

Eric Lindros

Dave Babych

Reggie White

Keith Jackson

Richie Allen

J.D. Drew

Scott Rolen

PLAYERS WHO BECAME LOCAL ANNOUNCERS
Richie Ashburn

Larry Andersen

Tim McCarver

Doug Collins

Steve Mix

Stan Walters

Tom Brookshier

Mike Quick

Bobby Taylor

Gary Dornhoeffer

Bill Clement

Brian Propp

Vai Sikahema

PLAYERS WHO SHARE FAMOUS NAMES
Don MacLean

Jim Lampley

Paul Neumann

Keith Jackson

SIGNATURE CALLS

Dave Zinkoff: "Julius Errrrrrrrrrving."

Richie Ashburn: "He looks runnerish."

Merrill Reese: "It's Gooooooooooooooooodddddddddddddd."

Gene Hart: "He shoots, he scores—for a taste of Tastykakes."

Harry Kalas: "That ball's outahere. Home run, Michael Jack Schmidt."

Bill Campbell: "He made it. He made it. He made it. A Dipper dunk. He made it. The fans are all over the court. One hundred points for Wilt Chamberlain."

Don Earle: "He skates right on in, he shoots. Oh, no, he hit the f — post."

FAMOUS DADS, FAMOUS KIDS

Joe and Kobe Bryant

Tug and Tim McGraw

Bob and Brett and Aaron Boone

Rick and Jill Arrington

Mike and Mike Dunleavy

Henry and Mike Bibby

Julius Erving and Alexandra Stevenson

Joe and Marvis Frazier

Ruben Amaro Sr. and Jr.

Tito and Terry Francona

Bill and Jake Bergey

Gene and Lauren Hart

Dolph and Danny Schayes

Bill and Kevin Dineen

Ed and Jay Snider

Jimmy and Dei Lynam

FIFTEEN

JUST PLAIN BUDDY

I wore a white Wes Hopkins jersey as I stood to ask the question, and I imagined me him, a tunneling, snorting safety looking for someone to hit to please the coach that stood before me. We were in the old Channel 10 studios on City Line Avenue, back when Channel 10 was WCAU, and the coach sat with that Kentucky horse trainer smile next to anchor Big Al Meltzer. So I asked about the blitz responsibility for the safety in a particular formation of the 46 Defense, and hoped a teenage hope the coach would respect the question and perhaps invite me to practice.

"Buddy," I began, "you're a genius. I know you're a genius . . . ."

The first question of my impending career as a journalist, I cringe now at my suck-up blather. But I was 16, and puny, portly James David Ryan was bigger than God. He was Buddy.

Buddy.

How perfect. For in hindsight, he was friend to fan like no other this city has witnessed. Buddy Ryan embodied sports Philadelphia better than a breathing boo wit'. Pudgy, garish, brash, loyal, wrapped in a cussing swagger, and he loved a defense that gulped glass shards and bopped the beans out of players, particularly quarterbacks. Mean Crow Green he was, and he didn't care because he believed in sucker punch football and so did we. Football is a game without couth, we believed, so why should our coach wear a tweed fedora and speak softly and pander to the Redskins?

Buddy was y'all and we were youse, but we ate him up like a greasy pork chop. God bless sentimental Dick Vermeil but he fell to burnout and we to Marion Campbell's Bend But Don't Break Defense, which broke like a promise in passion. We went from the Super Bowl in '81 to Cowboy porridge in five years, and we longed for lost Sundays. Enter the coach whose defense maimed like the Huns and who screw-you'd head coach Mike Ditka while they won a Super Bowl together and who pronounced three days later at his first Eagles press conference that he'd go unbeaten in the division. A breath of fresh hot air that we aggressively inhaled, Buddy made the city forever with a complex feel good and, despite his crass over class approach, proud. Everyone with insecurities looks for an identity other than loser, and the dastardly the better. Witness Raider Nation, whose inhabitants wither outside of their skulls and spikes and dress-up scowls. We wanted to be bad, because the Cowboys were blue bloods and the Redskins had their hogs and history and the Giants wore NY on their helmet. Buddy was our long-lost love, our kindred chunky spirit who gave the stodgy NFL the finger and sent out young toughs like Wes Hopkins and Seth Joyner and Reggie White and Andre Waters to do his dirty work.

There was no better example of this than the infamous Bounty Bowl, which transpired before a nation on Thanksgiving Day, 1989. In a game the Eagles won 27-0, Ryan offered cash bounties for players to knock quarterback Troy Aikman and kicker Luis Zendejas out of the game.

Linebacker Jesse Smalls went after Zendejas on the opening kickoff, prompting the former Eagle kicker to say afterwards: "It wasn't enough to get cut by Buddy Ryan. He had to try to knock me out of the game. That tells you what kind of man Buddy Ryan is . . . I got a call from one of my friends and he said, 'They're coming after you.' I didn't make much of it, then (a coach) told me about it before the game. He said, 'You know how Buddy is. He's going to put somebody on you on the first kick-off that you do.' All I could do was duck because he was going for my legs, and he just came straight at me."

Supposedly there was a $200 bounty on Zendejas and a $500 bounty on Aikman, who was tackled once long after the whistle, a hit that led to a fight and the ejection of tackle Mike Pitts. Ryan's bounties on players became lore around the league, as did his gory defense that resembled a band of bloodthirsty pirates, drunk on the village pillage.

In Washington, they still talk about the Body Bag Game with a queasy stomach. It happened on a nasty Monday night in 1990, and running back Brian Mitchell, who finished the game as the last Redskin quarterback standing, said recently, "I never seen nothin' like it. Guys were falling all over the field. I remember thinking, 'Damn, I'm going in there? I'm just gonna run for my life.' I can't believe nobody died that day."

"I've never seen a game like this," said Redskins Hall-of-Famer Bobby Mitchell. "Not even in the old days."

Perhaps the most frightening moment came when Hopkins knocked out the Skins' Joe Howard with a helmet-to-helmet head-on that resulted in wince and worry. Bubba Tyler, Washington's trainer, said, "For a long time, he wasn't moving at all and you could barely see him breathing."

"Man, he was snoring," Hopkins crowed of the concussion.

Skins' quarterback Jeff Rutledge, an old and poky sort, left the game broken and tortured, his throwing thumb swollen to the size of a baby's foot. When Ryan didn't send five rushers, he sent six. Except when he sent seven. That was the aim of Ryan's 46 Defense, feast on the weak and forget the football war crimes.

The 46 technically evolved from a nickel defense with extra run support in its early stages to a blitzing pass defense that at times left only three men in pass coverage. In Ryan's system, there were sometimes eight pass rushers close to the line of scrimmage, and the blitzers would come from a variety of positions and angles. It was designed as a football's version of shock and awe, a weapon of mass destruction that terrorized like a tornado, and defense-crazed Philadelphia reveled in the carnage it left behind.

The defense's only problem was being susceptible to the big play, typifying its inventor's bravado. Like his defense, Ryan left himself open for mass criticism. He didn't care, of course.

"I came up with the Jets, and I was there when Joe Namath guaranteed a win in the Super Bowl," he said. "To me, it showed a lot of confidence. Intimidating people is all part of it, and I know we intimidated teams. They were afraid of that defense."

In the end, Ryan's genius as a coach lay more with his handling of players than stratagems, particularly those on offense, where his axiom consisted of telling Randall Cunningham to make one or two big plays a game and let the defense win it. Ryan had the uncanny ability of making his players love him. He was as loyal as a blood brother, purposely positioning himself on the side of player in the player/management contract rift, often to the ire of management. His players responded in an almost cultish manner, transcending racial or generational barriers, Joyner and Simmons and Hopkins and Waters most of all. "Buddy say, we do," was their mantra, much like the marine to his commanding officer.

Ryan got into constant serious rifts with owner Norman Braman, whom he mockingly referred to as "the guy in France" because of Braman's penchant to vacation in the French Riviera. Whether it was over tight end Keith Jackson's contract or refusing to coach the Birds' "scab" team during the '87 strike, Ryan tweaked Braman like a man with his maker on his side.

Ryan's strategy during the strike solidified his standing with his players and with this union-laden city. Like his entire tenure, the move proved endearing but costly because the Eagles' replacements lost all three games they played, badly, too, and the team wound up narrowly missing the playoffs that season. And yet, the Eagles did extract some revenge on the Cowboys, whom the Birds accused of taking use of an unfair advantage of veterans during the strike game played between the teams.

With the Eagles leading 30-20, Cunningham twice sat on the football as the clocked ticked down to the final 15 seconds. However, the quarterback faked a final kneel down and heaved a bomb to Mike Quick that resulted in a pass interference penalty and a 1-yard touchdown run by Keith Byars on the final play.

The play left the Cowboys fuming, especially defensive tackle Kevin Brooks, who said, "It's a shame Buddy Ryan has no class at all."

Tom Landry issued only a terse statement: "I wouldn't even justify that with a comment. Everybody has his opinion of what it was."

Of course, Ryan relished the moment, and mock-mimicked a Landry quote from the replacement game: "I just played the hand that was dealt me." He also said, "The last touchdown was very satisfying. I had it planned all along."

Our odd couple — Randall and Buddy.

Buddy.

He was so anti-establishment, this man who told Tom Landry and his owner and members of the media and anybody who didn't like his players, his team, his fans, his ways, to simply piss off. He did it without fear of repercussion, born without the gene that says to care what others think of you, so rare in life and in sport, where the goal now is to say nothing using as many syllables possible. It won him love and loyalty, but never a playoff game.

In the end, the Buddy Ryan Era was the great tease, bluster and luster wrapped in one gigantic bust of a bust. Funny, we hated the Rich Kotite like he stole our milk money and he won more playoff games than Buddy Ryan. So did Ray Rhodes and Andy Reid, whom we bemoan for being boring despite two championship games. It's the great Philadelphia fallacy, or is it? Were his playoff sins of the Fog Bowl and the terrible home losses to the Rams and Redskins forgiven because he gave something more important to the city than a Lombardi Trophy? Was it all about an identity for us with Buddy Ryan? Did he—this kooky Kentuckian and Korean War veteran—get us better than any other coach?

Sure, he had his detractors in town, those who viewed him as the gutter's coach who perpetrated a fraud of X and O, who ruined and wasted the freakish talent of Randall Cunningham, who managed a mere 13 points total at home in the two biggest games of his career, who perpetrated the awful stereotypes of the Philadelphia bloodlust and boo and boor, ultimately giving Braman enough rope to hang him and not renew his contract after the disappointing 1990 season when the town cried to give him one more chance. But most of us somehow still skew history because we feel the need to cherish his memory instead of curse it. Buddy charmed us. He got us.

That's why what seemed like 1,000 people flocked around Buddy Ryan that night he received the Bert Bell Memorial Award at the Marriott Hotel in December 2002—more than a decade after he left Philadelphia for good. As he entered the ballroom, the crowd gave him a standing ovation, chanting, "Buddy! Buddy! Buddy!"

"Hell-owe," Buddy answered the phone recently.

"Buddy?" the caller asked.

"Yee-ep," he said.

"I'm a writer from Philly, and I need to ask you something . . . ," the caller said.

"Yee-ep, I still love your town," he interrupted. "It's a blue-collar town and I was a blue-collar coach. I remember this girl, cute thing, coming up to me at my radio show and she said, 'Buddy, I root for two teams—the Eagles and whoever's playin' the Cowboys.' So the first thing I said on the air was, 'I hate them Cowboys.' And you know what? I really did. I felt the vibe from the fans and it overtook me. Best years of my life there, even better than when I won the Super Bowl in Chicago. We were made for each other."

We talked some more. His voice sounded weak and life-worn. Still, I gushed like I did almost 20 years before. I couldn't help it. He's Buddy.

BOBBY VS. BOB

There is an image of a boy who is becoming a man sitting at a barstool among men. Real men, whose fingers are knobby and black from digging in the earth's belly and clutch the neck of a beer bottle, whose bristly faces are imperfect, scarred by lifelines but seemingly always adorned with a smile. It is a Friday evening, mid-summer in Flin Flon, and the zinc mine has closed. The boy listens to the room, as though it is a lecture hall and God is the lecturer. Hard work wholes a man's soul, he is taught, and beer is the reward.

"It was the best education I could ever get," he would say later in life. A high school dropout, he found his gumption in that mine, from those men. Those men had nobility, and if hockey hadn't worked out, he would have gladly rejoined them.

There is an image of a night in Rexy's, and everyone is there. It is not one particular night but the encapsulation of many nights spent at the homey tavern just over the Walt Whitman Bridge, across from the old Korvette's on the Blackhorse Pike. It is the '70s, obviously, judging by the bushy hair, the bushy beards, the caterpillar mustaches of his friends, Chief and Hound and Benny. The boy is now a man, and he is smiling a toothless smile. For this is what a team does. It plays together and eats together and drinks together, and occasionally breaks balls. It does it in public, with the public, which is the way it ought to be.

It is easy to do so in these days of the Snider Flyers and Carpenter Phillies and Tose Eagles and Dixon Sixers, before the great boom that brought gated golf communities with lots of landscaping and manmade lakes and all kinds of expensive buffers from the public. You could argue that the great boom, however lucrative, proved forever apocalyptic. It spoiled the players, sullied the fans, who became more fanatic, more clingy the more they were rebuffed. It destroyed a sentiment.

"If you think back, there was a time when all the athletes lived here," he says. "We used to have a softball team. Played 40 games a summer all over the Delaware Valley. Who we played kept the money and used it for kids' fields, stuff like that. When the game was over we'd go out with the people and have sandwiches and drink beer. It was just an unbelievable time."

There is an image of the man, much older now, and a press conference. His face is flushed. A droplet of sweat hunkers on his forehead, which is crinkled from furrowed brows. He clears his throat uncomfortably and he begins to speak inaudibly until he clears his throat again. The bliss of the past seems to have burned off like a spring morning fog. Life is no longer simple, and so resentment takes on a form now, as though it is growing wings and a snout. Because times have changed and people have changed and it's hard to relate anymore, which is probably the biggest reason for this raging rift that has developed between a city and a son.

Bob Clarke, Flyers general manager, is not Satan, as some would have you believe. He does not muse of today's players in chains or own a Voodoo doll of Eric Lindros. He is, however, the fallen angel of Hockey Philadelphia, which is akin to housewives turning on Oprah.

For so long, forever in my life, Bob Clarke has played ice icon, on it, off it, levitating above it, embodying the Flyers and the success of the Flyers and the notion of the Flyers as family. Of course, that was before the Flyers of recent years, before the revolving door of coaches, before all the failed high expectations, before the feud with Lindros, before the clumsy utterances that often sounded callous, perhaps even vindictive, before the fans' growing sentiment of unsentimental disdain toward, of all people, himself.

Hell, Glen and I do a radio show, and the public view on Clarke, my boyhood hero, is kind of distressing, though perhaps not without merit. It brings me back to a recent interview I did with him.

"People are going to call me an asshole, I know," Clarke said. "People have called me an asshole, I know. Nobody likes criticism. But it doesn't keep me up at night. It comes with the territory, I know."

The territory, he meant, is being management. Crossing over. The very second one removes the skates or sneaks and replaces them with shoes by Dolce and Gabbana, perception goes askew. That three-button single-breasted Paul Smith pinstripe suit represents authority, which represents bottom line, which represents cost, which represents ticket prices, which ultimately represents the notion, "You're screwin' me."

The Law of Sport says fans will always side with players, unless, of course, they quip something like: "For who? For what?" Otherwise, it's player over management, whether management is former player or great former player.

Clarke was right when he said, "Young people don't remember any of us. They don't know us. Nor should they." An entire generation can't recall 1975, or how Bob Clarke became beloved, or why. In a sports community often accused of pimping the past, nobody talks of Bob Clarke's legacy. And in a Flyer fan base often accused of sipping company Kool Aid, nobody talks of Clarke's achievements as GM: three division titles, four second-place finishes, three conference finals, two Stanley Cup finals.

Bob Clarke now seems defined by one person: Bob Clarke, the suit.

The first time he came to me, I was six. I can still see him, swathed in aura, which I guess is normal. They say children draw auras around people because they see divinity in people. Naked of Original Sin. Of flaw. That is how I viewed them all: Clarke, Doc, Bergey, Schmidt. Such is growing up boy in bicentennial Philadelphia.

I drew Clarke in 1975, copying it from a grainy picture in the *Evening Bulletin*. His arms were raised high, celebrating a goal, the Cup-winning goal, and I stood in line at a golf course in Jersey to hand him my sketch. He took it, patted me on the head, said, "Thank you, son." I knew then it didn't make it past the trash can near the eighth tee. But it was better to believe that he framed it, which is why that moment remains indelible in my reels of memory.

Imagine me back then, pretending to be him as I clopped up and down Gladstone Street on feet with a plastic orange puck, the iridescent Safe Shot puck, and my cousin Joey's Koho stick. Most kids on Gladstone Street pretended to be Clarke. One, I remember, loved Bernie Parent, the Flyers goalie, fearless in all of our eyes, a pillar of a French Canadian whose jersey No. 1 seemed more exclamation mark. But Bernie wore a mask, and Clarke, in those helmet-less days, wore only a raw cerement of emotion.

A plodding diabetic, Clarke was Rocky before Sly Stallone. He personified his sport. And if football, with its bombs and blitzes and attack formations, denotes war, than hockey denotes work, old-fashioned, hearty labor. After all, players play in shifts, and they dig in the corner and grind along the boards and muck like they do in the mine.

Bobby Clarke introduced me to this sport, and did the same for an entire town. A quarter of a century later, he is sitting before me trying to defend himself. I study him to see if there's anything similar from that day on the golf course. Of course, not. Time and circumstance alter all, even my perspective, which is now colored by hosting an afternoon sports talk show.

The callers speak out. Most are unforgiving. They talk of the executive Bob Clarke, how he doesn't connect with them, how he doesn't connect with the times, how he has failed to make the big trade to win a Stanley Cup, how he clings to a plodding style of hockey—"your muckers and grinders"—in a era of speed, how he is resentful of today's salaries, how he lies, how he should be fired.

Such public sentiment echoes tirelessly in radio rant and taproom talk and stream of cyber consciousness. A sampling of one caller's complaints: "Clarkie (sarcastically) and Mr. Snider (sarcastically) are the only common denominators over the Flyers' recent past. They've fired a bunch of coaches. They've gotten rid of Lindros. They've gotten rid of everybody but Clarke and Clarke's been the one making all of the decisions on the team. Clarke signed LeClair to all that money. Clarke gets all of those guys who can't play anymore with Mr. Snider's money. The Flyers have the second-highest payroll in the NHL and it's the same old sad story. When are they going to wise up and get rid of Clarke?"

Ask Flyer fans why they feel the way they do about Clarke and the response always begins with an exaggerated sigh. It is followed shortly by reference to losing and then to Lindros, the franchise player who, unwittingly, nearly splintered a franchise. And if there is a debate as to "who is at fault" in that bizarre Hockey Opera—there are more suspects than in one season of Ellery Queen, including the most obvious: just bad bleepin' luck.

Oh, don't forget Roger Neilson, the charming old hockey lifer who was diagnosed with bone marrow cancer as coach of the Flyers and wound up losing his job to assistant Craig Ramsey in the playoffs. If the point is made of Neilson's drawn, pallid look after his courageous fight for life as proof enough he wasn't right to coach, a grunt follows.

Then it's, well, look Ramsey didn't work out and Bill Barber got knifed in the back by the players and Clarke stood by idly. Flyer fans may then talk of a particular Clarke gaffe, the crowd favorite being the non-trade for Brendan Shanahan, the sniper forward who many thought would have put the team over the top, or the costly signing of free agent bust Chris Gratton, or the decision to stick with Roman Cechmanek. But every good general manager has a couple of those. Fact is, such mistakes would be overlooked, for sure, if Flyer fans didn't all allude to a certain chill that emanates from Bob Clarke's office.

Fact is, Bob Clarke is judged more on demeanor than on duty. "If there's one thing Bob doesn't get," says Flyers chairman Ed Snider, "it's public relations. He sucks at public relations."

The root of all the ill will, say what you want, dates back to The Failure of Eric Lindros. It is hard to say when Eric Lindros and the Flyers became a bad idea. Perhaps it was that draft day an arbitrator awarded him to Philadelphia over the New York Rangers. Because, obviously, the storybook hero thing wasn't meant to be. Nobody likes to cop out to fate and hear that answer, but what else is there?

Only Melpomene, the Greek muse of tragedy, could have made sense of the Saga of Eric Lindros. From the beginning, when the Flyers gave up the world to obtain his rights, to that deflating Friday night when Lindros lay in a heap on the First Union Center ice with his seventh concussion—following a grisly body check from the Devils' Scott Stevens early in the Flyers' Game Seven loss to New Jersey in the Eastern Conference Finals—the Next One proved to be a fitful one.

The "Can't Miss" missed, because he did not win a Stanley Cup. Because he did not complete the trinity with Mario Lemieux and Wayne Gretzky. Because he was not the next Bob Clarke. Because injuries mounted and pressure mounted and concussions got the best of him.

It's long been over now, and Eric Lindros eventually landed with New York, where he was a disappointment with the Rangers, too. It didn't matter, obviously, that Clarke got the best of that trade by landing speedy young defenseman Kim Johnsson, when a bucket of pucks would have been a successful deal.

There was a time not long ago when that would have been absurd. Prior to the 1998-99 season, Clarke challenged Lindros publicly to play worth his pay, marking the first outward sign of the Flyers' displeasure with their franchise player. Clarke's point was that it was time for Lindros to fully blossom into his billing. A motivational tact, like when he made Lindros the captain of Team Canada on a team with Gretzky and Lemieux, and it worked.

Lindros played impassioned hockey for the most prolonged stretch of his career. But toward the end of the season, in a game in Nashville, he suffered a near fatal lung injury that, in hindsight, had as much to do with this divorce as anything. Lindros' father and agent, Carl, alleged the Flyers recklessly endangered his son's life and that he could have died if he had flown the team charter.

Clarke, who was already growing weary of Carl Lindros' involvement in team affairs, scoffed at such a notion. Clarke's contention was that the organization had "bent over back-

Bob Clarke faces the media.

wards" for Lindros on numerous occasions, among those being a cover-up of a knee injury that Lindros sustained during a fight at a nightclub early in his career, the dismissal of coach Terry Murray, who often complained of Lindros' practice habits, and the dismissal of public relations director Mark Piazza over Lindros' alleged relationship with Joey Merlino.

The situation grew more uneasy during a playoff series with Toronto that spring, with Lindros still sidelined by the lung injury. Before one game, then-assistant coach Wayne Cashman made a crack to Lindros about Jeremy Roenick of Phoenix attempting to come back from a broken jaw. Cashman pointed to the television and said, half-jokingly, "You're not going to let that American come back before you come back, are you?"

Clarke laughed. Lindros seethed. Moments later, Lindros voiced his displeasure rather loudly in Clarke's office. He felt as though his leadership had been undermined by Clarke's going along with the joke and that his commitment to return had been questioned.

Lindros felt the climate around him changing. After a summer of trade rumors and innuendo, Lindros came to training camp for the 1999-2000 season on edge and confided to one person close to the team, "I don't know if I can take it another year."

Lindros again played well, but again was befallen by injury and the events surrounding it. In March, he suffered the sixth concussion of his career, and that marked the beginning of a bizarre stretch of infighting and backbiting. Lindros's contended that Flyers trainer John Worley did not recognize the symptoms and Carl Lindros's questioned team physicians on the diagnosis of the severity of the concussion, which led to Lindros leaving Philadelphia for his home in Toronto and being stripped of his captaincy.

"The team was put in a bad position because Lindros comes out with those statements and then our only defense is to either say nothing or say Lindros is wrong, and then we're fighting with our own guy," Clarke said reflecting back. "He had the medical reports. Our trainers didn't mess up."

The day after Clarke vowed the team would not name an interim captain, the Flyers announced Eric Desjardins as the new leader, a move that came about, according to Snider, because the players wished it. That night ESPN led its SportsCenter report with video of the symbolic "C" being sewn on Desjardins's jersey, an obvious affront to Lindros.

The players remained mum on the situation, with very few coming out in public support of Lindros. Word filtered quietly that they were upset at Lindros's denouncing Flyers trainer John Worley, a no-no in the uniform world of hockey.

"The whole thing really infested the city," Snider harrumphed. "When we got Rick Tocchet back [in a late-season trade with the Phoenix Coyotes], he said to me, 'What the hell is going on in this town? What happened since I left?' Then *Sports Illustrated* writes that story and says we're dysfunctional. When I read dysfunctional, it pissed me off. We weren't dysfunctional. It was all the Lindros thing."

Perhaps the most astounding thing of all, however, was that the Flyers kept winning and going deeper into the playoffs that year, the deepest they've been since. They beat the Sabres and their stonewall goalie, Dominic Hasek, in the first round. Against the Penguins in the second round, they lost the first two games at home. They won the next two in Pittsburgh, both in overtime, one that lasted five extra periods. They finished off the series in six.

The lasting memory of that playoff run was not goalie Brian Boucher, on his back, making the save of a lifetime. It was not the Flyers leading 3–1 in the conference finals against the eventual Stanley Cup champion Devils and blowing it. It was Lindros returning from the rubble for Game Six, and returning to it in the early moments of Game Seven. It was Eric Lindros unconscious, strapped to a gurney, which might as well have been a gladiator's shield.

Snider growled of Lindros, and what transpired: "Had Lindros had his head screwed on straight and just wanted to play hockey, I don't think we could have been defeated," he said. "Fact is, we were up 3–1 in the conference finals. He came back and we lost."

Obviously, Snider was bitter. He was bitter about how it all turned out. How it affected his team. How it affected Clarke. "Eric Lindros and his family had a major problem with the Flyers organization for years," he said. "In particular, they tried to portray Bob Clarke in a negative light, an issue that is very wrong . . . How come Bob Clarke isn't defined by other players? Guys like Rick Tocchet and Mark Recchi, who couldn't wait to get back to this organization? If it were a continuing issue with many of the players, I'd say there was a problem."

Clarke still tried to make the situation work before Lindros sat out the entire season and was dealt the following summer. In the end, Clarke said, "We did everything we felt we could to help Eric. It just never worked out between his family and our organization."

It finally ended, but somehow the ghost of Lindros has remained, through the first-round exit to the Sabres and the one to the Senators, through Ramsey and Barber and finally Ken Hitchcock. The Flyers did everything they could do to wash away the Lindros hue—they even removed his likeness from the walls in the First Union Center and the SkateZone practice facility—but the only thing that can truly chase away the past is a Stanley Cup.

Hitchcock's homecoming helps, because, finally, there's stability in the coaching realm. But the fan base feels scorned, ultimately because of failed promises on the ice than anything Bob Clarke did off it.

Bob Clarke would have been a good military man. It is what makes him honorable and pitiable at the same time, the fact that he says, "I wouldn't know how to act if Mr. Snider said, 'You're done, you can't come back.'"

"I was lucky when I quit playing," Bob Clarke said. "I never had to face life alone. I stayed a part of the team. I'd hate like hell for it not to be a part of my life. All of a sudden, being on my own? It would be very, very hard after thirty years."

We are all defined by something. We all point to something to identify our being, who we really are. After all, just being is rather pointless. For Clarke, it is hockey as long as it will have him.

Clarke and his wife, Sandy, have raised four children, two of whom they adopted. They have a grandchild, which doesn't seem plausible if only because I can still see that photo—the one I copied as a child from *The Evening Bulletin*. They keep a condo in Voorhees, but their main home is in Ocean City, N.J., beachfront.

But Clarke still needs the Flyers, and he isn't the only athlete to feel that way. The locker room is a safe place for a lifer, much like in a strange way prison walls are for a real lifer. "You know," Clarke said at the time, "we got a man's gym. My daughter kids that she's going to sue me if we don't let women in. When you go in there it's men of all ages, and they're all the same. They like to sit around, work out, swear if they want, discuss sports. All you need is three-four women to walk in and it'd ruin it for everybody. Change the whole atmosphere." He realizes this sounds funny, and feels the need to add, "Not that anybody is against women or anything."

It is this mentality that makes him look back with an odd fondness on his days in the zinc mine. "I thought it was great, cleaning up spills, working in the crusher room. I don't see how a young person could get any better training for becoming a man. You were working with men. You're watching how they act, what they did. Then Friday everybody goes for beer after work. I fit right in."

This is who Bob Clarke is. Objects, to him, always have a shape and basic color and are tangible to at least three of the five senses. A man, to him, is the man in the mine. His thoughts are not governed by modern tenet, and so emotion is a response that comes only after a job is done.

It is this mentality that makes Snider say, "If I were in a dark alley, nobody I'd rather be with than Bob Clarke. He's not gonna dump ya. He gets it." And his longtime friend Parent say, "There was nobody I met who wanted to win more than him."

It is also this mentality that prompted Bernie Parent to say, "If there's one thing I'd like to see him do is have more fun. I'd like to see him stop and smell the flowers."

It is also this mentality that has caused some to criticize his management style. There always has been a notion that Clarke is envious of the great boom because he missed out on escalating salary, which doesn't make sense when considering his great pride in those old Flyer teams for not losing one player to significant raises in the World Hockey Association. What fits, according to his critics, is that he abhors the great boom not for the money but the fall-out.

"He's the type of guy that if you asked for a million dollar loan he'd write you a check out of his own pocket and say, 'Whenever you pay it back,'" said ESPN hockey analyst Al Morganti. "But if you asked for a $100 raise and he questioned whether it was warranted, he'd fight you tooth and nail for it."

Clarke said, "For all of us, there has to be better balance of what comes in, what goes out. I think as great as individual players are it's the players who make $8-9-10-12 million a year who put you over budget. You can't have one or two players taking up half your salary and expect to be a good team."

His eyes beg of you: Why can't you understand that?

In hindsight, Clarke turned out to be correct. The league is heading toward financial oblivion, and the Flyers still can't get back to the Finals, despite the second highest payroll. The Rangers, who have the league's highest payroll, can't even make the playoffs.

Meanwhile, for Bob Clarke, it's all so simple. Like after his first season in the NHL, he had to borrow three hundred dollars from his girlfriend to get back to Philadelphia. He spent his salary on a new Plymouth with the biggest engine he could find. That's what you did, and he would do the same now.

It's all so simple. It's when you dissect and analyze and whittle to the molecule that you distort Clarke. There was a belief that when Clarke retired and assumed his lot in the front office that he underwent a sort of metamorphosis. That he mutated from Bobby, a selfless player who smiled a lot and whom a city loved, into Bob, this Western Canadian cold, stoic creature of a front office fellow. That he orchestrated this change from Bobby to Bob literally.

"I was always Bob Clarke," he said. "When I got to the NHL, there was Bobby Hull and Bobby Orr, so they started calling me Bobby Clarke. But I never use that term about myself. I never signed it that way unless I was asked to. I've always been Bob Clarke.

"Bobby? I always thought it was kind of feminine name. I mean, a grown man being called Bobby? That's for a kid 5-6 years old. At least they didn't spell it with an I-E."

He is smiling a very toothy smile now. Those missing front teeth are back in his mouth, permanently bonded to his gums. He pops his eyebrows just a little. "Guess what? They could call me 'asshole,' that's fine," he says. "Oh, yeah, they already do."

SEVENTEEN

WING BOWL: THE ULTIMATE PHILLY EVENT

Elvis has entered the building. He is sitting on a toilet—all 350 pounds of him—waving a plunger and wearing enough sequins to make a Mummer blush. His "throne," complete with a toilet paper stand, is hoisted by four jumpsuit-wearing Elvii courtiers who, in turn, are trailed by a pack of nearly naked women, one of whom lifts up her skirt to flash some cheek as thousands go berserk.

Hey, what's not to like?

We are here at the Wing Bowl, Philadelphia's paean to gluttony, and, truth be told, the grandest and most extravagant eating contest in the nation. Whether or not this is a sporting event is debatable (we'll argue that it is), but this much is certain: There is no single spectacle that reveals as much about the id of the Philadelphia fan as this once-a-year contest in which 20,000 crazies watch 75 underdressed women feed chicken wings to 24 obese guys.

Don't even try to understand it. Just bathe in this orgy of the grotesque. The procession of eaters, dressed as dead rock stars, biblical figures and, in one case, a giant fried egg. The sexy—if occasionally skanky—"Wingettes." The halftime show of a guy cracking beer cans over his head until he passes out. The guest celebrities, including Phils manager Larry Bowa and world middleweight champion Bernard Hopkins. And, oh yes, the competitors—cheeks bulging with chicken meat, faces smeared with sauce, fighting (and sometimes losing) the battle against the gag reflex.

Wing Bowl is the marriage of Mardi Gras and the 700 Level. It's a bit "Rocky," a bit pro wrestling, a bit "The Man Show." Think of Hooters on hallucinogens and you're getting warm.

"It's like the Mummers Day parade but better, because we have girls, not guys dressed as girls," says Al Morganti, the WIP morning show genius who conceived the idea for Wing Bowl. "I don't think it would work in any other city. In fact, when I explain it to out-of-towners, they don't get it. 'Guys eat wings at 6 a.m. and 20,000 people watch?' There's no reasonable explanation for this. It's just one of those Philadelphia institutions that defy logic."

On second thought, the popularity of Wing Bowl is not that hard to comprehend. Consider the timing: the Friday morning before each year's Super Bowl. It's not like our Eagles are ever going to make it that game, let alone win it. So, we have to create our own championship event. While other cities hold victory parades, we host one huge bacchanal. It is, to a large degree, an Irish wake, where we celebrate the death of our sports hopes by drowning in sex and sauce and beer.

Lots of beer. State law allows the First Union Center taps to flow at 7 a.m.—an hour after the opening of Wing Bowl—and by 10 a.m., beer receipts topped $115,000 in 2003, according to Peter Luukko, the man who runs the building. "We've probably done more in beer sales at a few other events," Luukko says, "but never that much, that fast, that early." And that, of course, does not include what goes down in the arena parking lots, where tailgating for Wing Bowl begins shortly after midnight. Better get there early because the spaces fill up.

Is there anywhere else in the nation where traffic on two highways would snarl at dawn, where normally sane people would call in sick from work, where folks would brave January ice storms just to watch fat men fight the urge to regurgitate?

Wing Bowl is the largest eating contest, in terms of attendance, as well as the largest radio promotion in the country. Still, it remains our little secret.

"If this was in New York, it would be listed in travel magazines," says Morganti. "If it was in Boston, it would be considered chic. But in Philadelphia, it's overlooked, just like the city itself.

"I don't know if you want to want to hold it up for acclaim like the Cherry Blossom Festival, but, hey, this is us, for better or worse. Twenty thousand people can't be wrong."

In the beginning, there were no 20,000 people. There were no Wingettes. There just two fat guys, quietly chowing down in a hotel lobby.

There was no great plan at the onset. There was just a slow week of radio.

It was 1993, and the two-week gap between the NFL conference championships and the Super Bowl was creating a deadly lull on WIP's morning show. With the Eagles out of the running—again—it seemed the only way to create excitement was to invent something.

Kicking around ideas, morning show producer Joe Weachter suggested an eating contest. Morganti seized upon Buffalo chicken wings, because the Buffalo Bills, as always, were in the Super Bowl. And while Morganti was the idea man, morning show ringmaster Angelo Cataldi was the salesman who made it work.

"I may have conceived it," says Morganti, "but Angelo built it up. It's like an eggs-and-ham breakfast. The chicken is involved. But the pig is really committed."

The pig, er, Cataldi, recruited two callers who vowed to out-eat each other. So on the Friday morning before the first Dallas-Buffalo Super Bowl, the original Wing Bowl was held in the lobby of the Wyndham Franklin Plaza Hotel in Center City before a crowd of 50, mostly quizzical hotel guests. History records that "Carmen, Jr." ran up such a big lead on "Doc," that he spent the last five minutes leaning back and enjoying a cigarette. For his efforts, he won a $10 portable hibachi that had been pulled from the WIP prize closet that morning.

As one-time radio promotions go, it was moderately entertaining. No one had thought of making it an annual event. But at the end, WIP midday guy Chuck Cooperstein, who officiated the contest in a referee's outfit, stuck a mike in the victor's face and shouted, "Carmen, Jr., you've just won Wing Bowl! What are you going to do now?"

Unfazed or unaware of the ubiquitous Disney World campaign, Carmen mumbled, "I'm going to start preparing for Wing Bowl 2."

And with that great pronouncement, recalls Cataldi, "We sat up and said, 'What the hell, we could do this again.'"

(A quick interlude: Wing Bowl's success prompted the Morning Show to try another gluttonous stunt at the hotel—a hot-dog—eating challenge. On July 4, 1994, six contestants vied in that affair, until one got so sick that he ran from the lobby to throw up. He ended up heaving outside a plate glass window right next to the WIP set, which set off a chain-reaction puke-athon among contestants, hosts and spectators that resembled the pie-eating scene from the movie "Stand By Me." Just at that moment, a Wyndham Corporation vice president happened to be walking through the lobby.

"Soon after that, our association with that hotel came to an end," recalls Cataldi. So did the hot dog competition.)

Anyway, Wing Bowl 1 led to Wing Bowl 2 (no pretentious Roman numerals here!), which eventually led to one of the annual highlights of our city's calendar. The crowd swelled every year so that Wing Bowl kept being the gold fish that outgrows its tank—from the hotel to a nightclub to a concert hall to the Spectrum to, finally, the First Union Center. It was Mayor Ed Rendell who initially granted WIP the use of the city-owned Spectrum, ostensibly in exchange for a charitable donation but also, in large part, because Hizzoner knew that the wackos who filled the joint were potential voters who might be impressed seeing the Mayor onstage, handing the sauce-spattered winner his chicken-bone tiara. Mayor John Street, on the other hand, wouldn't be caught dead anywhere near Wing Bowl and would probably be heckled more lustily than "Uncle Buck," the 2003 contestant who showed up in a full Tampa Bay Buccaneers uniform.

With growth came new wrinkles. Starting around year three, prospective eaters had to audition at WIP studios. That not only weeded out the impostors, it also gave the station a full month of easy promotion. The stunts have grown more outrageous over the years—witness the fool who ate a Sno-cone made of the slush stuck in a car's wheel well, or the vampire who swallowed a pig's ear with a chaser of pig's blood. I once watched a 600-pound man devour a Melrose Diner cake designed for 35 people. He kept it down. Another time, I witnessed a guy named "Corn Boy" slurp down six cans of Del Monte creamed corn in six minutes. He spewed.

Somewhere along the way, the trenchermen began showing up at Wing Bowl with processions—floats and thrones and entourages and sight gags that would make the World Wrestling Federation cringe. The highlight came in 1997 when the "Golden Buddha," a five-foot-six, 400-pound wise guy, led a 50-piece string band onto the stage at the Electric Factory. His raucous followers not only threatened to collapse the rickety set-up; they also managed to kick out the plug, sending the show off the air for ten minutes.

That was around the time Cataldi started recruiting pretty women to help dish up and hand out the wings. The "Wingettes" started out as fairly demure listeners of the station who wanted to be involved. Over time, they have been displaced by a parade of silicone—models and dancers from local strip clubs who realize that a Wing Bowl appearance means great exposure, and so exposure—of thighs, butts, cleavage and occasionally more—became what it is all about.

"They started out as the girl next door," says Morganti. "Now, they ain't the girl next door at all, unless you're living in certain downtown neighborhoods."

Wing Bowl had its formula. What it needed was a superstar. That guy, Kevin O'Donnell, showed up in 1994.

O'Donnell is an earnest, somewhat shy mortgage banker. Put him in a business suit and he can blend into the crowd, not an easy task for a six-foot-six, 350-pound man. Put a plate of food in front of him, and he turns into Godzilla.

Actually, he turns into "Heavy Kevy," the all-consuming alterego who swallowed down a dozen jelly donuts in four minutes to initially qualify for Wing Bowl. His eating style is spectacular; he developed the twist-and-strip method of devouring a chicken wing that allows him to rip the flesh off the wing, swallow the meat without chewing and discard the bone in one sweeping motion.

Heavy Kevy took speed eating to a new level in Wing Bowls 2 and 3. Most of the other early contestants were merely huge, slovenly guys who could consume food all day, although not at any great pace. Kevy was a speed eater, who—in his prime—averaged six wings a minute, one every ten seconds. His prowess at the plate became a draw for the event.

Think Babe Ruth here. There is more than a passing resemblance between the original Bambino and this Sultan of Sauce. Kevy, like the Babe, has that barrel torso, the huge head, even the spindly piano legs. While Ruth brought the home run to baseball, Heavy Kevy brought power eating to Wing Bowl. He also brought personality. While Kevin O'Donnell is a quiet man, Heavy Kevy is articulate, charismatic and a great trash talker—in other words the perfect guy to help advance a radio promotion.

Kevy lapped the field in those early Wing Bowls. He retired for a while, came back for one more try (finishing fourth in Wing Bowl 10) and then did what all great ex-jocks do, left the sport to go into broadcasting. In recent years he has served as Wing Bowl's expert analyst.

He also engaged in one of the great stunts of Wing Bowl back in 1997. Moments before the competition was to begin, Heavy Kevy invited his girlfriend onstage and—before thousands of screaming witnesses and tens of thousands of radio listeners—dropped to his knees to propose. She accepted. He got too choked up to compete.

The proposal was one of many strange Wing Bowl moments—planned and unplanned. In 2001, one couple actually went a step further, holding their wedding at the start of Wing Bowl. The First Union Center crowd, more geeked up for mayhem than matrimony, booed the whole time. That was the same year the National Anthem was sung by a woman bouncing on a trampoline. She, too, was booed because (a) her voice didn't carry, and (b) her outfit wasn't skimpy enough.

Respectful? No. But, hey, this is Philadelphia.

El Wingador – Philadelphia's most consistent champion.

And then there was the time that an eight-month-pregnant woman named Angela qualified for the contest. Cataldi insisted that a doctor verify that neither Angela nor her unborn child would be in any danger. She showed up at Wing Bowl, gobbled down more than 40 wings and then announced she was in distress.

"We used spicier wings back then to make it more of a battle of survival," Cataldi recalls. "She started sweating and turning colors. They rushed her to the hospital. Sure enough, she calls a few days later and tells us she delivered twins four hours after Wing Bowl. What a sideshow."

Other sideshows have been tried, with varying degrees of success. Standup comedians and hand-farters were heckled off the stage. One year, WIP personality Big Daddy Graham was set to grapple with professional women wrestlers (in a ring strewn with the excess chicken wings), but spectators started throwing so much debris at the ring that the brawl was called off.

"I guess there are some standards even our audience won't sink to," says morning show producer Joe Weachter. In fact, the event inspired Wing Bowl's motto: "We've upped our standards. Now up yours."

This year—2003—the gang decided to play it safe by holding a Miss Wingette contest. ("Nobody's going to boo women in bikinis," offers Weachter.) The winner turned out to be a statuesque, if vacuous, blonde whose talent is twirling a hula hoop while reciting nursery rhymes. Needless to say, she was a crowd favorite.

The audience for Wing Bowl is a fair cross section of Philadelphia sports fans, assuming that 99 percent of those fans are male. Certainly, the 700 Level maniacs are out in full force, shot-gunning beer in the aisles and lifting their T-shirts in hopes that the Wingettes might do the same. They're the ones that television cameras always find (and, yes, there is coverage by every local station), just like the moron who strips off his shirt at Eagles games when it's 10 below.

But around them are perfectly presentable people, just out for a good time on a dreary January morning. In my own case this morning, I've driven down my brother-in-law, a button-down public policy wonk who's more often found in the halls of Harrisburg than the bowels of a hockey arena; my 16-year-old son, skipping a day of high school for a much higher priority; and my 69-year-old buddy, Hilary, a dignified gentleman who has actually put on a tie this morning. Somehow they wind up in seats right next to the rooting section for a competitor named "Southwest Philly Junkyard Dog," who punctuate every sentence by barking in unison. My other son, 19, has driven all night from Boston in a van packed with college buddies determined to bathe in the lunacy.

"It's the cross section of fans that make it work," says Cataldi. "See, we just started this as a lark, but people adopted it as an extra holiday. They schedule a day off of work for this. We also didn't anticipate the high school and college kids coming out, because they're not the people who listen to our show. They've just heard that it's a nutty, out-of-control party. And who doesn't want four hours of that?

"I'd love to tell you we had these master plans to grow Wing Bowl into this huge event. But, you know, it just sort of happened on its own. Someone started the processions, and we lucked into processions. A couple of sexy women showed up, so we lucked into sex—well, sexiness, anyway. It just kept growing and getting more fun, and it's really the people, not us, who pushed it along.

"The fact that it's free doesn't hurt either."

Wing Bowl is a festival that comes two days before every Super Bowl, or just when the city's sports fans need it most. The Eagles season has invariably ended, often in bitter disappointment. The Flyers and Sixers are in that lull when their seasons are no longer new, but the playoff push has not yet started. We need something—a reason to party, an event to celebrate. And, we need a hero.

In recent years, that hero has been El Wingador, the monstrous alter ego of South Jersey trucker Bill Simmons. If Heavy Kevy was Wing Bowl's Babe Ruth, El Wingador is its Barry Bonds—an amazingly powerful athlete who keeps getting better with age. Headed into today's contest, he has won the event three times. In a city without dynasties, that makes this 41-year-old the clear favorite of most of the fans who pack the arena.

There is more pressure than ever this year. Wing Bowl has become known among a strange circle of men who travel the competitive eating circuit and call themselves "gurgitators." Our hometown event has now attracted competitors from New York and Ohio and Connecticut. They are here to gorge for the glory, and also to make off with the winner's prize. This year, that is a new Subaru, quite an improvement from the original winner's hibachi.

The morning show team has masterfully shaped today's affair into an "us versus them" contest, in which carpetbaggers have come to steal our honor. The outsiders are cast as villains no less heinous than the Dallas Cowboys. In this plot line, it is up to one of our local heroes (read: El Wingador) to keep the trophy—and our pride—from leaving town. And Simmons understands his role. Today he is wearing a Chuck Bednarik No. 60 Eagles jersey, a 1960 vintage reminder of a time when our teams were champions.

Unlike some of the other blobs in the contest, Simmons is a certified athlete, a star football and baseball player in high school who had tryouts with two Major League teams. He also takes an athlete's mindset into Wing Bowl 11. For weeks before the contest, he works on strengthening his jaw by chewing on frozen Tootsie Rolls. In the days leading up to it, he expands his belly by drinking three gallons of water a day. At six-foot-five, he normally weighs an athletic 285 pounds. For Wing Bowl, he bulks up to 310.

While the pageantry of pre-contest hype is taking place on a First Union Center floor, Simmons begins to turn into El Wingador in a private room backstage. He is psyching himself up, and here comes Bill Bergey, the great Eagles middle linebacker from the 1980s, to lend a hand.

"You want a pep talk?" offers Bergey.

"Sure, that would be good," says El Wingador.

"Okay," says Bergey, and suddenly he, too, is transformed. His eyes open wide, his face reddens and his head goes back and forth like he's searching for a quarterback to clothesline.

"You're the hope, you're the hero," Bergey spits out, his face inches from El Wingador. "The Eagles are done for the season! Philly fans are depending on you! Keep the title here! Make the city proud!"

Bergey swats El Wingador on the head a few times, an old football tradition, albeit usually done while the guy is wearing a helmet.

"Let me out there, let me at them," shouts the greatest eater Philadelphia has ever known.

All 23 other contestants have been introduced. The First Union Center lights dim, the music stops, and here he comes. The crowd goes wild. What Dr. J. was in basketball, what Richie Ashburn was in baseball, that is what El Wingador is today—one of our truly beloveds.

He is up to the challenge. In the first 14-minute round, he devours 86 wings, giving him a ten-wing lead over the closest competitor, Don "Moses" Lerman of New York. One of the out-of-towners, Ohio's "Coondog" O'Karma, has already pushed away from the table in disgrace.

The top 10 finishers compete in a second, 14-minute round; then the top five stay for a two-minute sprint. They may sip water. No napkins are allowed, to prevent bones from being smuggled out with the trash.

As the competition moves on, El Wingador's lead grows larger. The only real challenger is Lerman, a 150-pound retired grocer in his sixties. On the First Union Center's huge scoreboard, the camera focuses on a close-up of Lerman, who covers his mouth and appears to gag.

This is all the crowd needs to see.

"Puke! Puke! Puke!" The chant grows louder. Everyone is reminded of one of the all-time

Wing Bowl highlights, from 2002, when a contestant named Sloth seemed to be having trouble keeping his wings down. Seeing himself on the arena's big screen, Sloth seized the moment. He unleashed a projectile vomit far beyond anything seen in "The Exorcist." The arcing flow of half-digested chicken was replayed, again and again, in slow motion and stop action, much to the delight of the audience.

Sloth was disqualified from the event. Rule No. 1: If you heave, you leave.

Lerman does not lose control. The crowd is disappointed.

El Wingador, however, does not disappoint. Seeming to be in the kind of competitive zone that only great athletes find, he just keeps eating and eating. In the end, he has swallowed 154 wings—25 more than Lerman and an all-time record for Wing Bowl.

As he is fitted with the crown of chicken bones, El Wingador has his two young daughters on his lap. He has saved the title for the city, thanks to Bergey's pep talk, the months of chewing on Tootsie Rolls and his amazing capacity to just keep eating.

The crowd is thrilled. This may not rank up there with other sports titles, but in Philadelphia, well . . .

"This is our Super Bowl," says Morganti. "And it probably always will be."

EIGHTEEN

THE GOOD DOCTOR

I had a hero, and I mean it the most honest sense of the word. By the way, that word alone—hero—stands there like a pillar, sturdy and robust, and it's a natural magnet to a kid. For a kid needs to believe the outside is as safe as the inside, because the world seems tenuous at 10. It seems like it can go all bust overnight. A kid needs a hero because they need to believe in something. Belief is paramount to kid survival, whether it's in Santa Claus or the good fairy or the notion of heaven as an actual, physical place with a pool and a Marriott. There has to be something or someone out there that represents goodness or hope.

So, yes, I had my guy. By the way, a hero can't be a parent or a relative or a teacher, or anyone we interact with on a regular basis. Surely, we want it to be so, because we can usually control the action of such people and because it seems so pure that way. But we kid ourselves. We buy into nobility that a kid can't, not then, not looking up with starry eyes, an unweathered brow and unbridled naiveté. So while my mother was certainly hero-worthy, if only because of her brimming kindness toward others and all of her saintly ways, I did not choose her then because I could only choose her now. Then, I needed a stranger, whom I deemed larger than life, some immortal being. I didn't care much for superheroes or Westerns or history. Seriously, when I was 10 and my teacher assigned the obligatory essay on our hero, why in the world did she offer up as an example George Washington, boasting that, after all, he was the father of our country? I mean, why not Ben Franklin? I knew he had bad hair, too, but at least his likeness appeared on the hundred instead of the measly buck.

My hero had to be in sports. Honestly, that's all I really cared about then. I used to quiz myself on the roster of the teams, writing as many names as I can remember—their positions and jersey numbers—in the last pages of my math notebook. There were players I really liked. Bobby Clarke. Bernie Parent. Larry Bowa. Greg Luzinski. Bake McBride. Mike Schmidt, though mostly I'd just like to count his home runs and RBIs because I deemed him too steely. Bill Bergey. Wilbert Montgomery. Ron Jaworski. Loved them all.

But my main man was the Doc.

Julius Winfield Erving II, born February 22, 1950, in Roosevelt, N.Y, 6-foot-6, 210 pounds, star forward from the University of Massachusetts. He got drafted by the Bucks in '72 but didn't play, opting to sign with the Virginia Squires of the ABA. He later starred for the New York Nets before the Nets fell into financial woe and sold him to the Sixers. I knew all of this by heart, because my first real book I remember reading on my own was *The Legend of Doctor J*, by Bill Guttman. I read that book had to be fifty times, and flipped the rippled pages with the same fervor every time, especially the middle break with the montage of photos. I remember how cool he looked, skying over the rest of the players, like he was flying.

I was eight when the Sixers bought him the year of the Bicentennial, and I remember all of the excited talk. I had seen him play once, but I was enthralled by everyone's zeal. The Nets sold him for $3 million 24 hours before the start of the season following a contract dispute, and Sixers GM Pat Williams said, "We got the Babe Ruth of basketball." He was a show by himself, and he had the coolest nickname. Funny, what attracts kids. I remember cutting a picture out of the *Bulletin* of the press conference and sealing it with glue stick to red construction paper for a nice border. In the picture, Doc stood next to Sixers owner Fitz Dixon, and Doc wore this jacket and thick matching bowtie, I believe checkered. I distinctly remember making my mind up that anytime anyone ever asked who my all-time, all-time favorite player is—and Richie the Barber, who used to cut my hair at his place with the safari motif in Southwest [Philly], with the *Playboy* magazines on the coffee table in the waiting area, would always ask me that question—I'd say, Doc. Yep, Doc was my guy. Little did I know at the time that Doc was everybody's guy.

It didn't matter, of course. Because I had dibs on Doc with my friends, and my older cousin Joey, who also loved Doc, allowed me to claim him. It's vital at that age to stake claim to your own player. So anyway, I watched Doc dutifully that first season, and I remember being so angry at George McGinnis for what I thought blowing the series against the Blazers. I remember Game 6, the fourth straight Sixer loss after winning the first two. It took place on a Sunday afternoon, in Portland. I remember going outside on a warm spring day afterwards, bouncing my basketball by myself, hysterical in tears. But I was hooked.

Years later, I read an interview with Erving done in Las Vegas in 1992 for a publication called *Basketball Legend*, and he reflected back on that season with astute introspection. "In Philadelphia," he said, "our team was put together and I became the last component of that team. It was sort of parallel to what happened with the Yankees: George Steinbrenner getting all these players together and winning the World Series. There were a lot of assumptions that, in basketball, that's how things worked: if you put together a lot of high-priced talent, they were going to win.

"The first year that we were together, we were the second-best team in the world. But when we lost the four straight, the team suddenly became stigmatized. It was like, those guys are good, but they're not winners."

I loved basketball. To this day, I have hard time saying which I loved the most back then—football, basketball, baseball or hockey—for fear of slighting the others, like what would happen after naming your favorite parent. I truly followed each with a rabid fork. But remember, basketball in the late '70s wasn't anywhere close to as popular as it is now; in fact, the NBA was in dire straits—until Doc bailed them out, acting as the savior, the highlight bridge to Magic and Bird and later Jordan. Basketball was also highly black, and what did I know of race? I loved Doc, and I never once thought it odd that I had tan skin and he had a slightly darker brown hue. I did, however, think it was cool that I had an afro like Doc's, and it made feel better when Andy's older brother called me barbed-wire or Brillo pad because of my bushy hair. It wasn't until I got older did I realize the absurdity of the world when it came to color or creed. Not that that's any big deal, because I think it lessens the lesson to speak of it in this manner, but I am grateful that I was called to sport at such a young age because the only color I saw was home or away, jersey color. Sport kept my heart pure when it came to any ethnic group. I just saw players and teams, guys who I either liked or disliked because of their court or field prowess.

So I loved it when the Sixers traded McGinnis for Bobby Jones, an unselfish sort who'd let Doc be Doc and not fight him for the ball or the accolades. I remember looking forward to the games with such anticipation. I'd know the television schedule by heart, which the days the Flyers would be on 29, the Phillies on 17 and the Sixers on 48, so I'd make sure my homework was completed by tipoff and I fetch my pen and pad and watch the game while keeping track of Doc's points and rebounds. The next day, I'd cut out the game story and the boxscore from the paper. I had a scrapbook that went for volumes. I pestered my parents to sign me up for *Sports Illustrated* and *Basketball Digest* and *Sport Magazine*, and I'd wait with bated breath for the mail.

I tell you all of this because I know you did the same thing, or something like it. We all had a guy. My guy wore No. 6 so of course whatever sport I played—basketball, baseball, football—I had to be No. 6. I had to have the red satin Sixers jacket and the basketball charm that hung next to my Saint Anthony medal and the sneakers, yes, Doc's sneakers were big. The red and white Converse All-Stars with the star inside the sideways arrow, leather of course, and I made my mom polish them with shoe polish. And speaking of Doc's sneakers, I recall the time in third grade that we had to write a story giving life to an inanimate object, and I chose Doc's sneakers, writing that speak in squeak because of the basketball floor.

As I grew older, I appreciated Doc even more. I noticed how he acted, as well as how he played. Certainly, his game remained electrifying, and I swore he could walk on water, or at least a great lake like it was the free throw line, but he handled himself with a grace that I deemed the ultimate cool. Lots of people have waxed on about Doc, but perhaps coach Billy Cunningham said it best, "As a basketball player, Julius was the first to truly take the torch and become the spokesman for the NBA. Julius was the first player I ever remember who transcended sports and was known by one name—Doctor."

I think back to how foolish I was, however, endearing. Alas, I did more than try to mimic his bank shot or the way he shot fouls, I tried to copy his walk—arms dangling, moving with a cadence, guided by an ever so slight strut. I was proud of my arms because they were abnormally long, like Doc's, and truthfully, they were the only part of my body that was made for hoops, my shoulders broad and my legs thick. I had a linebacker's physique that didn't help when I tried to do Doc's finger roll at Poe Schoolyard.

I recall Doc talking of his physical attributes and saying that basketball picked him. "I think I was chosen by basketball, although I never really physically got drafted to any team that I played for," he said. "I think that my God-given physical attributes, big hands, and big feet, the way that I'm built, proportion-wise, just made basketball the most inviting sport for me to play. And from the first time I picked up a basketball at age eight—I had a lot of difficulty when I first picked up a basketball, because I was a scrub—there were things that I liked about it. When I was a freshman in high school I was maybe 5-9. And as a sophomore, 5-11, approaching 6 feet. As a junior I was 6-1, and when I graduated high school I was 6-3. When I got out of college, I was pushing 6-6. And I continued to grow until I was 25 years old."

I barely grew after eighth grade, topping out at 6 feet, and yet I wore the chintzy No. 6 jersey that was really a tank top cotton shirt with decals on it. I see the throwbacks now, and I am immediately envious until I see who's wearing them. For that was a time before hyper marketers dulled our senses with stuff like that, with too many games and too many sideline shots of players' wives and kids. Sport wasn't necessarily for everyone back then. It wasn't about a fashion statement, and it wasn't a subset of entertainment alongside movies, music, and foreign entanglements. Honestly—and I wholeheartedly admit it's quite pathetic—but I blanch when I see an 18-year-old kid wearing a Doc throwback today because they haven't the slightest idea.

Because I know they've never tried that move—you know, THE MOVE—and took 17 steps while trying to get past a fake Mark Landsberger on one side of the backboard and wind up on the other side scoring with that swoop of scoop. It went like this, and I swear this moment is indelible in my memory and has been since that very moment of Game 4 of the Sixers-Lakers Finals: First he drove past Landsberger along the right baseline and left his feet on that side of the backboard with a layup in mind. Doc's route to the rim was quickly blocked by Kareem Abdul-Jabbar's outstretched arms, so he brought the ball back down and just continued to float, seemingly forever, passing behind the backboard while appearing to glide slightly to the left in midair. He finally cleared all the way to the other side of the hoop, reached back in toward the court and put up a soft, underhanded scoop for the basket.

"Here I was, trying to win a championship, and my mouth just dropped open," Magic Johnson will say. "He actually did that. I thought, 'What should we do? Should we take the ball out or should we ask him to do it again?'"

I swear Doc had wings.

I know, I know, Connie Hawkins performed his own tricks, but Jordan and every modern mid-air maestro were merely the children of Dr. J. "When handling the ball," Doc said, "I always would look for daylight, wherever there was daylight. Sometimes there's only a little bit of daylight between two players, and you'd find a way to get the ball between those two bodies and you make something happen. Having good peripheral vision, I would always see daylight. Maybe I could see daylight that a lot of other players couldn't see."

I know a lot of things about Doc today that never made Bill Guttman's book. I know that he retired at age 37, having scored more than 30,000 points in his combined ABA and NBA career. I know that he scored 22.0 points per game in his 11 NBA seasons with the Sixers and 28.7 points per game in his five ABA seasons with Virginia and New York. I know that he was elected to the Basketball Hall of Fame in 1993. I know that he got the best of Larry Bird in that fight at the old Boston Garden on November 9, 1984. I know that he fathered illegiti-

"Doc" scores on some anonymous Celtic.

mate children. I know that his kids had to endure terrible ordeals. I know that he had marriage difficulties with the lovely Turquoise.

I know that he was a serial womanizer.

I know all about the frailties of man now.

Do I feel scorned or suckered? No. Did I discard my Doc memories? No. Honestly, do I really give a damn? No. To the contrary, I'm glad I made Doc my guy. Now I'm grateful nothing came out back then to tarnish the way I saw my hero, for at 10 we see things in black and white. But today I do believe that his gray was mostly good, and his basketball was absolutely great. Regardless, I've never met the man and don't particularly care to because he's best served where he is.

Today I don't have dibs on Doc alone anymore. I share him with my buddy Joe Ben, who only trumps me because he was born on Doc's birthday. We talk about the days of idol worship as kids, and once in a great while we make a late night pilgrimage with a quart of beer to Doc's mural just north of Center City. We toast him for the memories.

They've come through our town as superstars and bums, players of great promise and untalented frauds. Some played better before coming here, others improved after leaving. Many deserved our wrath, a few were unfairly targeted.

Regardless, all found themselves in our crosshairs.

Here is a gallery of the players we loved to hate:

Scott Rolen. We didn't always boo Scott Rolen. And we certainly didn't run him out of town—he macheted that path on his own. But it's tough to find a personality that ever fit the city worse than that of this dour, whiney third baseman from Jasper, Ind. Philadelphia requires players have to hide as thick as a rhino's. Rolen's skin was as thin and brittle as papyrus.

He came here as the great Midwestern hope; a slugging, slick-fielding prospect who would replace Schmitty. Hey, we *wanted* to like him. We cheered as he won Rookie of the Year, marveled when he got the Gold Glove in his second full season. Rolen played the game with a keen mind and a dirty uniform. Sure, he struck out too often with men on base, but everything was going to work out.

Except Rolen wanted no part of us. He was an uptight Ayn Rand disciple misplaced in a city that actually demands a relationship with its sports heroes. An early inkling came in an *Inquirer* personality profile—and we use the word "personality" loosely here—in which Rolen said he had no desire to share his off-field interests with the fans. To anyone asking more, he said, "Sorry about your luck."

Rolen was a loner in a public business. Said Curt Schilling: "If nobody said a word to him from the day he signed, he would have been fine. He just wants to show up, put his uniform on and play."

Or not play. One of the clarifying moments of Rolen's six-year career here came when he took a day of rest on the Sunday the team had declared "Scott Rolen Day." Blame idiot manager Terry Francona if you like, but Rolen—if he was as brainy as he considered himself—should have understood that you take the field on the afternoon 30,000 fans pay admission to take home T-shirts bearing your image.

He never did seem to get it. When a scattering of fans began booing his lack of offensive production, Rolen blamed us all. He refused to take a curtain call after a game-winning homer in 2001.

"My feelings were hurt," he said of the booing. "That crushed me. I didn't feel good about it. I didn't understand it. I don't ever want to feel like that again."

Aw, grow up.

He always had rabbit ears. He sulked in 2002 after manager Larry Bowa said that a slump by Rolen was "killing us." He went ballistic a month later when senior advisor Dallas Green said on WIP, "Scotty is satisfied with being a so-so player. He's not a great player. In his mind, he probably thinks he's doing OK, but the fans in Philadelphia know otherwise. I think he can be greater, but his personality won't let him."

Green was taking aim at Rolen's habit of being the last guy to arrive at the ballpark and the first to leave. By the summer of 2002 Rolen's heart wasn't in it—at least not here. That's why a teammate anonymously described him as a cancer in the clubhouse.

Clearly, the player once promoted as the redemption of the franchise couldn't wait to flee. Rolen floated the notion that he was distressed by the franchise's lack of commitment, but you didn't need to be a mind reader to know that what he was really saying was, "I hate this town and its fans and I'm dying to escape."

Which is not to absolve the organization. Phils ownership never spent the money required to improve the product during Rolen's tenure here. It's just that when Scotty declared, "I think the fans deserve better," we didn't quite buy that he was suddenly looking out for us.

The loner in a public business: Scott Rolen.

Rolen put the poison pill in his contract demand. He and his agent went where no player had gone in history. Beyond his own salary, he wanted the club to commit to a certain payroll ranking among the Major League teams. If the team fell below that standing, Rolen would become a free agent.

The Phils said no. Divorce became inevitable. In August 2002, the club traded Rolen to the Cardinals for a bag of lucky beans. In one final insult, Rolen said, "I feel like I've died and gone to heaven."

Hey, if St. Louis is heaven, Scott, we'll stay here in purgatory, thank you very much.

Von Hayes. Twenty years later, Von Hayes's chief tormentor still won't let up.

"They should have given him the uniform number 541," cackles Pete Rose, repeating the joke he first uttered back in 1983 spring training. "Get it?"

Yeah, we get it. Five-for-one, the legacy of Von Hayes. Never mind that only one of the five guys the Phils traded to Cleveland for him in 1983 turned out to be anything (Julio Franco), the simple mathematics of the deal will follow Hayes to his grave.

Hayes was crushed under the weight of expectations. His sweet swing and lanky body had some scouts touting him as the next Ted Williams. Truth is, he played more like Vanessa Williams. A softer, nicer Major League player you never met.

But there was more. Hayes played with a weariness and a vacuous look that bordered on stupefying. At least a half-dozen times a year, he'd get picked off base, staring into space with the inattentive expression of a Little League rightfielder. He would strike out looking and stroll back to the dugout with all the emotion of a doorknob. That's why, years later, Phils fans came to believe that Hayes had been reincarnated as Travis Lee.

As the franchise crumbled from Hayes's arrival in 1983 (when the Phils went to the World Series) to his departure in 1991 (their fifth-straight losing season), Hayes personified the languor of the entire organization. He had a few good seasons, even making the All-Star Game in 1989, but his lack of passion and his failure to meet expectations were too much for fans to handle.

Give him this, though: He never complained about the treatment, saying, more than once, "I guess it's better to be booed than not noticed at all." And he never harbored a grudge.

I ran into Hayes at a charity bowling tournament outside Philadelphia in 2003. To my surprise, he had nothing but positive things to say about the city and its fans.

"It probably would have bothered me if I was the only guy they ever heckled," he said. "But I knew there was a long line of players before and after me who heard it from the fans. I really enjoyed my times in Philly, especially playing in the World Series. If I measure the bad times against the good ones, I'm fairly happy. I think it's a very special city."

Lance Parrish. The body-building catcher was a six-time All-Star and three-time Gold Glover before he got to Philadelphia. He played seven productive seasons after leaving us. But during his two seasons in Philadelphia, Parrish forgot how to play.

He showed up in 1987, our biggest free-agent addition since Pete Rose. The Phils, desperate to catch the Mets and searching for a marketing tool, offered up the slogan "Lance us a pennant." If that seems laughable in hindsight, it didn't sound much better at the time.

Parrish was going to be the solid defensive catcher that had been lacking since Bob Boone left six years earlier. Plus, he had averaged 28 homers a year in his previous five seasons in Detroit. He would protect Mike Schmidt in the order.

It never worked out. Parrish was coming off back surgery and couldn't find his groove. Not that we gave him any time. We booed his third at-bat of Opening Night (a double play), a local record for impatience that stood until we booed Donovan McNabb as he got drafted.

If that bothered Parrish, he went ballistic a few days later when a few boneheads heckled his wife and children as they sat in the Vet. In less than a week, the relationship had soured and it never recovered.

Parrish played with a permanent sulk during his two years here. He hit .230 and, for all the offensive punch he promised, averaged just 63 RBIs per season. Incredibly, he managed to make the 1988 National League All-Star team (hitting .215), the most mind-boggling honor of that sort since Eagles quarterback Mike Boryla made the NFL Pro Bowl in 1976.

Then he left, returned to the America League and regained his ability to hit. Hell, he hung on until he was 39.

"Friends warned me about Philadelphia," Parrish told me soon after leaving. "They said the fans would turn on me if I had a bad game; that little kids would curse me, that Philly doesn't give players a honeymoon period. But when people heckled me—and my wife—after one at-bat, that was more than I bargained for. That city has a bad reputation for one reason: It deserves it."

Andy Ashby. One good rule of thumb for aspiring athletes: No matter how much venom the fans may be spitting, never respond with an obscene gesture.

Andy Ashby couldn't follow that guideline. And soon enough, he was gone.

Ashby came to the Phils from San Diego before the 2000 season. Actually, it was a return visit. The Scranton native had originally come up with the Phillies and said he was eager to be home. The fans were excited, too. With Curt Schilling as the No. 1 starter and Ashby (who had made the All-Star team a year earlier) as the No. 2, the team seemed to have its best front to a rotation since Steve Carlton and John Denny.

Except Andy quickly made an Ash of himself. For whatever reason, he couldn't pitch at the Vet, going 1-5 with a 6.37 ERA in front of the home fans. Maybe we intimidated him. To be truthful, he wasn't much better on the road. And he continually whined, letting everyone know that, on the whole, he'd rather not be in Philadelphia. With his contract soon to expire, Ashby wouldn't talk to the team about an extension.

We jeered, he bristled. Ashby ripped the fans, saying, "I go out there for nine innings, make one mistake and get booed. It's not fair."

We tried to figure the math: One mistake, six runs. How was that possible?

Ashby went two months without a win. It all ended in a late June meltdown at the Vet. Ashby gave up five runs in six innings to the Milwaukee Brewers, baseball's weakest-hitting team. As he ambled off the mound, Ashby was hooted by the small but angry crowd of 13,520.

First, he smirked and waved mockingly at a group of fans sitting behind the Phils' dugout. Because he was being named in trade rumors at the time, it seemed he was waving goodbye.

As he reached the top step of the dugout, Ashby stopped to jaw with a group of front-row hecklers. The exchange was X-rated—on both sides—and it culminated with Ashby grabbing his crotch and inviting a few fans to, well, you know . . . .

It's tough to win back the folks' hearts after that. A week later, Ashby was traded to the Braves. Proving that God has a sense of humor, Ashby even got to pitch in the 2000 post-season.

"No one likes to get booed, but it happens," Ashby said after the trade. "I did something wrong. I said something I shouldn't have. I lost it, and I apologized for it. Everything just built up . . . . I deserved to be booed. Heck, my kids were booing me."

Mike Mamula. Every once in a while, the fans simply know more than the coaches. Early on, we realized that Mike Mamula was an underachieving fraud. Hell, other players around the league knew it too. Taking off on Mamula's jersey number and his inability to stop the run, they tagged him with the nickname "Highway 59." In other words, if you need to go far, just take "Highway 59."

But the Eagles refused to acknowledge the failures of this 252-pound defensive end. They kept telling us how he led the team, if not the entire NFL, in "almosts," as if getting close to a sack was good enough. For six years, Mamula was the guy you'd see just entering your television screen as the other team's quarterback threw the ball.

First Ray Rhodes and then Andy Reid tried to sell us that Mamula made the other players around him better—like Hugh Douglas would turn into Hugh Grant if Mamula wasn't on the other side. Rhodes even compared him to a young Charles Haley.

This, of course, drove us nuts. We may not be able to break down the tape like an NFL coach, but we could see the obvious. Mamula had one move, a speed rush to the outside. If the opponent's offensive tackle was conscious enough to stop that, Mamula would finish the day with his usual stats—one tackle, one assist, zero sacks.

Mamula was one of the first NFL combine prodigies, a guy who wowed the scouts with his vertical leap and ability to dance between orange cones. Never mind that he was a middling player at Boston College; his stellar performance at the league's 1995 tryouts shot his stock up so much that the Eagles actually traded up to snag him with the seventh overall pick. Two defensive linemen they passed up with that pick—Douglas and Warren Sapp—went on to have decent careers, near as we can tell.

From the start, Mamula was an enigma, to put it nicely. Once or twice a season, he'd put together a two-sack, five-tackle game. The rest of the year, he was Mr. Cellophane. He never seemed to add to his repertoire of moves. And his small size made him wear down over the length of a season.

Beyond all that, he was a surly fool. In 1998 he made headlines during training camp for exposing himself to a female bouncer in an Allentown bar. He didn't bond with fans, media or, most important, teammates.

But his coaches still loved him. When his initial contract expired after 1998, we all thought he was out of our lives. Instead Reid signed him to a new deal—at $2.7 million a season!—and said, "Mike's going to be a big part of this defense's future."

Oh please. Mamula played two more years, averaging seven sacks. His most notable feat was colliding with Douglas during a 1999 game and tearing his own teammate's knee ligament.

Finally, after 2000, the Eagles gave up and stopped trying to sell this pretender to the fans. They cut him. Final stats: six seasons, 33 sacks, no Pro Bowl appearances. This time, we knew best.

Doug Pederson. If only they had leveled with us. If only Andy Reid had been candid enough to admit that Pederson was merely a tackling dummy serving as starting quarterback until Donovan McNabb and his blockers had digested the graduate-level offense, maybe we would have cut the guy some slack.

Instead, Reid insisted throughout the 1999 season that Pederson could actually play. "Doug's doing a tremendous job," the straight-faced coach told baffled reporters at his weekly news conferences. "We're getting closer."

Now, that we weren't buying. Pederson's stats were hideous. His short-armed passes seemed aimed at seams in the Vet turf. He couldn't throw, couldn't run, couldn't read defenses. In the NFL, that's a trifecta of ineptitude. This guy was the team's worst starting quarterback since John Reaves in 1972.

The abuse rained down from the 700 Level. We were impatient. We wanted to see McNabb, the rookie with the pedigree. Instead, we were spending good money to watch this career third-stringer from Northeast Louisiana State.

Charges of nepotism didn't help. Reid and Pederson had been good pals at their previous gig in Green Bay. Even their wives were said to be close friends. It appeared, more than anything, that Reid was handing his buddy the chance to be an NFL starter, as well as a huge chunk of change, at our expense.

Reid described Pederson as "a professor out there. I can't pay Doug enough for what he's done this season." You know the expression: Those who can't, teach. And he sure couldn't.

After a while, Pederson got a bit touchy about our invective. "You're trying to do your best on the field and that's how a lot of people want to pay you back," he said.

When it finally came time to hand the job over to McNabb, Pederson may have been the only person in the Delaware Valley who didn't see it as a positive move.

"You're ticked off. You're dejected. But you move on," he said.

Yes, please move on. Right out of town would be okay.

In hindsight, Reid's strategy of breaking McNabb in slowly seems to have made sense. And teaching the offense to his blockers before throwing the rookie in there may have saved the kid's life. We might have even accepted it at the time if the coach didn't keep lying to us about how sterling Pederson was playing.

Hey, McNabb may have gained for Reid's patience. But we—at the time—suffered mightily.

Ed George. More often than the "E-A-G-L-E-S—Eagles!" chant, these words were uttered at Veterans Stadium during the early days of the Dick Vermeil era: "Holding, Philadelphia, No. 64." The offensive guard did more clutching and grabbing than an overeager prom date.

George also maintained a hold—however negative—on the Vet Stadium fans. As soon they saw the yellow handkerchief hit the air, a murmur of disgust would pass through the seats. As the referee turned on his microphone, they would warm up their throats. And before the ref's words came out, they knew the guilty party. "Booooo."

"Ed George's problem is his own mental makeup—he whips himself," offered Vermeil, ignoring that we were more than ready to whip him ourselves. "He gets so intense, so concerned about things that sometimes it affects the way he plays."

In 1978, the NFL liberalized its holding rule to allow offensive linemen to extend their arms and open their hands to stave off rushers. It wasn't enough for George. He needed the rules to go one step farther—strangulation, for instance.

Shawn Bradley. In another town, on another team, this seven-foot-six zombie might have been just another stiff. But in Philadelphia in the mid-90s, he became the Great White Nope. Missionary Impossible. The White Man's Burden.

Bradley, like Von Hayes, was another guy doomed by what had been expected of him. The Sixers took him with the second pick in 1993 (passing up Penny Hardaway), even though he spent most of his college career overseas, canvassing door-to-door for the mission of the Church of Jesus Christ of Latter Day Saints. Despite the inexperience, Shawnie was promoted as the solution to the center problem that had plagued the Sixers since Moses Malone left in 1986. If nothing else, his agent David Falk deserves points for chutzpah for negotiating a $44 million deal for a human praying mantis. Local basketball experts from Jimmy Lynam to Sonny Hill told us he would "revolutionize" the game.

The only revolution was taking place up in the Spectrum seats. Fans watched in amazed agony as Bradley played an entire game without scoring a point and followed it up with a game in which he did not nab a single rebound. To be 90 inches tall and that inept was inconceivable. Hell, he couldn't even master dunking.

Making matters worse was the Somnambulant Sixer's lackluster work ethic. He spent the entire summer after his rookie season on an extended honeymoon, even though coach Lynam wanted him to stay here and work on his game. He wasted $100,000 that the team paid a trainer to help build his physique by refusing to follow the exercise regimen. Even Pat Croce couldn't motivate this guy.

What he didn't understand is that great athletes have an internal desire that drives them. A little nastiness would have helped as well. Bradley was a gentle soul. In the NBA, they feast on gentle souls.

"There is no 12-step program to cure gutlessness," *Daily News* columnist Bill Conlin wrote in 1995. "This kid is more than an empty uniform. He is a thief who turned the bad judgment of everybody with a dream of what he could become into the biggest daylight heist since the Brinks Robbery."

Wow. Bradley, for his part, didn't get it. The boos rolled off his back like rain off the roof. He never cared—or never got—that we didn't like him.

"I have a lot of fans in Philadelphia," he once insisted. "It's just that none of them come out to the games. But I know there are a lot of people in Philadelphia who thought I was a bust, too."

You think? Forget the Phils' Jeff Jackson or the Eagles' Kevin Allen. Bradley became this town's gold standard of a bad draft-day decision. Even now, with him fading in our rear view mirror, he is recalled with contempt. Any dubious draft pick, trade or free-agent signing by any of the four franchises is always held up to comparison with his selection. Ultimately, any other botched choice falls short.

In the ultimate irony, the Sixers finally traded this Tin Man to the New Jersey Nets in 1995 in return for . . .

Derrick Coleman. Talk about a trade that hurts both teams. We finally purge ourselves of Bradley and wind up getting the only guy in the NBA with a lazier streak.

The joke about the 300-pound Coleman is that he liked Philadelphia's cheese steaks and pretzels so much that he came here for two tours of duty. Actually, the joke was on us.

The first time, Croce—then president of the franchise—threatened to suspend DC for weighing more than the Liberty Bell.

"You can't do that," Coleman's lawyer protested. "Are you a lawyer?"

"No," countered Croce. "Are you a physical therapist?"

In January 1997, Coleman cut his left pinky on the rim and missed the next 13 games. During this month of trauma he accompanied the Sixers to Detroit, his hometown, but neglected to attend the game against the Pistons. The team fined him $84,000.

He came back to play one game and then declared that the pinky, along with a new calf injury, would keep him out another month. Coleman insisted the decision had nothing to do with the fine, but shrugged when told that the team doctor had cleared him to play.

Coach Larry Brown looked at Coleman's innate talent and his $9 million-a-year contract and just shook his head. "This guy gets all this money. He gets a suite on the road. And he's never won a playoff series. He says he's the second-best player in the league, yet he wants to go to a winning team. That is mind-boggling."

What was most mind-boggling was that DC wasted the opportunity to be an all-time great player. If there's one thing Philadelphia fans can't tolerate it's an athlete who squanders his talents. So, we kindly and politely urged him to do better. Well, maybe not so kindly or politely.

"The majority of the criticism I've received probably is warranted," Coleman said, "but I don't worry about it. As long as my family is fine, and I'm playing and having fun . . .

"Do I care about the fans' perceptions of me? No. They judged Jesus Christ, so who am I? That's how I look at it."

Let's see: You play 50 pounds overweight, skip practices, battle with teammates and coaches, refuse to attend team charity events and cap a career with a few drunk-driving episodes, and you compare yourself with Jesus Christ? Very nice.

Mercifully, the Sixers dumped the six-foot-ten stiff in 1998. And that seemed like the end of our nightmare until Coach Brown, inexplicably, brought him back as a free agent in 2001. Brown even promised that Coleman would bring a winning attitude this time.

Let the record reflect that the Sixers won no playoff series during DC's first three-year term here, then won five series (even making a trip to the NBA Finals) during his three-year absence. In his first season in 2001-2002, they were one-and-done in the post-season. The following season they actually won a round, prompting management to re-up DC for another two years.

The following year, well, Derrick proved it's never too late. At age 35, he finally played with the hustle that had been absent his entire career. His body breaking down, he showed us heart and grit and—finally—became a crucial performer for the Sixers in their 2003 playoff run.

Some suggested that DC's critics owed him an apology. We'd counter that Derrick owes the apology—to his craft, if not the fans.

Matt Geiger. Even when he retired in 2001 with degenerative arthritis in both knees, it was tough to have much sympathy for this Mr. Clean look-alike. After all, how many pros would dare announce that: "Basketball doesn't mean that much to me"?

Never in their history did the Sixers pay so much to receive so little. They invested $53 million in this seven-foot-one free agent, or an astounding $343,000 for each of the 154 games he managed to dress for. Even when he was active, Geiger played with a shuffling apathy, punctuated by an occasional hard foul. His only moment of glory—at least in the fans' eyes—came when he was ejected for roughhousing Indiana's Reggie Miller during the 1999 playoffs.

The rest of the time he played soft. If there's anything Philadelphia fans can't stand, it's a guy who plays soft. If there's anything they can't stand more, it's a 260-pound giant who plays with all the swagger of Mr. Rogers.

But he sure could style. Sixers' fans lasting image of Geiger may be of him plopped down on the bench, resplendent in a $4,000 suit and $1,000 shades. The TV cameras would catch him during games, looking cool as he sprawled in the courtside seats while his teammates sweated on the court.

Even Larry Brown once noted that Geiger seemed more concerned with his appearance in street clothes than in his uniform. "Matt's got a new outfit, a new haircut, a massage and a facial," Brown noted during the 2001 playoffs. "Everything but a pedicure."

Toughness wasn't part of this Florida native's makeup. You don't often hear an athlete whine that the fans made him feel he had "committed a crime" by sitting when so many teammates gutted it through injuries. Nor do many publicly gripe about playing in Philadelphia because it means shoveling snow in the winter.

Geiger retired to his preferred lifestyle in 2002 (he had the distinction of owning the largest single-family home in Pinellas County), but still managed to haunt the team. He cost the 76ers an additional $17 million against the NBA salary cap in subsequent seasons, precluding them from signing any significant free agents.

Maybe after the Geiger experience, that was just as well.

Armon Gilliam. Here's all you need to know about this six-foot-nine forward's toughness: When they were teammates with the 76ers, Charles Barkley, thinking Gilliam too soft, used to call him "Charmin" instead of Armon.

The fans, meanwhile, nicknamed him "Gumby," a tribute to his sloping haircut and his fun-and-games approach to defense.

When Barkley got traded to Phoenix, Gilliam said he couldn't wait for the opportunity to play against his old tormentor, just to show how tough he could be. The chance came in November 1992, when Gilliam offered to cover Barkley in a Sixers-Suns game. In the first half, Barkley collected 25 points, 10 rebounds and the satisfaction of humiliating his opponent. For his part, Gilliam scored five points (two on a questionable goal-tending call against Barkley) and ended his performance by waving to the bench so that Sixers coach Doug Moe could mercifully pull him from the contest. Dispirited Sixers fans could only moan that the wrong man had been traded.

What an era that was. The 1992-1993 Sixers were a collection of mutts that included Gilliam, Charles "The Other Shaq" Shackleford and Andrew Lang. The biggest dog of all may have been coach Doug Moe, who sometimes cut out of practice to catch a matinee movie.

Chris Gratton. Once in a while, you find an athlete who shows great promise on a bad team, but can't keep his feet on a good one. Usually, it's a matter of wilting under the spotlight of attention and the pressure to produce in meaningful games.

Such a player was Chris Gratton, who starred at age 22 for the Tampa Bay Lightning, a team no one cared about in a city that didn't follow hockey. Gratton looked so good that Flyers general manager Bob Clarke lured him to town with a free-agent contract that included a $9 million signing bonus. Gratton promised to be a big, tough center who could anchor the second line or—in the unthinkable scenario that Eric Lindros ever left—take over the first line.

He couldn't have fallen on his face quicker had his skates been tied together.

Gratton stopped scoring before the ink even dried on his $16 million contract. Hey, everyone goes into an occasional scoring slump. But even worse, he stopped the banging that had made him such a valued player. Mostly, he skated around in circles.

Flyers fans rarely boo their own, but they let this underachiever have it. Even Gratton's uniform number set him up for abuse: He wore the No. 55. In the peculiar custom of the NHL, repeating double-digit jerseys are reserved for superstars like Wayne Gretzky (99), Lindros (88), Paul Coffey and Raymond Borque (77) and Mario Lemieux (66).

Big contract. Big number. No production. It was the perfect equation for abuse.

A year and change later, Clarke gave up and shipped Gratton back to Tampa Bay. Clarke even apologized to the fans—and team owner Ed Snider—saying, "It's my responsibility. I screwed up."

For his part, Gratton sounded relieved.

"I don't mind at all," he said. "It's going to allow me to play more, maybe, and allow me to play more in critical situations. They had superstar players in Philadelphia who take care of those points in the game."

In other words, why would I want to play for a contender?

Flyers fans don't heckle often, but at least they get it right when they do.

TWENTY

THE CURIOUS MR. SCHMIDT

He was, without question, the greatest third baseman in the history of the game. For 18 seasons, Mike Schmidt graced the hot corner at Veterans Stadium. When he finally left, his numbers were remarkable: 548 home runs, 10 Gold Gloves, three Most Valuable Player awards, a world championship ring, and a spot in the Hall of Fame.

So how come we never loved him?

Oh, we respected Mike Schmidt. Appreciated what he meant to the franchise. But we never really *liked* him. Our affection went to his teammates—scrappy guys like Pete Rose and Larry Bowa—or his peers from other sports—luminaries like Doctor J and Bobby Clarke.

Schmitty? Nah. He was the unadored superstar, the guy who was too cool for his own good. Too elegant, too detached. A stoic out of Ohio who, by his own account, would have connected better with fans in a place like Los Angeles than a clock-punching, row-home town like Philadelphia.

"I always felt that Mike would have been happier in a city where people didn't take their sports so seriously," Rose, a teammate for four seasons told me in an interview a few years back. "In some ways, Philadelphia made his career. Hell, they helped him become a Hall of Famer. But in other ways, that city was a really tough place for him. He had a hard time connecting with the fans. Some times he seemed so . . ."

Tortured?

"Yeah, that's right. I think he always wanted the people there to like him; it just never worked out that way."

Schmidt declined to be interviewed for this book. That's okay. He already said it all over the years, from his first outburst in 1978 ("I've just accepted my role as the guy the fans are going to take their frustrations out on") to his last in 1995 ("It's hard for me to have good things to say about a town that never did anything for me and made life miserable for me"). What more could he add now?

It was Schmidt who first uttered the line that best summed up the local media: "Only in Philadelphia do you have the thrill of victory and then the agony of reading about it the next morning." Perfect.

Just weeks before his 1995 induction into baseball's Hall of Fame, Schmidt hit the fans one more time in an interview with *Philadelphia* magazine. Typical. He always managed to stick a needle in our elation. Still, thousands of red-hatted Phillies fans attended the induction ceremony (it didn't hurt that Richie Ashburn was being honored as well), and they gave Schmidt one of the most rousing ovations ever to bounce off the hills of Cooperstown, N.Y.

How do you explain that? Who knows. Perhaps the fans were making one last effort to get some emotion out of this all-time stone face. Perhaps they were choosing to remember only the good times, which seems perfectly appropriate for the occasion. Perhaps they were trying to show that, in the end, we really did appreciate what a privilege it had been to watch Schmidt play all those years.

It is complex, the schizophrenic relationship between this all-time great and the people of our city. As the eminent psychiatrist Pete Rose says, "You could go nuts, trying to figure Mike out. And you'd go twice as nuts trying to figure the fans out."

Like all psychological phenomena, it has to be examined from its roots up.

Schmidt came to the Phillies in 1973, a shy 23-year-old whose biggest fear was walking through the clubhouse to get to the field. His teammates hazed him like a freshman frat pledge, needling him for his strikeouts, his Ohio Valley naiveté, even his acne-scarred marked skin. They cruelly called him "Titlelist Head" for having as many pock marks as a golf ball. It was nothing more than locker-room razzing, but Schmidt struggled to cope with it.

"Guys like Larry Bowa, Greg Luzinski and Willie Montanez were ragging me all the time, kidding me about striking out," Schmidt said years later. "There was plenty of jealousy there and I saw it as mean-spirited, no question."

Former shortstop Bowa, who spent nine seasons playing 50 feet away from Schmidt, insists that jealousy had nothing to do with it.

"We would all needle each other about everything," Bowa says. "(Garry) Maddox, Bull (Luzinski) you could kid with, but Schmitty took things personally. He was tough to get to know. I think he now realizes that if he had let his guard down, he might have had more fun."

Regardless, Schmidt struggled as a rookie, hitting just .196 and striking out in more than one-third of his at-bats. Phils fans, having been told that this phenom would help lead them out of six straight losing seasons, showed him no patience.

We booed.

He persevered. By 1974, Schmidt began to live up to expectations, winning the first of three consecutive home run titles. In those early days he could run as well, and his fielding grace approached that of Brooks Robinson. Anyone paying attention could see that this guy was the complete package.

In the playgrounds, the kids imitated that stance—the little rear-end wiggle, followed by the crisp, compact swing. We imitated Harry Kalas' great boozy-voiced home run call: "Long drive, Michael Jack Schmidt, watch that baby, outta here!" Still, fewer of us seemed to want to be like Mike than his more gregarious teammates—Luzinski or Tug McGraw—or the pesky Bowa. Even outside of baseball there were Philadelphia sporting icons stealing his spotlight.

For every Schmidt poster tacked up on kids' bedroom walls in the 70s, I'll bet you there were five celebrating the other megastars of the era, Erving and Clarke.

Doctor J was the cultured skywalker, all grace and magic on hardwood. And with all his dignity (we didn't know of the warts that came out in recent years), you almost felt like you were stepping up in class just watching him play for a few hours.

Clarkie, the gap-toothed rink rat, was the embodiment of what Philadelphia fans admire: 180 pounds of gristle and hustle, a guy who would butt-end Mother Theresa if she stood between him and the puck. Again, ignore "Bob" Clarke's recent relationship with fans as general manager of the Flyers. Remember the "Bobby" Clarke who broke Philadelphia's title drought in 1974, just as Schmidt was emerging as a star.

"Doc was class and elegance while still being approachable," says Stan Hochman, who covered them all as a columnist for the *Philadelphia Daily News*. "Doc would sit by his locker after games and answer every last question from every last reporter. Clarke was a different horse entirely—a skinny, diabetic kid from Flin Flon who spilled his guts on the ice night after night. The fans really connected with those two guys.

"But Schmidt, for whatever reason, couldn't connect. He was more introverted than Doc and less emotional than Clarke. He projected an image of a guy aloof, more cold than cool. When he struck out, he never threw his bat. He just always walked back and gently placed it in the rack. The fans wanted some emotion, a sign that he cared as much as they did."

The underlying problem, says Hochman, was Schmidt's demeanor: "He just didn't seem to enjoy playing."

For his part, Schmidt never disputed that assessment. He was cursed, he says, with a psyche that made him an undemonstrative perfectionist. He was almost afraid to enjoy the moment, lest he lose his concentration. Schmidt saw it as focus; we saw him as a guy with all the emotion of an accountant.

Meanwhile, he was surrounded by a circus of teammates who could rouse the crowd by the sheer force of their personality. Consider the image of certain Phillies in your mind's eye. There's Rose, sliding home head-first. There's McGraw, leaping off the mound after a save. There's Bowa, throwing his bat and starting a fist fight.

There's Schmidt, standing stone faced at third.

It doesn't even look like he cares, said the fans.

"A real part of the problem was simply the way he looked," says Hochman. "He was meticulous about his uniform—the crease in his pants always had to be perfect. He never got dirty. He made great plays, but he always came up clean. The fans' image of their third baseman was a guy who was dirty and rumpled."

As Schmidt saw it, why dive in the dirt when smart positioning would get you there standing up? And why fling your bat after a strikeout? What good would that do?

Funny thing. Years earlier and a few miles north, another superstar was celebrated for that stolid demeanor. Joe DiMaggio—twice as dour as Schmidt—was immortalized for his detached grace. Schmidt, meanwhile, was nicknamed "Captain Cool" by his teammates, and they didn't mean it in a flattering way.

In interviews after his retirement, Schmidt said he regretted his unemotional persona, his joyless approach to his craft.

"There's no question at all that I didn't enjoy my professional life like I wished I would have," he said in 1995. "I didn't allow myself to enjoy it because of my obsession for succeeding, my obsession for wanting to be the best.

"There was always something gnawing at me, something that wouldn't allow me to free myself up to enjoy that whole ride. I would have loved to have been able to play the game like Rose and (Gary) Matthews, get the crowd involved whenever I felt like it."

There's a lot of self-examination there. And, like most middle-aged men rummaging through their regrets, he brings it back to his upbringing.

"I understood that I played the game appearing to not be emotional. That's not my fault. That's my mom and dad's fault. That's been handed down for years, apparently, in the Schmidt family."

That's his psyche. Our id and superego are this: Never mind how your father repressed you, we demand that our heroes be gritty and rumpled, perhaps with a broken nose and a little dried blood caked under their fingernails. Get off the shrink's couch and go get messy out there.

Consider a few of our heroes over the years—"Concrete" Chuck Bednarik, Dave "The Hammer" Schultz, Lenny "Nails" Dykstra. This isn't so much a sports town as a hardware store.

"I don't know if the fans liked me for my talent," says Bowa, who went from a slap-hitting shortstop to one of our truly beloveds. "I think they liked me because I played with my heart on my sleeve. And I always hustled, played with an edge and dived in the dirt a lot."

There it is again. If only Schmidt could have had a little Pigpen in him, we would have appreciated him more. And if only he had shown us his heart, we might have embraced it.

Once asked why he set his hit movie in Philadelphia, Sylvester Stallone replied, "Rocky is a Philly kind of guy. Not much finesse, but a lot of heart."

Look at the list of Philadelphia's all-time favorites: Guys like Rose, Dykstra and Ashburn (the hustling leadoff hitter type); Bednarik, Reggie White and the Broad Street Bullies (guys who could smack you into next year); Allen Iverson, Brian Mitchell and Tommy McDonald (little guys playing big men's games). Then add Doc for his grace, Clarke for his balls, Mo Cheeks for his dignity, Steve Carlton for his sneer.

Where does Schmidt fit in? His talent is unquestionable, his effort unassailable. But he never won our heart.

"I guess the best way to describe Philadelphia fans is that they have a strong toleration for the blue-collar player," Schmidt ruminated a few years back. "They like the player who seems to have a tough time of it on the field, the player who gets dirty. Someone who seems to have to work real hard to get the job done. Somebody they can really see sweating every day.

"But they have a very short fuse for players who glide. Players who rise to the top with what their perception tells them is less of an effort on the field. In other words, a player who is a bit unemotional, just get the job done, no frills"

He is, of course, describing himself.

And, too, Philadelphia fans have never tolerated players who shrink in the big moment. Fair or not, that became the perception of Schmidt.

There are folks in this town who swear they never saw Schmidt hit a clutch home run. Certainly, that ignores the monster blast against Montreal that clinched the national League East in 1980. Indeed, it ignores the entire 1980 World Series, when he hit .381 with two homers and was named Most Valuable Player. Hochman once sat down and logged all of 548 career blasts. He discovered that Schmidt hit as many in late innings of tight games as he did in early innings or in laughers. "Still," Hochman says, "nobody believes it."

What folks recall is that Schmidt failed to clear the park in his first 76 League Championship Series at-bats. Overall, he hit just four homers in 36 post-season games, a pace that projects to a Von Hayes-like 18 over a full season. His career post-season batting average of .236 is a lot closer to Turk Wendell than it is to Ted Williams.

The Phillies were 2-9 in their three Championship Series from 1976 through 1978. Schmidt, who twice led the league in home runs during that span, batted .182 in those play-offs, did not have a home run and drove in a total of four runs. So we made him our fall guy. The team's playoff failures became Schmidt's failures. We even nit-picked his great regular seasons: Never mind those 548 homers, what about those 1,883 strikeouts?

Even when the Phils won and he starred, we never really gave him credit. Test yourself. What are your memories of the 1980 Series? Perhaps Rose catching the ball off Bob Boone's glove. Perhaps Dickie Noles knocking George Brett on his hemorrhoid-laden keister. Maybe even the police horses ringing the field as McGraw whiffed Willie Wilson one more time.

How far down the list was the image of a joyous Schmidt leaping on top of that pile of flailing, screaming, celebrating bodies near the mound?

That jubilant act, in itself, seems a surprise in hindsight. Schmidt was so rarely just one of the boys. Like the Flyers' Eric Lindros a generation later, he was the superstar who couldn't fit in, the mega-talent who could never comfortably share a few beers and dirty jokes with his teammates.

A couple of years after he retired, Schmidt was asked to name an active player he admired. His answer, of all people, was John Kruk. Kruk? The anti-Schmidt? You couldn't come up with a more dissimilar player if you tried.

"I believe that if he and I melded together, we'd have a hell of a player," Schmidt said. "You take his jovial, relaxed, country-type attitude that the fans latch onto and love; put it together with my work ethic, my knowledge of the game, my experience with winning, and you'd have, without question, the makings of a tremendous player."

Interesting thing about Kruk: He spent a ten-season career growing increasingly out of shape, but the Phils couldn't wait to hire him back as a coach. Schmidt, meanwhile, remains in exile on a Florida golf course until the Phils finally called in 2003 to offer him a post managing in the low minors. Before that, except for an occasional appearance at spring training, the organization called on him about as often as they summoned Philadelphia Phil and Phyllis.

In other cities, they stay. Deities like Sandy Koufax, Stan Musial, and Hank Aaron found roles with the franchises they personified. But Schmidt, other than a one-year turn as a broadcaster (he was, by the way, a terrifically candid analyst), became persona non grata with the Phils. Maybe it was his suggestion that he move straight from the batter's box to the general manager's office, just as Clarke had with the Flyers. More likely, Bill Giles and partners never got over the luncheon speech in which Schmidt introduced a film celebrating his 500th homer by ripping the organization for a "depleted farm system" and the stench of "cat stink" outside the clubhouse.

He always managed to say the wrong thing at the wrong time. On Labor Day weekend 1983, just as the Phils began the charge that took them to the World Series, Schmidt opined, "We're the least likely of the four (contending) teams to get hot in September, because we don't have any kind of a foundation for the guys to build on." Gee, Mike, thanks for the pep talk.

His most famous sound-off came in 1985, when Schmidt told a Montreal newspaper that he had met the enemy and it was us. "It's a mob scene, uncontrollable," he said. "I can't say *spoiled* is the right word. They've seen me playing well more than badly. I've achieved excellence in baseball in front of these people. But I make a great deal, and there's a lot of jealous people in those stands. For their ticket price, they want to see excellence on a regular basis, and I can't do that for them."

Then, in the ultimate treason, he carped that, had he played in Los Angeles or Chicago ("someplace where they were just grateful to have me around"), his career numbers would have been better. That was like a guy telling his wife that he should have married the girl around the corner.

In that pre-Internet era, Schmidt never expected his words to cross the Canadian-American border. They did, of course. When the Phils returned from their road trip, he knew the angry rabble lay waiting with torches and pitchforks. So he showed up for infield practice incognito—in sunglasses and a long fright wig. The fans took one look and laughed away their fury. Never mind that the disguise was the idea of gonzo teammate Larry Andersen; it was Schmidt's first and only attempt at self-mockery and we all appreciated him for lightening up.

That's really all we ever asked from the guy, a little bit of humanity if not humility. He played 18 seasons here—the longest career of any professional athlete in our history. He once said that playing his entire career in Philadelphia was as much an accomplishment as those 548 home runs. So he never asked to be traded, never sought to escape us as a free agent. Yet we never really felt like we knew him. He never loosened up, never really let down his guard.

Until the end. By 1989, he was spent—weary from injuries and the talentless squad surrounding him, unable to make even routine defensive plays, older than the bumbling rookie manager (Nick Leyva) who kept asking him to take a few days off. Schmidt had learned from Julius Erving that it's best to leave sport on your own terms so, with no warning, he decided to announce his retirement. On the road, of course.

The team hastily called a news conference in San Diego and there, as folks back home interrupted their Memorial Day barbecues to watch on TV, Captain Cool broke down and sobbed. Uncontrollably. The cork came out of the bottle and all those feelings he had bottled up for years came splashing out. It was stunning to see the Great Stoic actually lose his composure and begin to blubber. He apologized for the show of emotion ("I usually only cry at weddings and funerals," he offered), but, in fact, we all appreciated it. Maybe real blood did course under that red-and-white Phillies uniform after all.

And suddenly, he was gone.

Only then did we truly realize how fortunate we had been to have him. For all of his whining, Schmidt truly is one of his sport's immortals, a blend of power and defense that is surpassed only by Willie Mays and Mickey Mantle. And if one world championship during his 18 seasons didn't seem enough, realize this: It's the only one the Phillies took in their 120-plus-year history.

"I think Phillies fans respected Mike more at the end than during his career," says Rose.

"There was a turnaround there. But he was hard to understand—not to me, I understood him, but to the fans who took everything he said literally. When they finally got a chance to look back at it, turns out he did pretty well, don't you think?"

Beyond that, his griping aside, Schmidt never did anything to embarrass his adopted city or his team. No arrests, no drug busts, no news conferences to question the merits of practice. It didn't seem much of an accomplishment at the time, but nowadays, well, you've got to appreciate that.

Now, Schmidt makes only sporadic appearances in town, like when the Phils honor their teams of the past. The applause is enthusiastic, but not quite up to the decibel level of a few teammates, Rose and Carlton in particular. A few years ago, he tried to recruit investors for a chain of hoagie shops with a radio spot in which he said, "I'll always be grateful to Philadelphia fans for their great support over the years." It didn't help that the spots ran just as the magazine article came out where he accused us of making his "life miserable."

Most interesting was Schmidt's attempt was in 2001 to counsel Scott Rolen, another dour Midwest-bred third baseman who had trouble relating to fans and teammates (boy, haven't we cornered the market on those?). Schmidt told the kid to relax, to enjoy the moment, to let things roll off his back a little more.

In short, to do everything he could not as a player.

It almost seems that Schmidt, through Rolen, was asking for a do-over.

And when it comes right down to it, that's what we all want with Schmidt—the chance for a do-over.

TWENTY-ONE

THAT GUY IN FRANCE

Here's my favorite Norman Braman story:

I was working for the *Inquirer* in 1992, covering the antitrust trial pitting NFL players against owners. I managed to get my hands on the Eagles' financial records which, until that time, had been as tightly guarded as the Pentagon's missile silo locations.

The numbers were staggering. They showed that the Eagles' operating profits were highest in the league and 12 times the NFL average. And, beyond all those profits, there was a single-line item revealing that Braman had paid himself a $7.5 million salary the previous year. This, at the same time he had raised ticket prices for a third straight season. At the same time he was dunning his players if they took an extra pair of sanitary socks.

So I called Braman—at his vacation villa in the Riviera—to ask for an explanation. After all, the guy had always insisted that he didn't profit a single penny from the Birds.

"When I'm out of the country, I don't comment on things," he told me before hanging up.

Okay. His decision. I wrote the story—which also noted that his coach, Buddy Ryan, was the league's lowest paid—and included his no comment.

The next morning, my phone rang at 7 a.m. Apparently, Braman—having seen the story in print—was ready to comment on a few things.

"You're an asshole," he barked. "You made me look bad. That was a cheap shot."

Then he handed the phone to his wife, Irma, who chirped, "It's people like you who are hoping to run Norman out of town. You're trying to make him look greedy."

Hey, I didn't have to try very hard.

Braman got the phone back, and piped in: "I don't own this club for fun, you know. Why would anyone have a problem with me making a few dollars?"

And then, after insisting he would outlast his critics, Braman hung up and returned to his life in the South of France.

I was left with two questions. First, exactly who defines $7.5 million as "a few dollars?"

Second, if—as he always insisted—he didn't own the Eagles to make money, and he didn't own them for fun, exactly why did he own them?

The only answer I could come up with was that he owned the club in order to torture us.

Norman Braman was a soulless, cold-blooded auto salesman who could have easily stood in for Lionel Barrymore in the role of "It's a Wonderful Life"s' Mr. Potter. While we saw our Eagles as noble heroes, he viewed them as depreciable assets. While we viewed the team as a community treasure, he seemed to regard it as chattel.

To us, football was about passion, about the quest for greatness, about frozen November Sundays huddled under blankets at the Vet, cheering and cursing and praying for Super Bowl glory.

To him, it was always about the ledger sheet. Stan Hochman of the *Daily News* tabbed him with the perfect nickname: "Bottom Line Braman."

Perfect, Stanley.

You would think it would be difficult to select the most hated person in the history of Philadelphia sports.

It isn't.

We've booed an entire alphabet of athletes—from Ashby to Zendejas—but no player to the degree that he stands above all others in facing our animus. And players, for any faults, were never accused of betraying and looting the fans who gave them their trust. Braman was.

We've despised our share of coaches—bumblers like Joe Kuharich and Doug Moe; snarlers like Bob McCammon and Jim Fregosi; company stooges like Rich Kotite and Terry Francona. But no coach ever came across as an imperious Scrooge McDuck who collected bottles of wine costing more than our cars. Braman did.

We've slung arrows at other owners. Harold Katz was a meddler who scrimmaged players on the asphalt of his driveway. Bill Giles and his anonymous partners choked the life out of baseball for a decade. Leonard Tose nearly snuck the Eagles away in the middle of the night to pay off his gambling debts. Each man had his faults, but each, as well, also had our adoration for at least a few brief moments. And each shepherded a team that either won or at least got to the championship round. Braman never did.

In our roll call of reviled rogues, he stands alone.

Not that he didn't try to fool us.

Braman bought the club from the bankrupt Tose in 1985 for what was then an astronomical $65 million. Revisionist history has it that Braman got involved in order to keep Tose from pirating the Eagles to Arizona, but that's patent nonsense. Tose and the city had already completed a deal to keep the Eagles here under a far-improved Vet Stadium lease. Braman was merely a wealthy buzzard able to benefit from that sweetheart deal and Tose's financial ruin.

Still, he called himself a "white knight" at his introductory news conference. And, like so many other rich men, he tried to bluff that he was one of us—holding up a green T-shirt with the words "Super Bowl '86 Eagles" emblazoned on it. Right away you could see he didn't look at ease with it.

Braman had grown up in working-class West Philadelphia. Although he had long ago left our city for one of the most prestigious addresses in Miami Beach, the auto dealer tried to sell us that his heart had always remained here. "The Eagles belong to Philadelphia," he said. "Norm Braman belongs to Philadelphia. I know these fans. We won't have a problem with them."

"That guy in France."

But even as he was introducing himself, he dropped clues of what was to come. The franchise would be run in a "businesslike fashion," he said. The fans were growing tired of the players' "ridiculous, absurd contracts." He had no intention of operating in the red because "I don't know what the words losing money mean."

Soon enough it became clear that he wasn't just talking about being thrifty. Braman was like a penurious Dickens character. Half the team, it seemed, held out during the first training camp as the new owner tried to redefine NFL economics. When rookie quarterback Randall Cunningham griped about his offer, Braman countered: "It looks very, very bleak that Randall Cunningham will ever wear a Philadelphia Eagles uniform. It doesn't appear that he has passed the test of character to put on a Philadelphia Eagles uniform."

Huh? We're looking at the kid as the savior of the franchise, and Braman's ready to drop the nuclear bomb.

A few months later, he raised ticket prices for the first time. Most other owners at least attempt to convince customers that they have no choice, that they need to jack costs to stay competitive. Not Braman. "Do you have to lose money to raise prices?" he said. "Look, you don't get rich from owning a football club. I'm glad I don't have to depend on the Philadelphia Eagles for my financial well-being."

And that was him in a nutshell: The powerful guy who knew he had you by the balls and had no intention of trying to make you feel good about it. What were we going to do? Cancel our season tickets? Stop watching the games?

I covered Braman a lot in those days and found him to be a paradox. He would, on occasion, award lush contracts to his top stars (including, eventually, Cunningham), but loved to nickel-and-dime his role players. Each year he treated about 40 front-office workers and their spouses to a weekend retreat in Florida, but he cut the scouting staff in half. He directed the NFL Properties committee and pushed it into selling high-end fashion wear, but he ordered that his own players be charged if they took more than their allotment of clothing from the equipment room.

He loved hobnobbing with the high-and-mighty, holding pre-game champagne brunches in his luxury suite. But when Joe Fan came by to shake his hand, Braman assumed the look of a man who had just discovered dog manure on his shoe.

As much as he insisted on calling himself a native son, Braman preferred to play the absentee landlord. He showed up in town the day before games, ensconced in a suite at the Center City Four Seasons hotel. The rest of the time, he ran the franchise from afar—his oceanfront home in Florida or the villa in France that he once boasted to me he had "bought on a whim." Hey, most people buy a lottery ticket on a whim, not a multi-million-dollar estate.

It was Buddy Ryan who tagged Braman with the nickname "the guy in France." Buddy was the needle who loved deflating Braman's balloon of pomposity.

And Buddy Ryan, looking back, was Braman's best move—even if he soon came to regret it.

Braman hired Buddy in 1986 after first flirting with Jim Mora and David Shula. He had read of Buddy's masterful 46-defense in the *New York Times*, and figured if it was good enough for the *Times,* it was good enough for him. What he quickly learned was that Buddy Ryan was the most un-*New York Times*-ish coach he could have found.

An odder couple never existed. Braman was the champagne-sipping, art-collecting snob who never got his hands dirty. Buddy was beer and bratwurst, with a little horse manure caked into the soles of his cowboy boots.

Buddy was also a far stronger personality than Braman had bargained for. From the start, the new coach told the novice owner to butt out of the football side. And when Braman's tight-fistedness prompted players to hold out, Buddy undercut the owner by squawking about how much he needed those guys to win. Hell, when Keith Jackson finally caved and ended a 50-day holdout in 1989, Buddy sent a limousine to the airport to pick up his star tight end. Braman nearly fired him that day.

Ryan didn't care. He ridiculed Braman and club president Harry Gamble every chance he had. Gamble, a nice but bland man, once told me that his biggest job responsibility was serving as a buffer between the other two—sort of the vanilla ice cream lodged between Braman's champagne sherbet and Ryan's rocky road. He broke up more than one potential fist fight.

The real acrimony began during the 1987 NFL players' strike. Braman was a hawkish owner who wanted to crush the players' union. He compared players' salaries to those of cops and nurses, and slammed the Eagles' player representatives. He was a big proponent of the plan to hire fill-ins to play the NFL games. He even sued the city over lack of police protection at the scab game.

Ryan infuriated Braman by wanting no part of the pretenders hired to wear Eagles uniforms. He mocked them, ignored them, barely coached them. He told his real players to stick together—even if that meant staying out. Braman considered that treasonous behavior and after the third and final replacement game—and in front of the scab players—went into the locker room to call Ryan "an asshole."

Still, what could he do? Buddy's teams kept winning—in the regular season if not the playoffs. Ryan took a moribund franchise and gave it life by designed an exciting aggressive defense that, in his words, "brought the heat." The fans loved it, and filled the Vet.

But you knew that Braman was only biding his time. In January 1991, three days after the third consecutive playoff loss, Braman made Buddy pay for all of his jabs and all of his backtalk. Citing the post-season failures and the team's arrogant, undisciplined image, Braman canned Ryan. He later told me that he thoroughly enjoyed the entire process.

With Gamble as his advisor, Braman opted to choose between his two coordinators as the team's next coach. Defensive coordinator Jeff Fisher was a bright and earnest young man, whose biggest sin was that he was a Ryan protégé. Offensive coordinator Rich Kotite was a bumbling idiot, whose biggest attribute was that he was willing to allow Braman to again play with his toy.

I don't need to tell you what happened.

Kotite had some initial success—even winning a 1992 playoff game with the talented players Ryan had left him—but we knew the rock was rolling downhill. Braman's cheapness made every summer a soap opera of holdouts. In five seasons, beginning with 1987, the Eagles had 72 players miss a staggering 1422 days of training camp. The annual hardball contest drove a wedge between management and players—and between Braman and the fans. In 1991, Vet Stadium "Sign Man" John Rodio unfurled a first-quarter message reading, "Wake Up, Braman," and then one in the second quarter that added, "Now Spend Some $$$$." Club security officials scampered over to rip the signs down. They reacted similarly a year later when Rodio hung one reading "Norm, You Make Me Sick."

You didn't need a sign to read the writing on the wall. One of Ryan's loyalists, linebacker Seth Joyner, said in 1992: "Buddy cared about winning and Braman cares about making money. Buddy did not get the chance to complete the job. Braman wanted a puppet and that's what he got (in Kotite)."

Ominously forecasting the future, Joyner added, "Free agency is coming and this team could be ripped apart."

Indeed, free agency was the undoing of Norman Braman in every way. The trial against the league provided a window into his finances. And the players' ultimate victory provided the door through which an amazing collection of talent left our city.

First, the trial. If nothing else, *Reggie White et al v. the National Football League* proved the adage that the guys with the most money tell the biggest lies. None of us ever believed Braman's claims that he made no money off his football toy, but the legal papers proved his nose was longer than Pinocchio's.

As part of the players' discovery process, each NFL owner was required to file his profit-and-loss sheets with the court. I was the first reporter to look at the Eagles' papers, and the numbers were stunning. They showed that Braman—even as he pleaded poverty—made a $35 million profit the first five years he owned the team. And that didn't include the $7.5 million he paid himself in salary in 1990. His enviable 21 percent margin could be interpreted this way: On every $30 ticket bought by fans, $6.30 was profit for the team.

As he was accumulating gold, Braman was also squeezing the franchise dry. The court documents revealed that the Eagles ranked 24th among the 28 NFL clubs in spending for training camp, equipment, and coaching and scouting staffs. Ryan's $273,000 salary in 1989 was at the bottom of the league's head coaches. Overall, the amount spent on coaches was 40 percent below the league average.

Similarly, the Eagles' spending for scouts was half the amount paid by division rivals Washington, Phoenix and New York. It was a third the amount spent by arch enemy Dallas.

The numbers were damning. And they clarified the extend of Braman's avarice. The man who had once spent $4.1 million for a painting by Jasper Johns actually placed a bounty on extra jock straps smuggled by his players. The man who seemed eager to skin us to the bone by annually raising ticket prices had profited more than any of his 27 colleagues.

Before the trial opened, Braman boldly predicted, "The day NFL players gain free agency is the day hell freezes over." Other, smarter, owners realized they probably would lose their stranglehold on player movement, and prepared accordingly. But Braman was the rigid martinet who neglected to see the inevitable outcome.

When the players won, the parade out of town began. First, Keith Jackson, the all-pro tight end, signed a four-year deal with the Miami Dolphins. Then defensive tackle Mike Golic departed. Then fullback Keith Byars. Then Joyner and defensive end Clyde Simmons left on the same day, just as they had come to the Eagles. Overall, 13 quality players left the team as free agents in little more than a year. Nearly every one made the same exit speech, saying the accumulated talent could have won the Super Bowl had Braman shown some dedication.

Instead, a powerful and exciting team fell into mediocrity. The Eagles finished 8-8 in 1993, their worst record in six seasons.

The biggest loss, of course, was Hall of Fame defensive end Reggie White, who was listed as the first plaintiff on the lawsuit. After White won his liberation, Braman made no contract offer to the superstar, which baffled and angered the fans. Mayor Ed Rendell told Reggie that he hoped he would stay in Philadelphia. Upon hearing that, Braman called the mayor "a schmuck."

White, of course, left for Green Bay, where he won a Super Bowl. Braman tossed his final volley in an interview in *Philadelphia* magazine, where he questioned White's sincerity, referring to his devout beliefs as "that religion crap."

At that point, Braman's heart wasn't really in it anymore. Unable to keep players under contract at his penny-pinching price, he lost whatever competitive spirit he had. And his war with fans and media became overwhelming. "There is a meanness of spirit up there that I don't recall when I was growing up in Philadelphia," he told me in 1993. By then his appearances here became more and more infrequent. He passed through town only to count the receipts.

And then, on a snowy March day in 1994, word leaked out—Braman was selling the team! He was on a cruise ship in the China Sea at the time, unavailable for comment as usual, but his loyalists put out the word that he had tired of the commute, the business and—perhaps most of all—the fans.

If there was a jackpot to be realized by holding onto the Eagles, there was more of a jackpot to be realized by selling them. Braman got $196 million for the club, nearly tripling his investment in nine years.

We didn't know anything at the time about this Hollywood producer, Jeffrey Lurie, who was buying the team. We just knew that he had to be better than Braman, right? The sale negotiations took weeks and nearly collapsed over Braman's insistence that Lurie buy his corporate jet as part of the deal. One last drop of blood to squeeze from the stone.

And then he was gone. Never to be heard from again. No reunions, no nostalgic visits to the Vet, no orchids or barbs popping up in the press.

And no one ever missed him.

TWENTY-TWO

GREAT MOMENTS 3: RALLY FOR REGGIE

There's a great scene in the classic comedy "Animal House," in which the demoralized college boys from Delta House decide not to take their suspensions lying down.

"I think," says frat playboy Otter, "that this situation absolutely requires that a really futile, stupid gesture be done on somebody's part."

"And we're just the guys to do it," echoes the drunken Bluto Blutarsky.

In March 1993, our friend Angelo Cataldi at WIP played the role of Bluto. In an entirely futile gesture, he spurred more than 2,000 Eagles fans to gather at JFK Plaza in an attempt to coerce Eagles ownership into re-signing free agent Reggie White. Ultimately, White left town for Green Bay without our team even making an offer, but at least the "Rally for Reggie" showed that the fans wouldn't take it lying down.

What else could we do? Every Eagles loyalist knew by 1993 that the franchise's recent success was slip-sliding away. Bumbling coach Rich Kotite had lived for two years off the strong nucleus left by Buddy Ryan, and now key parts of that nucleus were poised to leave. Owner Norman Braman, a real-life Ebenezer Scrooge, fought harder than any owner against the NFL players' court case seeking free agency. When the players won their case, Braman, basically snapped shut his silk purse.

And so White, arguably the best defensive end in NFL history, hit the open market. Eagles fans kept waiting for Braman to make him an offer, any offer. White toured the league like a VIP. Talk about being wined and dined, hell, the owner of the Atlanta Falcons gave Reggie's wife a fur coat just as a way of saying hello. Detroit, Cleveland and Dallas all flew him in on private jets.

Still, the Eagles did nothing. We gulped when Braman declared, "What's going on out there right now is a circus, and the Philadelphia Eagles are not in the circus business." We choked when Kotite predicted the club would "survive just fine" without White, an ominous foreshadowing of Andy Reid's words a decade later that the Eagles might be stronger without Jeremiah Trotter.

Finally, the fans knew they could not idly watch the club's top player just walk away. A year earlier Cataldi had organized a "Honk for Herschel" campaign. In that one, people drove around Vet Stadium blasting their car horns as a message to the Birds to sign free agent runner Herschel Walker. Whether Braman heard the horns is questionable (he was in France at the time), but the team did get Walker so, hey, give the little people a dose of credit.

Thus empowered, Cataldi called upon folks to lobby to keep White around. On a blustery mid-March morning, the Center City park jammed with people for what turned out to be part pep rally and part revival meeting. A stage was decorated in green and white, and you could go green-blind from all the Eagles jerseys in the crowd, most sporting White's No. 92.

The Rev. Herb Lusk, a former Eagles player, worked the crowd like his Sunday morning congregation, reminding everyone of White's charitable work as well as his football talent.

"He's been a minister to the poor," shouted Lusk. "What's his name?"

"Reggie!" the crowd roared back.

"He's been hope to children, single mothers and the homeless," said Lusk. "What's his name?"

"Reggie!!"

"We want Reggie signed," Lusk concluded. "Sign him now!"

White was not there, but sent a letter thanking the fans. He said he "looked forward to hearing from Eagles management."

That call never came. With no offer from the Birds, White signed with Green Bay and helped lead the Packers to a Super Bowl victory. The Eagles went 8-8 the next season and the free-agent exodus was on. Keith Jackson, Keith Byars, Clyde Simmons, Seth Joyner and other key players soon followed Reggie out of town. The team eventually collapsed.

Braman, meanwhile, sat on his money. Finally, mercifully, he sold the franchise in 1994 and left our lives forever.

Ultimately, the "Rally for Reggie" accomplished nothing, really. But, it felt good, at least for a moment, for fans to bond together in an attempt to pressure management to do the right thing. Hey, it was a really futile, stupid gesture. But somebody had to do it.

And who knows? Maybe we helped make Braman's life miserable enough that it helped persuade him to get out. Well, that plus Jeff Lurie's $196 million.

Months after the rally, White saw a video of the gathering for the first time.

"When I saw how many people were at that rally, it made me almost want to cry," he said.

"They had that whole plaza crowded. I never thought people would appreciate me that much. I'll never forget that. I'll show that to my great-great-grandchildren."

That's all we're left with as well. Memories.

TWENTY-THREE
CHARLES, RANDALL, AND ERIC: TRINITY OF OUR DISAPPOINTMENT

This has been our Groundhog Day story:

The fledgling superstar arrives in town as our next savior. We have champagne dreams and parade fantasies. The tease comes next—a deep playoff run, maybe an MVP season.

"Next year . . . ," the fans proclaim. They don't even have to finish the sentence.

But, ultimately, it all falls apart. A rift develops between the star and management, sometimes between the star and the fans. Poisoned by frustration and desperation, the relationship turns toxic. Next year never arrives. It is replaced with this:

"You'll never win a title with _____ (fill in the blank)."

And we don't.

Eventually, the superstar leaves. Packs his bags for Phoenix or Minnesota or—worst of all—New York. And we are left wondering. Is it us? Did we overrate the guy? Were we sold false promise? Did we somehow contribute to its all falling apart?

There is no answer. There is just the same old song, repeated again and again. And when then the music dies, we are left alone on the dance floor.

Charles Barkley. Randall Cunningham. Eric Lindros. The Holy Trinity of our disappointment.

Each was to fill Mike Schmidt's role as a Hall of Fame Philadelphia lifer. Each would lead us to a championship. Each fell short. And each left before we could measure him up for the bronze statue that was to be added down at the South Philly sports complex. We had reserved a spot right there between Rocky and Doctor J.

So we are left only with the memories—good and bad. Barkley's one-locomotive fast breaks, which ended with dunks that shook windows in Conshohocken. And Barkley dismissing Philadelphia as "a racist town."

Cunningham cartwheeling into the end zone to beat the Giants or unleashing that buggy-whip arm to throw for five touchdowns against the Redskins. And Cunningham, sullenly wearing his team jacket inside-out in protest of being benched for Bubby Brister.

Lindros bulling by the Rangers' Mark Messier in the 1997 playoffs to score the series-winning goal. And Lindros, in Game Seven against the Devils in 2000, concussed again, crumpled on the ice in the fetal position. He would never play for the Flyers again.

Where do the scales balance out? Certainly, each man made it fun to be a Philadelphia sports fan. You'd catch a stranger's bleary-eyed look at the water cooler or corner newsstand in the morning and know he had stayed up the prior night watching the same magic as you. "Can you believe what he did?" you'd ask, recalling a slam or a scramble or a body check.

Among them, our Trinity had 15 all-star game appearances. Barkley ensured himself a spot in the Hall of Fame. Cunningham and Lindros carried away MVP trophies—hell, Lindros broke down and cried thanking the fans when he got his award. In their combined 27 seasons here, their teams had 18 winning seasons and went to the playoffs 17 times. Not bad.

But only one number really counts. That would be world championships.

And that would be zero.

Among them, they had just one appearance in a title round, when Lindros and the Flyers were humiliated by the Detroit Red Wings in the 1997 Stanley Cup Finals.

It stung more that the Trinity arrived following a decade in which our city had seen four championships, as well as the Eagles' only appearance in the Super Bowl. Back then, we assumed it was our birthright to see our teams win the Big Game.

Not any more.

So much promise. So much disappointment.

Barkley was the first to arrive, coming to the 76ers in the great 1984 NBA draft that included Michael Jordan, Hakeem Olajuwon and John Stockton. He was already a national figure, "The Round Mound of Rebound" out of Auburn, a clown prince who stood six-foot-five and weighed close to 300 pounds. Cracked general manager Pat Williams, "His bathtub has stretch marks."

He wasn't deemed the savior at first. Indeed, Charles (the last name soon became super-fluous) was joining one of the NBA's elite teams. The nucleus of the 1983 championship squad—Doc, Moses, Toney, Cheeks, Bobby Jones—was still here, and still playing well enough to get to the conference finals his rookie season. Charles was simply part of the mix: a good rebounder who would help Moses under the basket and an energetic player to come off the bench to provide offense.

"When Charles is in there, our whole team picks up," said coach Billy Cunningham. "He's like adding a lit match to a few sticks of dynamite."

It seemed then that he would be part of the continuum that great franchises boast—like Kareem Abdul-Jabbar to Magic Johnson to Shaquille O'Neal in Los Angeles. So when Erving, the 13-year pro, took Charles under his wing ("He just needs to be given some sneakers and pointed in the right direction," Doc said), we were confident that things would be great in Sixer Nation for years to come.

Except they weren't. By 1985, Andrew Toney's foot problems essentially ended his career. In 1986, owner Harold Katz dealt Malone in the second-worst trade in franchise history (we'll cite Barkley's departure as the worst). And in 1987, the great Doctor J retired. Instead of being

"The Round Mound of Rebound" on his way to a thundering dunk.

surrounded by Hall of Famers, Charles's teammates now included Cliff Robinson, David Wingate and Albert (The Wrong Brother) King. The more Katz tinkered, the worse things got.

One night, management woke Charles up to inform him the team had just signed "Shack." In his half-conscious state, Barkley heard it as "Shaq," as in Shaquille O'Neal.

"I was dancing around the house, saying, 'We got Shaq, we got Shaq,' " Charles later recalled. "And then Gene Shue had to tell me it was Charles Shackleford." That would be Charles (5.5 points per game) Shackleford.

Of Shue, the taciturn general manager through the early 1990s, Charles said, "Gene Shue is a clown whose only ambition is to caddie for Harold Katz." Actually, we had to agree.

During Barkley's last four seasons here, just one other Sixer (Hersey Hawkins in 1991) played in the NBA All-Star Game. Charles would look down the bench and see non-entities like Armon Gilliam and Ron Anderson and know the team didn't stand a chance. And he wasn't shy about ripping his teammates.

"The only reason Dave Hoppen is on this team is that he's white," he once offered up. "A lot of fans won't come out to see an all-black team."

But the fans didn't see Dave Hoppen as the problem. When teams go bad, all eyes go to the guy making the biggest paycheck. And that was Charles. Somehow, *he* became the problem.

"They'll never win the title with Barkley," folks would say. How come no one ever said, "You'll never win the title with Johnny Dawkins?"

If you looked at him fairly, he was nothing short of terrific. Not just the floor-length Buffalo-herd dashes, but the artistic passes and the incredible ability to out-rebound men eight inches taller than he. Charles was all about effort (well, maybe not on the defensive end), and the scratches and bruises on his arms and shoulders were like medals he earned in battles under the basket. And remember the perspiration? Some guys sweat rivers, Charles would sweat the Amazon.

He could feed on the crowd and do impossible things. And he would show the full range of human emotion on the court, sometimes smacking himself in the forehead in disgust, other times flashing that great smile that reminded us that the game was, after all, supposed to be fun.

Charles often proclaimed himself as "the ninth wonder of the world." Who were we to disagree?

Away from the court, Barkley was as accommodating an athlete as this town has ever seen. Yeah, he would throw a occasional heckler through a plate glass window, but if you were nice and respectful to him, he wouldn't just sign an autograph, he'd probably buy you a beer. I once watched at a Main Line restaurant called Al E. Gators, as he got up from dinner with friends to join the birthday party of a 10-year-old boy. Charles hung with the thrilled kids for 15 minutes.

But as the Sixers grew worse, Charles grew more frustrated—and more vocal. One season he wrote "April 18," on the locker-room chalkboard as teammates looked on quizzically. "There it is," he declared, "the start of the golf season." In other words, no playoffs to spoil their summer fun.

Ahh, the mouth. It was always there, right from the start. Problem with Charles was, it was tough to tell when he was being brutally honest or just trying to get a rise out of people. After one game, he told the assembled press to "kiss my black ass, even though your lips might stink."

Another time, after a tough win, he said, "This is a game that, if you lose, you go home and beat your wife and kids. Did you see my wife jumping up and down at the end of the game? That's because she knew I wasn't going to beat her."

When asked if he wanted to reconsider the comment, he said, "Nah, print it. Piss off those women's groups."

Most of us laughed that one off. And we didn't mind as he tweaked ownership or an occasional teammate. But then Charles turned on the town. Seeming to want to write his ticket out, he called us racists and said we had chased away the great players before him. Tired of losing, he bullied the Sixers into getting rid of him by taking shots at all of us. He transformed himself from a superstar we couldn't live without to a negative force we couldn't live with.

"Philadelphia is a stupid city," he said in 1991. "A lot of stupid people live here."

Yo, Charles. Thought we had each other's back here.

And then, on June 17, 1992, it happened. Katz swapped Barkley to the Phoenix Suns for Jeff Hornacek (who clearly didn't want to play here), Andrew Lang (who clearly didn't want to play anywhere), and Tim Perry (who just couldn't play).

Yecch. We're still wondering what was behind Curtain No. 2.

That was that. Barkley went to the NBA Finals with the Suns. The Sixers went from bad to horrible in the ensuing years, setting an NBA standard by having declining records in six consecutive seasons. Not until Allen Iverson came along in 1996 was there a new ray of hope.

Sometimes, you don't know what you've got until it's gone.

Cunningham came to the Eagles in 1985 as the 37th player chosen in the draft (the debate among team officials at the time was whether to take Cunningham over UCLA quarterback Steve Bono). He arrived at camp with long, jheri curls, a black leather jacket and a T-shirt that read, "Any Questions? Call My Agent." He seemed callow and distant and a bit spacey for a team that still had remnants of the straight-laced 1980 Super Bowl squad hanging around.

Mostly, he was just petrified and trying to put on a tough front. For all of his skills, Randall Cunningham was one of the most socially uncomfortable people you would ever meet. The kid who grew up in Santa Barbara, Calif., and went to school in Las Vegas, couldn't figure out the East Coast psyche. The more he tried to fit in, the more out of place he seemed. If women are from Venus and men are from Mars, Randall was beamed here from the Planet Plutonium.

But, hey, we've lived with strange characters before ("Paging Mr. Steve Carlton"). If the guy has talent, we've been able to overlook anything from the serial promiscuity of Wilt Chamberlain to the social misanthropy of Lenny Dykstra. And talent was what Randall was all about.

No quarterback in NFL history could move with the ball like Randall (as with Charles—and Madonna and Cher for that matter—no last name was needed). "He definitely brings another dimension to the game," said receiver Mike Quick. "He can take the snap and hand off to himself. Once he's in the open field, he's like a receiver or a back."

Randall would take the snap on third-and-15, roll out and pump fake, freezing the defense. He would wave a receiver downfield, then heave one 50 yards—usually off the wrong foot. More often than not, it got there.

Actually, more often than not, he would take off on foot. And you'd gasp—sometimes in terror, sometimes in delight—as he'd fly over the defense or snake through it like some Elastic Man. During his 11 seasons here, he was never the NFL's best player, but he was certainly its most exciting one. As a team, the Eagles were the same—never the best, but always the most exciting.

Of course, being the best running quarterback in the history of the NFL is kind of like being the best cook in the Miss America pageant. It's not exactly why you're there in the first place. Critics (including most of his beleaguered offensive line) fairly noted that if Randall would just stay put for another half-second, he would be able to find his receivers and the offense would be that much better.

But Randall never had the patience for that. He was more about the highlights. More about being a one-man marching band.

Everybody has their favorite Randall Cunningham highlight. Some cite the Monday night play against the Giants in 1988 when Randall went back to pass, ranged to his right and found linebacker Carl Banks drawing a bead on him. Banks took his best shot, cutting out Randall's legs. But Randall broke his fall with his left hand, sprang upright and flipped a nifty touchdown pass to Jimmy Giles.

Others remember, of all things, his franchise-record 91-yard punt against the Giants a

The "Ultimate Weapon" lets one fly.

year later at the Meadowlands. Randall always claimed he could be the best punter in the NFL if Buddy Ryan would just let him handle the job.

Me? My all-timer came against the Buffalo Bills in 1990. Playing dodge ball against the big boys, Randall eluded three sacks in his own end zone, ducked under a snarling Bruce Smith, and—running backward and left—launched one 60 yards. Somehow it landed in the hands of rookie Fred Barnett, who trotted home for a 95-yard touchdown.

Those kinds of plays led *Sports Illustrated* to put Randall on the cover of its NFL preview issue under the label "The Ultimate Weapon." At the time, we as fans were delighted to see one of our guys getting the recognition. In truth, it was a bit of a curse. Randall believed the hype. Believed he could do it all, based on his talent.

Believed, truth be told, that he didn't have to do the required homework.

There's a story about Randall that early in his career the team brought in legendary offensive coach Sid Gillman to teach the kid a few basics. Randall's mind would stray during the sessions. Once, Gillman told Randall to take home a film reel (this was before videocassettes) and study the techniques of great quarterbacks. On a hunch, Gillman stuck a little tab of paper halfway through the film, knowing it would fall out as the film rolled. When Randall returned the reel, the tab of paper was intact.

Certainly, Randall deserves criticism for his work ethic. I also blame Buddy Ryan, who failed to coach the young prodigy. Buddy distilled his offensive plan to this: "We got to let

Randall make five big plays a game, whether running or passing or kicking, and then have the defense finish the job."

In the regular season, that worked more often than not. In the playoffs, where the opposition is tougher and has more time to develop a game plan, it killed the Eagles.

Randall's record in the post-season was one win, four losses. Take away the 36-20 victory over New Orleans in 1992, and he averaged fewer than nine points a game directing the offense in the four losses.

For whatever reason, he could not execute in the playoffs. It wasn't for lack of individual skills or, certainly, lack of courage. But even after a decade in the league, Randall still could not read defenses or find secondary receivers when it really counted.

"Can't win the big one," critics scoffed. Eventually, we had to agree with them.

And there was another side of Randall that was so, well, un-football. We're not even talking here about the gold-tipped shoelaces or the "Let Me Be Me" baseball cap. We're talking more about the request to his teammates that they hold hands in the huddle. "I need a little love," he'd say. Ron Jaworski never asked Harold Carmichael for love. Chuck Bednarik—Philly guy to the core—would have bitten your hand off if you tried to hold it.

But that was Randall. In a sport where heroes are bubbling vats of testosterone, he was looking for a little emotional sustenance.

It is said in places that the fans finally drove him from town. Not true. Randall spent 11 seasons here and when he left it was because coach Ray Rhodes knew the guy wasn't about to start learning his new West Coast offense. Like a once-good relationship that went on too long, it just had to end.

And again, we are left with the question of what might have been. If Randall had been better coached from the start, would he have succeeded in the post-season? Perhaps. We're still not sure he could have won the Big One (read: Super Bowl), but it would have been nice to see him get there.

And then there was No. 88.

By quirk of fate. Eric Lindros was delivered to Philadelphia the same week that Barkley was traded. Lose one superstar, gain another.

Actually, Lindros's status at the time was above and beyond that of any other savior since Wilt Chamberlain came here in 1959. In the insular world of hockey, he had been touted since he was 13. By the time he was an 18-year-old playing junior hockey in Ontario, he had been nicknamed "The Next One," as in the guy who would succeed "The Great One," Wayne Gretzky. No one viewed this as exaggeration.

These can't-fail phenoms show up in hockey about once a decade—Gordie Howe, Bobby Orr, Gretzky, Mario Lemieux. Each of those four men delivered multiple Stanley Cups to their NHL teams. We had every reason to expect Lindros would do the same.

Oh, we wanted him badly. After being the most consistently excellent franchise in town (17 straight playoff runs), the Flyers had fallen into mind-numbing mediocrity under the leadership of Jay Snider and Russ Farwell. This six-foot-five square-jawed kid would be the answer. He could shoot, skate, pass and—best of all—crush people. We like our hockey heroes best when they smack an opponent into next week.

He wanted us as well. Lindros had sat out all of 1991-92 after being drafted by the Quebec Nordiques. He wanted to play in a major market. When he finally touched down in Philadelphia, he said, "This feels like paradise."

His initial contract cost the team $23 million over five years. That doesn't include the $15 million the Flyers sent to Quebec, as well as the six players and two draft picks.

Goalllllllllll!

(Sometimes, in a "Back to the Future"-type way, you wonder what would have been had the trade had never occurred. What if the Flyers had kept Peter Forsberg, Chris Simon, Ron Hextall and the others? What if they had drafted Jocelyn Thibault or, better yet, swapped the pick for Patrick Roy, as Quebec-Colorado later did? It is our curse to live in the world of what-ifs.)

But we didn't know all that back then. We were thrilled when he scored 41 goals as a rookie, and delighted (foolishly so, in hindsight) when he was named the franchise's youngest-ever team captain in 1994. The Spectrum, and later the First Union Center, was packed with fans wearing No. 88 jerseys (at $100 a pop) in three color schemes.

In the shortened 1994-95 season, he tied for the NHL lead in points and carted home the Hart Trophy as most valuable player. He also led the Flyers to the Eastern Conference Finals against New Jersey that season. You remember that heart-breaking series—it ended with Hextall allowing a 60-foot floater by Claude Lemieux to flutter over his shoulder.

But even as we looked forward to "next season," there were signs of trouble. This Adonis of a man always seemed slowed by injuries—a knee here, a shoulder there and, starting in 1998, the first of six concussions. How could such a tough guy be so brittle?

Behind the scenes, things were even worse. Lindros's parents—Bonnie and Carl—had been regarded as meddlers since the time he refused to play for the Canadian junior team in Sault Ste. Marie, Ont., at age 16. You figured by the time he hit his twenties they would back off. But they never did. Behind the scenes they tried to lobby general manager Bob Clarke on who should be Eric's linemates, who should be traded, what coach should be hired or fired. And when negative stories about their son hit the press, they urged Clarke to control the flow of the news.

Foolishly, the Flyers went along with it for years. When Lindros got busted in Toronto for a silly beer-spitting episode, the Flyers spin was that it was just a gaggle of Lindros haters trying to bring down a good kid. They used the same logic to defend Eric's acquaintance with mobster Joey Merlino.

"We ended up trying to baby Eric all along and do whatever his parents wanted, and it backfired on us," Clarke later said. "It was the wrong thing for us to do."

Finally, in 1998, the Flyers decided that the approach of protecting Lindros and building him up wasn't working. The first schism came when Clarke challenged Lindros to play better if he wanted to be among the league's top-paid players. Seems innocuous enough, but it infuriated Bonnie and Carl.

Thus began a three-year cold war that made both sides look terrible. It escalated into ridiculousness after Eric sustained a collapsed lung in 1999. In the months that followed, Lindros's parents claimed that the Flyers tried to "kill" their son by attempting to put him on a plane before the injury had been diagnosed.

It all culminated in a memorable visual on national television: Flyers equipment manager Turk Evers strips the captain's "C" off Lindros's jersey and sews it onto that of defenseman Eric Desjardins. It was like Chuck Connors having his military stripes ripped off and his saber broken in half in the opening credits of the 1960s television show "Branded."

But it didn't even end there. Even after that, Lindros came back to play, his tragic Flyers career ending with him twitching on the First Union Center ice after the crushing hit by Scott Stevens. Another year of wrangling, sitting out and arguing about potential trades and finally, mercifully, he was swapped to the New York Rangers. The best player in that deal turned out to be Kim Johnsson, a solid puck-moving Swedish defenseman. Lindros, in his post-Flyer career, turned out to be just an average player in New York, a guy trying to skate away from the expectations that doomed him.

No controversy between player and team ever split the Philadelphia fan base like this one. By the end of his career here, the First Union Center was divided between the people who still defiantly wore their Lindros jerseys and those who put an "X" through the number or replaced his name tag with one reading "Cry Baby."

While it is fair to say that Lindros never lived up to the lofty predictions and that his parents' meddling often put him in a straightjacket, the Flyers, too, must take some of the blame. By the end, Clarke's incessant raging certainly tarnished the legacy of his days as the team's gaptoothed captain.

Even at his worst, Lindros was one of the NHL's top five players during his career here (at least when he played). That the Flyers failed to win the Cup during that eight-year era was more a reflection of the weak supporting cast than any of Lindros's shortcomings. We would argue that the biggest flaw was not No. 88, but rather the team relying on Hextall, an over-the-hill John Vanbiesbrouck and then rookie Brian Boucher in goal—rather than going after Mike Richter or Curtis Joseph when they were available.

But that's just sorting through the rubble now. Whoever is to blame, the result is the same. We find our savior, we believe in our savior, we are crushed by our savior.

Remember the sight of Lindros and Clarke in their Flyers jerseys, being paired together and skating the final lap around the Spectrum ice back in 1996? How ironic it all looks right now.

We cheered, and we believed that, just as Clarke had skated the ice before carrying the Stanley Cup, so too would Lindros one day.

Charles Barkley. Randall Cunningham. Eric Lindros.

The Holy Trinity of our disappointment.

TWENTY-FOUR

GREAT MOMENTS 4: BILLY TIBBETTS: GOOD RIDDANCE TO BAD RUBBISH

They have been called "Stepford fans," an allusion to their robotic loyalty. Whatever moves the Flyers make, whatever propaganda the front office spins, the team's supporters have always saluted—sometimes blindly so.

But even Flyers fans have their limits.

In 2002, those fans showed class when the organization did not. They refused to accept a convicted rapist on their team. They rejected the lame justifications of team founder Ed Snider and general manager Bob Clarke. They booed a bad move and shined a rare heat lamp on the front office.

Twenty-three days later, Billy Tibbetts was gone. The fans did themselves proud.

The episode started when the Flyers, in one of their annual scoring slumps, traded for Tibbetts, a 27-year-old goon who had one goal and 188 penalty minutes on his resume. But Tibbetts's Cro-Magnon playing style wasn't really the issue. His criminal record was.

Tibbetts' rap sheet was longer than his NHL bio: Rape, assault and battery on a police officer, disorderly conduct, intimidating a witness, shooting a friend with a BB gun. Not to mention 40 months in prison.

When he was 17, Tibbetts raped a 15-year-old girl at a party in Massachusetts. The crime meant that he had to register as a sex offender under Pennsylvania law, and was not allowed into Canada at all. Adding to the mix were a few follow-up brushes with the law—one just weeks before his trade to the Flyers—which suggested that Tibbetts had not been rehabilitated to the point where he would win life's Lady Byng Trophy.

Details of the rape cannot be printed in a family book such as this. But they became common knowledge around Philadelphia and, rightly so, disgusted most fans.

Unfortunately, the same could not be said for team management.

Snider tried to defend the move with a boys-will-be-boys approach.

"When I was 17 I took out a lot of 15-year-old girls," he offered.

Then Snider added, "Our take on the whole situation was that he got somewhat of a bad deal and didn't rape the girl even though it says it was rape. If he had actually raped the girl he would have been put in jail right there. What you have to do is go back and read the transcripts of the trial—which, admittedly, I have not done."

Hey, way to do your research, Ed.

Clarke insisted that Tibbetts was "a good kid who is trying to do what's right now. He made some mistakes but he's trying to live his life properly."

Turned out, Tibbetts was not living the exemplary life. In his brief NHL career he had been suspended twice, once for kneeing and once for sucker-punching an opponent sitting on the bench. And, a month before the trade, he was stopped by police after being clocked driving 120 mph on the Pennsylvania Turnpike.

Those escapades raised the question of whether Clarke hadn't done his research or knew of Tibbett's discipline problems but chose to ignore them. Either way, the Flyers image was tarnished.

When Tibbetts suited up for his first game here, there was one more insult to fans. He was dressed in No. 17, last worn by Rod Brind'Amour, a class guy and fan favorite. The fans wouldn't have it. They booed the newcomer's first appearance on First Union Center ice, and let him have it every subsequent shift.

Local papers were swamped with angry letters from fans.

"I've cheered for the orange and black for 25 years," Chris Antolik wrote to the *Daily News*, "but now I plan on sitting behind the home bench and pelting Tibbetts with beers and epithets."

"I think it is a disgrace that the Flyers, an organization that has had nothing but class until now, went out and got a guy like this," wrote Bill Jensen of Clifton Heights. "It is yet another black eye for the city, a convicted rapist. I am ashamed to be a Flyers fan today."

The team hoped Tibbetts' play would mollify angry fans. It didn't work out that way. He took stupid penalties, started fights at the wrong time and displayed no apparent skills beyond coughing up the puck. Tibbetts cost the Flyers one game when he grabbed Carolina winger Craig Adams and threw him down on top of Flyers goalie Neil Little. A goal was scored as Little tried to dig himself out from the tussling pile.

The whole episode lasted 23 days. In the end, this was Tibbetts' scorecard:

Games played: 9.

Games suspended: 2.

Total minutes played: 60.

Penalty minutes: 69.

Assists: 1.

Goals: 0.

Plus/minus: -3.

When the Flyers finally cut him, they insisted the reason was much too depth at center. But no one was buying that. Clarke and Snider had made a poor judgment—in terms of hockey and public relations. How were folks supposed to forget this guy's sordid history if he still acted like a knucklehead every time he stepped onto the ice?

Sometimes, the fans just know better.

We sat around one night over a few too many beers and came up with the quintessential Philadelphia sports fan's question: Who was the best-ever Eagle whose last name began with the letter "S"?

"Duce Staley," said Glen.

"Clyde Simmons," trumped Anthony.

"Nah, Torrance Small," offered our radio producer Dave Breitmaier. We immediately cut off his beer supply.

We kicked it around for a while . . . Norm Snead . . . Corey Simon . . . even Vai Sikahema got some support.

"I got it," said Dutchie (DeGaetano), another producer. "How about that Jerry Sisemore?"

Tough to argue. Sisemore played more than a decade for the Birds and was a rock at right tackle. For his fine effort, we made Dutchie buy the next round. And we continued to the next debate: The best-ever Sixer whose name began with the letter "D."

We've got too much time on our hands. If you, as well, find yourself engaged in such lofty discussion, here's a little crib sheet you can use. We listed whom the four of us we came up with as the top Flyer, Sixer, Eagle and Phillie since 1960 for each letter of the alphabet.

A – Barry Ashbee, Ron Anderson, Eric Allen, Richie Allen.

B – Bill Barber, Charles Barkley, Chuck Bednarik, Larry Bowa.

C – Bobby Clarke, Wilt Chamberlain, Harold Carmichael, Steve Carlton.

D – Eric Desjardins, Darryl Dawkins, Brian Dawkins, Lenny Dykstra.

E – Pelle Eklund, Julius Erving, Byron Evans, Jim Eisenreich.

F – Bob Froese, World B. Free, Irving Fryar, Woodie Fryman.

G – Simon Gagne, Hal Greer, Roman Gabriel, Greg Gross.

H – Mark Howe, Hersey Hawkins, Wes Hopkins, Von Hayes.

I – Gary Inness, Allen Iverson, Mark Ingram, Pete Incaviglia.

J – Kim Johnsson, Bobby Jones, Ron Jaworski, Jay Johnstone.

K – Tim Kerr, John Kerr, Keith Krepfle, John Kruk.

L – Eric Lindros, George Lynch, Randy Logan, Greg Luzinski.

M – Rick MacLeish, Moses Malone, Tommy McDonald, Garry Maddox.

N – Simon Nolet, Paul Neumann, Al Nelson, Dickie Noles.

O – Joel Otto, Doug Overton, John Outlaw, Johnny Oates.

P – Bernie Parent, Tim Perry, Floyd Peters, Lance Parrish.

Q – Dan Quinn, none, Mike Quick, Paul Quantrill.

R – Mark Recchi, Clint Richardson, Pete Retzlaff, Pete Rose.

S – Ron Sutter, Eric Snow, Jerry Sisemore, Mike Schmidt.

T – Rick Tocchet, Andrew Toney, Bobby Taylor, Manny Trillo.

U – none, none, Morris Unutoa, Del Unser.

V – Ed Van Impe, Tom Van Arsdale, Troy Vincent, Ozzie Virgil.

W – Joe Watson, Chet Walker, Reggie White, Rick Wise.

X – none, none, none, none.

Y – Dimitri Yushkevich, Barry Yates, Roynell Young, Floyd Youmans.

Z – Peter Zezel, none (unless you'll accept Dave Zinkoff), Mike Zordich, Todd Zeile.

TWENTY-SIX

MY SECOND FAVORITE
SEASON: THE 1993 PHILLIES

In looking back, the season almost seems an apparition, one of those dreams of half-consciousness that you're not sure afterward was fact or fiction.

Did they really even exist? That collection of greasers and bandits, muscle heads and fat men—did they really pass through town in 1993 and give us one joyous year of baseball?

They did. They came, they won, they stole our hearts, they broke our hearts. All in the span of six months. Hard to believe, Harry.

Look at what surrounded that Phillies season. The franchise had finished under .500 the previous six years with three last-place finishes. After '93, it returned to seven straight losing years, never even finishing with in 20 games of first place. That's not a dry spell, that's a crawl through the Gobi Desert.

But for one joyous summer, everything fell right—clutch hits, sterling defense, consistent starting pitching. More than three million of us jammed the Vet to watch our kind of players. These were not skilled and graceful high-pedigree stars, but rather an unshaven group of slobs that reflected our own community—and we mean that in a positive way.

"Lightning in a bottle" became the cliché, and it was right. Once Joe Carter shattered the bottle with one swing in Game Six of the World Series, the lightning never could be recaptured.

That gloomy SkyDome ending, with reliever Mitch Williams stalking off the field before Carter had even circled the bases, left millions of us staring at our TV screens, cursing the pitcher or the manager or the heavens. But it was, in a sense, perfect Philadelphia. The scrappy underdog—long on heart, short on style—scuffles all season to get to the title match. There is hope, but also a sense of foreboding, the deep-rooted knowledge that we can never escape our history.

In the end, Rocky loses. But he never leaves his feet.

There was no sense entering 1993 that the team would be anything special. Manager Jim Fregosi was back, this after personally directing seven straight losers in three cities. Who had faith in him? Fregosi was a dour, grumpy guy who hedged the frailty of a manager's security by living in a hotel suite near the stadium. When this team bonded with the fans, rest assured it was not through Fregosi, who would go on the next year to suggest that South Philadelphians sleep with their sisters. A couple of boys from the neighborhood later expressed their disagreement with Fregosi's opinion by roughing him up in local tavern.

But give him credit for this: He knew the right tone for this clubhouse. Given the strong personalities of his players, Fregosi was smart enough to step back and let the players govern themselves.

The roster itself looked like nothing to get excited about entering spring training. After unsuccessful runs at free agents Kirby Puckett and David Cone during the winter, the Phils brought back the same nucleus that had lost 92 games in 1992. Role players had been added—Pete Incaviglia, Jim Eisenreich, Milt Thompson, Danny Jackson—but none had Cooperstown stamped on his luggage.

Writing in Street & Smith's *Baseball Annual* that spring, forecaster Maury Allen wrote, "The famous fans of Philadelphia, known to boo Santa Claus, the Easter Bunny and the Thanksgiving parade, are gearing up should this team dare to finish behind the expansion Florida Marlins."

Ignore for a moment Allen's cheap shot at the fans. His prediction, hackneyed as it may have been written, was not far from what most people expected.

"Not many people outside the team had much faith," recalls Larry Bowa, who was the third base coach in 1993. "The players all saw that, and they decided to turn it into a positive. If the world was going to treat them without respect, they would go out and earn that respect."

Us-versus-them is the oldest motivator in sports, but it still works. And chemistry on a team can be vastly overrated, but, in 1993, that alchemy created a glue that brought together a diverse group of characters: the brooding, seemingly psychotic third baseman; the primping, matinee idol catcher; the cantankerous, beer-swilling first baseman; the tobacco-spitting, pain-in-the ass centerfielder.

The tough-guy veterans who set the team tone lined up their lockers on the back end of the clubhouse. "Macho Row" is what former WIP host Mike Missanelli brilliantly termed it, and it became the weigh station to hell for anyone who didn't fit in—nosy reporters, gawking guests and, sometimes, younger players like outfielder Wes Chamberlain, who was condemned for his lack of dedication.

The boys played together and partied together. They even fought together. A pre-season brawl against the Cardinals, in which the burly Phils manhandled their opponents, was often cited as a springboard for their season-long success. Foolish me, I always thought it was the strong starting pitching.

Whatever, they got off to a great start—sweeping the Astros in a three-game road series—and never looked back. By June 15, they had a 45-17 record and an 11-½ game lead over the Cardinals. From there on in, they put it in cruise control and wound up with a record of 97-65.

There were some tense moments, such as a four-game losing streak in July that dropped the lead to three games. Suddenly, every fan in town had visions of 1964, when the Phils blew a 6-½ game margin with 12 to play. The players would have none of the fatalism.

"Most of us weren't even alive in 1964," said catcher Darren Daulton. "I think the fans should just relax and enjoy this. We'll be fine."

And so they were.

There were no Hall of Famers on the 1993 Phils, unless Curt Schilling continues to pitch into his fifties. There were not even any perennial all-stars. But somehow the pieces fit together as assembled by Fregosi and general manager Lee Thomas.

Centerfielder Lenny Dykstra was the catalyst, a leadoff hitter who could shrink to the size of a toy poodle in the batter's box to force a walk. Dykstra was like a mosquito bite to the other team—the more you tried to scratch it, the more it got on your nerves.

Behind him was a solid if unspectacular power lineup—first baseman John Kruk, third baseman Dave Hollins, catcher Darren Daulton, and the lefty/righty combo of Incaviglia and Eisenreich—"Inky" and "Eisy" as the fans affectionately called them. None was anything close to a superstar. But that year . . . .

"It was one of those magic seasons where you press any button and it works," recalls Bowa. "Everybody produced in the clutch. I've been in baseball for decades and I never saw anything like it."

Remember, for example the Mother's Day game in which the Phils trailed St. Louis 5-2 with two outs in the bottom of the eighth inning. How many in the Vet Stadium crowd of 43,648 expected anything? But Daulton scratched out a single, Chamberlain doubled and reserve outfielder Thompson took a walk. The Cards' huge reliever, Lee Smith, stared down Mariano Duncan as he came to bat. Duncan was anything but a power hitter, and certainly no one's choice to be up in that situation. But he turned on Smith's first-pitch fastball and jacked a game-winning grand slam.

It was Duncan's eighth season, and his first career grand slam. As Bowa said, you press any button and it works.

The backbone of the squad was its starting pitching. Each member of the five-man rotation—Schilling, Danny Jackson, Tommy Greene, Terry Mulholland and Ben Rivera—won at least 12 games in 1993. Each made between 28 and 34 starts. That kind of depth is a rarity in modern baseball. Even more unusual was that none was homegrown. Each came to the Phils via trade, prompting Schilling to term the rotation "The Five Drifters," like some corner bee-bop group.

Schilling was the anchor (and the last surviving member of the '93 team), winning 16 games and leading the staff in starts, innings and strikeouts. Unfortunately, too many fans remember him that season for nervously wearing a towel over his head as Mitch Williams struggled to save his World Series game against the Blue Jays.

My recollection of Schilling? How about the 16 brilliant innings he tossed against the favored Braves in the National League Championship Series? Schilling didn't win either game, but the team won both and he was named Most Valuable Player of the series. When he opened

Game 1 by striking out the first five Braves he faced, we knew then that Atlanta was not invincible.

Williams—brilliantly nicknamed "Wild Thing"—was the guy who always ended up on magazine covers and highlight shows. Remember his famous leap after closing out the NLCS? He was infuriating in that he would enter a game with a two-run lead, promptly walk the bases, and force himself to escape a jam. More often than not, he did. When he didn't—i.e. the World Series—it was death.

Sometimes watching Williams felt like torture. "Just throw a bleeping strike," you'd scream from the seats. In the dugout, his teammates were screaming the same thing.

"Mitch doesn't have ulcers," Fregosi said of him. "But he's one of the biggest carriers there is."

Ah, but the memories. The greatest of all came in the back end of a doubleheader that started at 4:30 p.m. on July 2 and ended 12 hours and five minutes later. Six hours of rain delays didn't chase most fans from the Vet. They were rewarded when the Phils rallied from a 5-0 deficit in the second game to take it into extra innings. Sent up to bat for himself in the 10th because Fregosi had used up every pinch-hitter, Williams singled home the winning run. It was, of course, his first at-bat of the season.

And that's what it was about that team. You wished for a miracle, you got a miracle. Beyond that, they were just fun. The 1980 championship Phils had been a miserable lot who hated the manager, hated each other, hated the fans. This group, says, Schilling, "loved going to the stadium every day and seeing 40,000 screaming maniacs.

"I think that year's club really personified Philadelphia," says Schilling. "It was a work-hard group of guys who never loafed and embraced the ethic of the city we represented. It was one of those brief moments when a team and a city come together with a shared identity."

Maybe so. And Schilling's sincerity is reflected in his decision to keep his permanent residence in the Philly suburbs even after he was traded to the Arizona Diamondbacks.

Truth be told, however, the '93 Phils were not as lovable a lot as they came to be described. I covered several road trips with that team and found some to be not quite as gregarious as they were portrayed. Kruk, the scruffy country hick, was a first-class grump who brightened up only when the TV cameras came on. Hollins was nasty and homophobic and so moody that teammates avoided him after losses. Dykstra was a lowlife who treated most people with no respect. If fans didn't learn his foibles after the 1992 car accident with Daulton, they should have as stories continued to drip out—like the time he drunkenly challenged a state senator to fight in an upscale Main Line restaurant.

Maybe that's what people liked about Lenny: he would thumb his nose at big shots. My opinion of him changed during a shared cab ride in Atlanta. The cabbie, thrilled over his famous fare, handed Lenny a bat that had been autographed by other players he had driven to the ballpark.

"It's for my kid," said the cabbie, perhaps lying. He handed Dykstra a Sharpie and asked, "Sign it?"

"Sure," said Dykstra. He smirked a bit, wrote on the bat and showed me his handiwork.

"Eat Me!," he had written.

But, hey, it really doesn't matter in hindsight if the players we adore are truly paragons of virtue or have feet of clay. We don't really want to know their human flaws when we engage in serious hero worship. From the viewpoint of our bleacher seats or our Barcalounger, they're all our best friends.

So leave it this way. The 1993 Phils may not have been the best baseball team the city has ever seen. Certainly the 1970s clubs had more collective talent. The 1980 team won its World Series. And the 1983 team had a stable of future Hall of Famers.

But the '93 squad, warts and all, was the perfect group for this city. Full of personality, dedicated to a work ethic. Majestic enough to keep you glued to the television at 4 a.m., human enough to fall short in the end. For one year, baseball owned the city.

The farther away it appears in the rear-view mirror, the more you remember how good it was.

TWENTY-SEVEN

GREAT MOMENTS 5: AMAZING GRACE

We don't cheer the other guys in Philadelphia. We don't admire their grace and their grit. Philadelphia may be "the city that loves you back," but if you come from New York or Boston or, especially, Dallas, we love you only flat on your back, preferably unconscious. You would never hear supportive chants of "Beat LA" in this town, unless, perhaps, Larry Allen was engaged in a tussle with Corey Simon.

This is a good place to live, but a nasty place to visit. Larry Bird once said that a day in Philadelphia was like a day in purgatory. We think he was being too kind. A visiting player, Hall of Famer or not, should consider this a road stop through Dante's Inferno, complete with the rivers of blood and showers of fire flakes.

Hell, I was in the Spectrum seats once and heard a group of guys rain down cries of "sissy" and "pretty boy" on Wayne Gretzky, then with the Los Angeles Kings. Gretzky craned his neck to find the critics. Who heckles God, anyway?

There's us and there's them, and we don't like them. Period.

Except that, every once in a while, real life creeps in. And then, we're smart enough to see the difference.

One such moment came on March 2, 1993. On that night, we showed that our heart was as powerful as our passion. We gave comfort and support to a guy who had tormented us for years.

Mario Lemieux didn't regard the Flyers as his personal play toy; it only seemed that way. In 65 career games against our team, the Pittsburgh Penguins superstar scored 50 goals and added 68 assists, most, seemingly, achieved with Woody Acton's stick lodged between his legs. The Flyers tried jamming, clutching and poking Lemieux, never with much success.

In Lemieux's prime—1988 through 1993—the Flyers mustered a 13-21-5 mark against the Penguins. Most gallingly, the orange-and-black had a losing record at home. The Flyers would grind and sweat for two periods and then Lemieux would effortlessly bury a goal and steal the win.

It drove us nuts. That, plus his elegant style. We like our hockey heroes best when they're dripping blood and dragging their knuckles on the ice. Lemieux is the NHL's version of Joe DiMaggio, and his grace never played to fans in this town. Perhaps the only player who annoyed us more over the years was his androgynous teammate, Jaromir Jagr, whose entrance was always greeting with a few chords from Aerosmith's "Dude Looks Like a Lady."

So we abused the Magnificent One. Through his great years and his greater ones, through his run at Gretzky's records and his debilitating back injuries. And then, on a cold March night in 1993, we stopped.

Two months earlier, at the age of 27, Lemieux had been diagnosed with Hodgkin's disease, a form of cancer that attacks the lymph nodes. A lump was removed from his neck. Many believed he would never play again. Lemieux was not among that group. He underwent 22 debilitating bouts of radiation treatment and, on the day of the final treatment, chartered a plane to Philadelphia and dressed to play against the Flyers. He wore a turtleneck under his jersey to cover the areas left tender by the radiation.

Mario in action against the Flyers.

One by one, the Penguins walked through the tunnel and stepped onto the Spectrum ice. One by one, they were booed. But when Lemieux appeared, the last player out, the partisan fans rose and gave him a 90-second standing ovation. A welcome-back message appeared on the big screen, and the fans cheered some more for their long-time tormentor.

Some fans carried signs: "Get well, Mario," and "Welcome back, Mario. Slip us a puck."

As the roar persisted, Lemieux stood on the blue line, shuffling his skates, pretending not to notice. Finally, he raised his stick in appreciation, which stirred the fans even more.

"It would have been nicer to start at home in Pittsburgh with all the excitement," Lemieux after the game. "But the fans in Philly were great when I stepped on the ice. It's a great feeling when something like that happens on the road."

In the second period, Lemieux slipped a soft goal by Flyers goalie Dominic Roussel. The Spectrum crowd rose for another standing ovation. A few minutes later, he set up linemate Kevin Stevens for another goal. This time, the crowd was more muffled. Hey, welcome back and all that, but we'd rather you not beat us tonight.

From that night on, it seems, we forged a new relationship with Lemieux. Our boos were replaced by a respectful appreciation, the type other cities' fans showed Julius Erving late in his career.

In 1997, Lemieux announced his impending retirement before a playoff series against the Flyers (okay, the departure didn't take, but who knew that at the time?). When the series ended with a Flyers' win in what was then the CoreStates Center, Philadelphia fans broke into a chorus of "Mario! Mario!" and stood in tribute to our opponent. The game ended with public address announcer Lou Nolan introducing "No. 66, Mario Lemieux, tonight's first star and only star."

If he ever retires again, we'll give him another fine send-off. Now would seem a good time.

TWENTY-EIGHT

OUR TEN MOST EMBARRASSING MOMENTS

Sure, this book is designed as a celebration of Philadelphia fans and their heroes. But in the spirit of full disclosure, we must admit there have been times when we were ashamed of our own behavior.

Here's a list of the ten most embarrassing moments in Philadelphia sports history, with contributions from players, coaches, owners and, yes, the fans.

10. Prep School Brawl Mars Phillies Opener.

It became one of the rites of Opening Day in the late '90s—like "Rocket Man" and "Kite Man" and booing the manager. But the annual rumble between rowdies from St. Joe's Prep and Bonner High wasn't exactly what the Phils had in mind when they promoted the product as "family entertainment."

The most-publicized brawl occurred in the centerfield bleachers on April 13, 1999. Students from the two schools, both of which had dismissed classes prior to the 3 p.m. game, began taunting each other. Chants of "Bonner sucks!" and "Prep sucks!" filled the 700 level.

It would seem difficult to top that clever repartee, but the boys managed, by pitching beer, ice and pretzels at each other through the early innings. Problem was, most of the debris hit innocent fans stuck in the same sections as the wannabe British soccer hooligans.

The first punch was tossed in the fourth inning. Within moments, the crowd of 37,000 was treated to the sight of shirtless high-schoolers clobbering guards and tumbling down rows of seats while flailing away at each other. The action was so intense that players stopped the game to gawk into the stands.

"True Philadelphia," lamented Curt Schilling. "Make a city proud."

The fracas involved about 40 teenagers and lasted more than ten minutes. That night, it was run—blow by blow—on CNN, ESPN and Fox. David Letterman even worked it into his nightly "Top Ten" list.

Afterward, an inquiry by the city slapped the stadium concessionaire for selling beer to minors and cited the police department for not having enough cops on duty. Investigations by the two schools resulted in eons of detention and, presumably, a few raps on the knuckles from the thin edge of a ruler.

Not everyone got the message, however. One Bonner student interviewed a few days later, told the *Inquirer*, "We got in some trouble, but it was worth it. We kicked some major butt."

9. Rich Kotite's Chart Runs in the Rain.

This much you expect from your head coaches: If they don't know the right call instinctively, at least they know how to look it up. We didn't even get that from Richie the K.

On a rainy October Sunday at Texas Stadium in 1994, Kotite's Eagles scored a touchdown with six minutes left, bringing the score to 24-13, favor of Dallas. As Eagles kicker Eddie Murray waited to be sent in for the extra point, Kotite and offensive line coach Bill Muir conferred on the sidelines. Muir pulled from his pocket the standard chart that all coaches use when trying to decide whether to try a two-point conversion.

Television cameras captured the scene: the two men in a furious pantomime, struggling to read the chart as rain gushed through the hole in the stadium roof. Finally, Kotite opted to go for two. He sent in his offense, which was promptly snuffed. Momentum gone, game over.

It would have been just another questionable call in a bad coaching career had Kotite not admitted the next day that the problem was mostly a lack of lamination. "To be honest with you," he said, "we should have gone for one. That's what the chart said, but we misread the chart. It was wet and everything."

Wet and everything?

"Yeah, the ink was running and we couldn't read it."

For lack of a horse the kingdom was lost. For lack of a plastic coating (or waterproof ink), so were the Eagles' chances. Wags joked that Kotite must have borrowed the blackjack chart that former owner Leonard Tose used in Atlantic City when he used to hit on 18, but for the fans it was no laughing matter. It was just one more nasty reminder that the boob who was directing our football team wasn't even bright enough to stay out of the rain.

Making matters worse was our knowledge that the chart was authored by former Eagles coach Dick Vermeil. No way Vermeil ever blows that call.

8. Wes Hopkins's Wife and Girlfriend Tussle at the Vet.

You think No. 48 was tough? You never met his wife.

In a 1992 game between the Eagles and Denver Broncos, the crowd of 65,000 was brought to its feet by what looked like a prolonged catfight between two attractive women in the 200 Level. What the fans didn't realize was they were watching Erika Hopkins take out years of frustration over infidelity on Wes's latest squeeze. Or, a "sis-boom-bimbo," as Mrs. Hopkins later termed her target in Mark Bowden's book, *Bringing The Heat.*

The incident began after Erika introduced herself as Wes's wife to a newcomer in the private Vet lounge reserved for players' families.

"That's funny," said the newcomer. "I just met another woman who told me she was Wes Hopkins's wife."

Erika Hopkins was no dummy. She suspected her husband was having an affair, and quickly searched out the section where players leave complimentary tickets for guests. She located her prey and—as the wives of Reggie White and Eric Allen stood by for support—clobbered Wes's concubine with the full wrath of a woman scorned.

The girlfriend fell, rolled down nine rows of steps and began to flee. But the Eagles' wives, loyal teammates that they were, grabbed her and pushed her back. Erika flailed away.

Eagles fans are accustomed to seeing fights erupt at the games. But the sight of attractive, well-dressed women gouging each other was something else entirely. No one knew at the time the story behind the scrap; they just knew they were witnessing something they would talk about for years.

The franchise, appalled by the incident, never publicly acknowledged it. Nor did Wes Hopkins, who was separated from Erika a few days later. But the players' wives—many of whom had their marriages interrupted by "sis-boom-bimbos"—celebrated the fight for years.

7. A Flare Gun Fires on Monday Night Football.

We've had our share of idiot fans over the years—the slob who dived into the penalty box to tussle with Maple Leafs enforcer Tie Domi in 2001 comes to mind. But no bigger moron may exist than the man who sneaked a flare gun into the Vet and then fired it into a fully packed stadium.

The 1997 season was slipping away from Ray Rhodes's Birds. They were 4-5 headed into a Monday night game against the San Francisco 49ers. When the game turned ugly early, so did the crowd. An all-out brawl in the 500 Level got the attention of ABC's broadcasters and, by final count, more than 60 fistfights punctuated the night. This was, in fact, the game that convinced the city to start holding Hanging Judge Court at the Vet.

The captain of the Stupidity Squad was Robert Sellers, a 29-year-old Jersey guy who left home that night, according to police, with his ticket, driver's license, two marijuana joints and a standard-issue flare gun. How he got past stadium security guards is one question. How he took it from inside his jacket and set it up with no one interceding is another.

Regardless, as unhappy Eagles fans left early from a game their team would lose 24-12, Sellers locked, loaded and launched from his seat in the 200 Level. The flare arced over the field in a stunning fireball and landed in an unsuspecting section of folks in the corner of the end zone. Amazingly, no one was hurt.

The ABC broadcasters, seeing more action in the seats than on the field, responded with awe.

"Did you see that?" asked Al Michaels.

"I'm not sure what just went off," responded Dan Dierdorf, "but this is very, this is very frightening."

Sellers was arrested and charged with eight counts, including felony arson and drug possession. Interviewed by WPVI-TV Action News, he explained why he did it:

"I was just caught up in the moment, you know? Everybody was screaming and yelling. Everybody was fighting all around and then . . . I just, I set it off."

He admitted to being drunk at the time. We're not sure if that became the cornerstone of his defense.

6. Gary McLain Ruins the Fun.

It's rare enough that this town ever wins a championship in anything. So why did Villanova's Gary McLain decide he had to spoil the celebration?

McLain was a talented senior point guard on the 1985 miracle team that won the NCAA Tournament. We don't need to remind you of the details—Nova entered the tourney as a lowly eighth seed with ten regular-season losses and then rallied its way to four nail-biting wins to get to the finals. There, the Wildcats shocked Patrick Ewing's Georgetown team, 66-64. Rollie Massimino's boys made 78 percent of their shots that night and needed every one of them.

What endearing theater. The players cut down the nets and draped them over the head of ancient trainer Jake Nevin, his body bent by Lou Gehrig's disease. A few days later, the disheveled Massimino smiled alongside President Reagan at a Rose Garden reception.

Overall, it was such a great underdog story that snooty Nova even won the hearts of Big Five rivals who always rooted against them on principle. More than 100,000 people showed up for a ticker-tape parade down Broad Street. The team had earned a spot in our roll call of heroes.

And then McLain turned the thrill of victory into the agony of scandal. He sold an 18-page story to *Sports Illustrated* saying he used and sold drugs during his days at Nova; that he played many of his games on cocaine, even that he was stoned when he met President Reagan. The most damning allegation in the story (for which McLain was paid $40,000) was his charge that Massimino knew about but ignored his drug use.

Massimino denied the charge and a university investigative panel cleared the coach of any wrongdoing. Still, the story rocked Villanova to its conservative foundations and placed a stain on a magnificent achievement.

Many of McLain's former teammates continue to believe he made the whole story up for a paycheck. Regardless, he scarred the memories of everyone in Philadelphia who cheered him and his teammates through an incredible climb to the national championship.

5. Owners Who Are Guilty of Rampant Stupidity.

It's tough to choose between two legendary episodes in which our franchises' stewards acted like bumbling fools. So we decided to cite them both. In both cases, the guilty parties later denied the incidents, but the body of evidence (and some loose-lipped underlings) suggests otherwise.

First, we believe that Sixers owner Harold Katz, as part of his interview with prospective draft pick Brad Daugherty, had the seven-foot center out to his Main Line manse, where they played a little one-on-one. Afterward, Katz declared Daugherty "too soft" to play for the 76ers. That precipitated the June 1986 Draft Day Massacre in which the team traded Moses Malone and Terry Catledge to the Washington Bullets for Jeff Ruland and Cliff Robinson, and also shipped the top overall pick in the draft to the Cleveland Cavaliers for a bag of magic beans.

The Cavs took the "too-soft" Daugherty, who went on to average 19 points per game over an eight-year career. The Sixers went into the toilet during those same eight years, struggling with a roll call of centers that included Tim McCormick, Christian Welp, Rick Mahorn, Mark McNamara, Kurt Nimphius, Manute Bol, Charles Shackleford, Andrew Lang, Eddie Lee Wilkins and Shawn Bradley—the ultimate Mr. Softee. They didn't contend for the title again for 15 years.

Second, we absolutely trust that Phillies general partner Bill Giles referred to our fair city as a "small market" in 1994 when rationalizing why he didn't want to spend big money for free agents. Never mind that Philadelphia was the largest city in the nation playing home to just one baseball franchise. Giles later amended his statement to call us a "small-revenue" market, but the damage was already done.

His gum flapping hurt on two levels. First, Philadelphians consider our town the rival of places like New York and Boston, not Cincinnati and Milwaukee. That term—"small market" —sticks in your throat like a fish bone.

Second, Giles's mindset condemned the Phils to losing for a full decade. It meant that our team was the one with no chance to compete for big-time players, and allowed stars like Curt Schilling to skip town. It took until 2003, when the Phils signed free agent Jim Thome, for the taint to wear off.

4. Eagles Fans Celebrate an Injured Irvin.

Whether it was half the crowd that cheered as Michael Irvin lay unmoving on the Vet Stadium carpet, or one quarter of the crowd, or one tenth, the bottom line remains the same —some of our fans partied as a man lay temporarily paralyzed.

We will not defend that here. We will lay out some facts, however. Irvin was hurt on a crushing tackle by Eagles safety Tim Hauck—the kind of hit that fans across the nation cheer and the league celebrates on its own highlight films. As Irvin lay there, teammate Deion Sanders danced around signaling to the heavens, to Irvin, to himself. This annoyed the crowd.

The incident came months after Irvin was arrested in a sea of crack cocaine, exotic dancers and sex toys. Irvin then showed up for court in a full-length fur coat and jewel-encrusted glasses. He was, in short, the kind of player that fans love to see get crushed. We don't think the reaction would have been the same if it were Art Monk laying there.

Still, it was very wrong. Cheering Hauck's hit was fine. Raising the decibel level as the ambulance rolled onto the field was something else entirely.

The incident, of course, contributed to our reputation as America's barbarians. It prompted jokes, like the one that the city's motto is "Philadelphia: The City That Loves (to Cheer When You Break) You(r) Back." It made us the target of every behavioral expert in the nation, never mind that both Irvin and Cowboys owner Jerry Jones said they received hundreds of get-well messages from our city's sports fans.

Look, worse incidents have occurred in other cities and, no question we get condemned more than we should. But the bottom line is this: The minority of people who cheered as Irvin lay motionless were stone-cold wrong. The entire city needn't be embarrassed, but those people should be.

Governor Ed Rendell probably captured the essential truth of it all when he said: "The reality is, nothing's going to happen in towns with no pulse. Philadelphia is a passionate city. More things are going to happen—positive or negative."

3. Police Dogs and Horses Nip at Phillies' Heels.

The Phils had been in business for 97 years and never won a World Series. So when the time finally came, on October 21, 1980, no one was sure how the city's fans would react. Would there be chaos on South Broad Street? Would we tear the Vet apart?

Mayor Bill Green wanted to take no chances. So as the ninth inning began, a long line of mounted police officers pranced their horses onto the field, like cavalry troops awaiting battle. Dozens more cops jogged out to the outfield wall, tugging at leather leashes to restrain their snarling German shepherds.

It was done in the name of safety, but it just looked wrong. On national television, it made Philadelphia appear like an armed prison camp. And while it may not have dampened the mood in the stadium (we had waited so long that nothing could spoil our fun), it did succeed in frightening the players.

Phils closer Tug McGraw recalls that as he started to warm up in the bullpen before the ninth inning, "I went to reach for my glove and a German shepherd had fallen in love with it. That dog went 'Grrrr' and I said, 'Hey, you're supposed to be on our side.'

"The cop snatched the dog away and I went out there. I knew I had to pitch good; otherwise that dog might come out and bite me."

McGraw pitched good, er, well enough, loading the bases before getting Frank White to pop out (off Bob Boone's glove into Pete Rose's) and then striking out Willie Wilson. As the crowd went wild, the horses reared in fear. And as the jubilant Phils danced off the field, several players got nipped at by the nervous K-9s.

Baseball's use of riot-control animals in Series-clinching games has become almost standard in recent years. The Eagles even rolled out the infantry in 2003 for a playoff game against the Atlanta Falcons. Still, it appears wrong to us. A championship should be time for jubilation, not a call to arms.

2. Eagles Dis-Honor Mike Quick.

In nine brilliant seasons he caught 363 passes and scored 61 touchdowns for the Eagles. Teaming up with Ron Jaworski and later Randall Cunningham, he created reel after reel of highlights. The 99-yard reception against Atlanta in 1985. The three-touchdown game against the Raiders in 1986.

So when chronic knee problems forced Mike Quick to retire early, even clueless owner Norman Braman realized that this graceful star needed to be honored. This was a good idea—a year earlier Braman had been slammed for ignoring the tenth anniversary of the 1980 Super Bowl squad.

The Birds held a ceremony at halftime of a 1991 game. A highlight film was played on the Vet scoreboard while Nat King Cole's "Unforgettable" played in the background. There were a few speeches, and the Eagles announced a $1,000 donation in Quick's name to Big Brothers. And then, as a reward for all his years of service Quick was presented with a green-and-white golf bag. An empty golf bag at that.

The fans felt Quick deserved more and booed the presentation. The empty bag was a perfect metaphor for Braman's cheapness. After all, the guy also owned more than a dozen car dealerships. He couldn't have let Quick drive off in a Cadillac? Or at least a golf cart?

Quick, to his credit, never griped about the insulting gift. When I asked him about it in 2002, he said, "You know, more people ask me about that stupid bag than anything I did in my career. But that's okay. The way I figure it, the franchise was nice enough to honor me. They flew in my family, treated us first-class. I didn't expect anything."

Besides, he said, he still plays out of the bag—even if he had to buy his own clubs to fill it. "And I'm a six-handicap," he added. "What's so bad about that?"

It's nice to know that Quick has class, even if the owner who honored him did not.

1. Fans Boo the Selection of Donovan McNabb.

There's no avoiding it. For all of the extenuating circumstances and all of our rationalizations, this is our most embarrassing moment as sports fans. And every time we think we've moved past it, there are the TV networks, eager to play the whole sordid episode again.

First, the background: With the sorry Eagles holding the second pick in the 1999 draft, fans were itching to see someone come in who could have an immediate impact. That someone (for most of us, anyway) was Ricky Williams, the Heisman Trophy-winning University of Texas running back. Local newspapers lobbied for Williams, Mayor Rendell presented him with an Eagles jersey during the Maxwell Club dinner, WIP-AM campaigned for his selection.

The Eagles said little, but it was obvious they planned to go another direction. New coach Andy Reid planned to build his team around a quarterback, and Syracuse's Donovan McNabb was his guy.

As the day grew closer, our colleagues at WIP hired a bus to take fans to New York City to watch the draft live. About 30 fanatics piled in for the trip, fueled by beer and the excitement that the Eagles could grab a franchise-maker with the second pick. Maybe it was the alcohol talking, maybe it was bravado, but by the time the bus rolled into the Marriott Marquis parking lot, the boys had irrationally convinced themselves that the Eagles would take Ricky Williams.

The time came. NFL Commissioner Paul Tagliabue strode to the podium to announce the choice. The fanatics began palpitating.

"With the second pick," said Tagliabue, "the Philadelphia Eagles select Syracuse University quarterback Donovan McNabb."

"Boooooo!"

The cameras quickly found our boys, faces painted green and silver, reacting in shock and anger. This was foolish and, in hindsight, downright rude, but at the time it was just a cathartic release of disappointment. No one there actually had a grudge with McNabb; they were venting their anger over the team's passing on Ricky Williams.

The fallout was overwhelming. We got a national scolding, with everyone from John Madden to Miss Manners saying we needed to have our mouths washed out with soap. McNabb's mother expressed outrage and, truth be told, has never seemed to forgive the city. McNabb himself never griped about the affair but, no doubt, it had to sting. Everyone involved—from Mayor Rendell to WIP's Angelo Cataldi—has apologized repeatedly over the years.

Booing at the NFL draft, we learned, isn't like booing in your living room or at the stadium. It's like booing at an awards banquet. It's bad etiquette.

Hey, Donovan. We'll never boo you again. We promise.

TWENTY-NINE

THE VET

I write this during the Vet's last leaky days, the place now condemned to memory. Soon it will be smoothed-over rubble and tarred black, a good spot to park for the replacement stadiums that we have watched take form with the eagerness of a Powerball drawing. They will be aesthetically beautiful structures with God's grass and lots of luxury suites and character and charm, the beloved antithesis of the building that stood on Broad and Pattison for a generation.

Mostly, the masses will toast the dawning of new digs. Good riddance to bad rubbish, they will say.

For the Vet, I am told with the frequency of the Philadelphia boo, was the bane of stadium architecture, the mobile home in a Victorian burg. It was impersonal, synthetic, trite, a brickless, colorless, multi-purpose mess that never indeed had a purpose, born unto a time in America when modernism was viewed as being first and foremost functional, forsaking all style and taste. Panache gave way to suburbanism and strip malls and silver Christmas trees and ligament-tearing Astroturf. So you see the Vet never had a chance. Fate said the Vet could never have been a fixture like a Lambeau Field or Wrigley Field in the same way placebo cities like Charlotte or Denver could never matter as much as Philadelphia. Even on the Vet's first official day in April 1971—when the Phillies' Dallas Green stood awestruck on the field during the pregame pageantry and thought, "It's the most beautiful thing I've ever seen. So huge. So majestic. So new."—the place seemed constructed to be destructed.

Hell, it wasn't even original, merely one of the cousin Concrete Charlies that were erected in Pittsburgh and Cincinnati and St. Louis around the same time. But a few, like myself, will mourn. We will feel the loss of a constant in our lives, over 32 years, which means life is growing short. The last thirty years have seemed shorter than a Steve Carlton complete game. We will look to the deeper meaning, yes, and also to the times spent there. All of those Sunday afternoons and twi-night doubleheaders, 5:35 p.m. start time, usually on Friday nights. All of those games, yes, I understand, mostly with the sour ending. "But still," I respond, fumbling for a salient argument to check mate. Apparently it's my turn now. The Vet is my Baker Bowl, a place some kid will never know—or care to know about. It is during a moment like this that a man must reflect. Forgive me but my life is forever tied to that stadium. My mortal timeline intersects what transpired there: Black Friday, Black Sunday, Pete and the popup, Horses on the Field, Wilbert's run, The Body Bag Game, Mitch Williams (against the Braves), 58-37 over the Lions, Black Sunday, Part Tampa.

Beyond the cinema, I befriended the Vet. Like most bred from within its shadows, I bonded with my mother there, and my father, separately in fact, particularly the time when she flirted with Lou Brock so I could get his autograph. I followed around my cousin Joey who was really a brother there. I sought refuge there. I got lucky there. My friends all worked there, Vinny and John as security guards, Boo, Bobby and Andy in the Nylon Brothers concession stands. They got their jobs after a guard at Gate B got so tired of them sneaking in that he left behind a pile of applications. The easiest way to sneak in was dart past the old guy who stood watch at the Will Call entrance. He'd care only to mutter something under his cracking breath. If you were looking for style points, there was the broken turnstile outside Gate C, the ramp that connected two sections and wasn't encircled by barbed wire, the electric garage door where they funneled out the garbage. One part of the door was always off the track.

The Vet was our fort in the backyard. We explored every crevice and cubbyhole, and more than a few times came face to face with one of our heroes. Bobby once mooned Larry Christenson after he faked throwing him a baseball. Like each other, it was a constant in our lives. I don't remember the old South City Drive-In or nearby Beaver Street, the place where young men parked with young women after a movie. The screen, I was told, was right about where homeplate came to be. For us, the Vet has always peeked from over the trees from the edge of South Philadelphia. We drank sodas that were covered by only Saran wrap and ate hot dogs with yellow mustard they'd swipe on with a stick and snuck sips of Schmidt's beer and loved the batting glove the Phillies gave away on a particular Sunday and ogled the Hot Pants girls in cherry red boots.

Parochial Philadelphia understands this, and so in the end, it's not about banners and titles and wins, but experiences that went beyond butt in a seat with binoculars. The place houses stories, legends, tales, of those who played there, worked there, rooted there. Some of the tales are sordid at the core, though passing days have somehow amended them cartoonish, non-threatening because of sheer outlandishness, sort of like gangsters in wide Capone pin-stripes. I was told tales of riots and orgies and complete lawlessness. I was told tales that pick-led and tickled. Some of the tales I could not substantiate, others I chose to leave for the after-life. Tales of the past are easy to come by as the protective barrier that encases them dulls and tatters through dust and time.

There was the one of the mother in her late thirties who taught her teenage daughters how to be a groupie in the early '80s, how to infiltrate that world and go to bed with it. One person who was there recalls that he "couldn't count how many players and guards they slept with. I remember I sneaked one of the daughters into the clubhouse well after a game. She had a crush on Von Hayes. He never messed with her. But she saw the athletic shorts he wore under his uniform hanging in his locker and she went over and sniffed the crotch."

There was another, like the player who emerged from the stadium with his wife and two babies and whispered to a security guard, "See that pretty blonde over there? Tell her to wait here while I take my family home and that I'll be back." He gave the security guard a wink. Later he told him he spent the night across the street at the Hilton, and bragged he didn't spend a nickel on her, save for the plane ticket from San Diego to Philadelphia.

Then there was the security guard who used to make a fortune forging ballplayers' signatures. He had every notable name down pat, down to every loop and squiggle. There was the time a producer for "All My Children" during a pregame softball game between rival soaps pined for Steve Carlton's autograph on a ball that included fellow 300-game winners Nolan Ryan's and Tom Seaver's, and the security guard boasted that he signed it for $100.

Perhaps the most infamous tales came about because of the Goon Squad, a faction of security guards who worked for the Phillies during the early part of the '80s and were known for their overzealous enforcement of crowd control in the pre-Judge Seamus days. They consisted of mostly neighborhood boys who lifted weights and loved to fight, puffy-chested sorts who could have secured Rikers Island and were paid at their peak $37 a game. So the story goes, after almost every home game workers had to hose down the elevator that led to the police holding room because of the amount of spilled blood.

"Of the guards, there was one contingent who took the job to watch baseball and the other who went there to beat the fuck out of people," says one former Goon Squader. "When you came into security, you wanted to be a part of that gang. Some of them were schoolteachers who wanted to earn a few extra bucks, passive guys during the day but who'd come to the games at night and fuck people up. And guess what? It worked. People knew not to fuck around at the Vet. We'd take people into utility closets, closed concession stands, remote parts of the 700 level. There are big steel swinging doors that lead to the holding room. I opened that door with the faces of more people . . . ."

Vinny and John worked security in those days. In fact, the Phillies fired Vinny after he punched out a drunken fan in full view during a game with the Dodgers. He was in charge of watching the visiting owner's box that day. Some college-aged kids had trespassed. They began fighting with stadium security. The melee spread and grew, so much that play on the field momentarily ceased. Players pointed to the section. One fan swung a bottle of vodka at an usher. Vinny caught him with a short right to the jaw. Later, former Phillies infielder Mariano Duncan applauded Vinny. "That's right!" he said. "You don't take no shit! That's the way we do it in the Dominican!" Smokey Lasorda, brother of Tommy, told him, "You knocked the fight right out of that guy!" Smokey even wrote a letter on Vinny's behalf, saying his action was warranted. Vinny petitioned to get his job back and won.

Whether it's an Opening Day skirmish between students of rival Catholic high schools or an anarchic post-game Robert Hazard concert or the time Met fans attacked the Phillie Phanatic—one receiving a bloody nose from the paw of the mascot, the stands of Veterans Stadium have hosted more battles than Russia's outer terrain. Of course, the most infamous acts of maim have occurred during Eagles games. If a full moon inspires madness, then football and alcohol and a fan in division enemy garb represent a thousand full moons, beaming idiocy to those predestined to Hyde.

John worked that blustering Sunday when a Redskin fan in a pricey headdress provoked the green demons of the hardscrabble 700 Level and left beaten and bloodied, nary a feather intact. "I heard Joe Theismann reference it just the other day," he says. "To be frank, if there was ever a guy who deserved to get beat up it was him. He wasn't just cheering for his team. He was taunting everyone around him. We kicked him out the section but he didn't make it out of the stadium." During a different Washington game, three large men festooned in draping old ladies' cassocks and pig noses, saluting the Redskins' famed offensive line nicknamed the Hogs, appeared panicked at the police desk. "They were crying, I mean, bawling," says Eagles chief of security Anthony Buchanico, then a decorated Philly cop. "They got beat up. You ain't seen nothing until you see three 300-pound fat guys in old ladies' dresses in tears."

Certainly alcohol is the stimulus for such mayhem. And what is it about football and booze? Why after hours of tailgating do some fans suddenly exhibit a brilliant cunning to sneak in a nip? According to Buchanico, there was a guy in a wheelchair pretending to have no legs sitting on a half keg of beer and another accompanied by his wife and baby who put vodka in one of the bottles—on a whim, an usher decided to test the formula. Buchanico has seen everything from cans of beer swathed in hoagie wrappers—so diabolically intricate that the price was scribbled on the front along with something like "no onions"—to people taping ziplock baggies of booze to their body to Juicy Juice containers filled with alcohol via syringes.

The souls of the living leave behind an aura as real as paw prints, and so the place is abuzz with flickering images. It is so ever strong in the Phillies clubhouse, where I can almost hear the old Pope, former GM Paul Owens, challenge the entire '80 team to a fight (okay, that actually happened in San Francisco but you get the point). "Half you guys might be able to beat me," he snorted from those cheese-grater lungs, "but I'll get some ice on it and I'll be knocking on your door tomorrow."

Bowa, Schmidt, Carlton, Maddox, "Looo-zin-skeee"—as longtime public address announcer Dan Baker would say, amid the glowing image of giant hands clapping on the bulby, graphic-challenged right-field scoreboard ("Polysyllabic names are the most fun to announce," Baker says)—were ballplayers in the way Andy Seminick was a ballplayer to my father. Indeed those ballplayers loathed Green right about then, but they got into a Fuck-You Fight and played harder just to spite the old bastard. Nobody's agent threatened the prospects of re-signing. Maybe it's unfair to compare. Maybe the Phillies are undertaking a renaissance, with a burgeoning farm system and fresh faces, baseball faces, like Jimmy Rollins and Pat Burrell and Brett Myers and Jim Thome. Maybe the tacit ban on baseball here has been lifted, and we're heading back to once in a blue moon with the Phillies. But know that until police horses return to the Vet—or to that dreamy new ballpark—It Always Goes Back to the '80s.

"Sheesh," grouses Green. "I live with '80. Nothin' like what we did in '80. They got there in '93 but they lost. Period. I tell that to Fregosi. I tell him: 'You didn't do that great a job, Jim. You lost.' It wasn't just the winning. It was how we went about it. Spittin' and spewin' at each other. Fought all year. Took 161 games to win the NL East. Four of five extra inning games to win the sonofabitch pennant. Can't go back to '80 though. Guys get coddled now. Yep, '80 is dead."

Steve Carlton would camp in the clubhouse swigging French wine and pondering life until five in the morning in '80, and the clubby couldn't leave until he did. Lefty tipped him big, of course. "This is for you, kid," he'd say and then keep him another half hour. Once in a while in '83, Schmidt and Sarge Matthews would share a beer and a smoke between innings.

During batting practice in '80, especially during those tense days, Tug McGraw would aim to take the edge off the fellas. He'd spot a looker in the seats and hoot: "Tits! Tits! Lay 'em on the rail!" And sometimes she'd lay 'em on the rail. Sometimes Pete Rose would be at the plate in '80 cursing his then-girlfriend Carol, the former Eagle cheerleader, because she would be hysterically banging on the plexiglass behind home plate, telling him she figured out the cryptic message that affixed to the crop plane flitting above the stadium. She would say it's from a girl and you're supposed to meet her at so-and-so's! The pitcher would be in his windup and he'd snicker, "Fuck you. Fuck you." Then he'd get a hit and she'd collapse sobbing in the corner near the grounds crew. Meanwhile, the grounds crew in '80 hung behind home plate with a barrel crammed with beer and marveled at Maddox tracking down a fly ball in dead center. "Look at the deer!" they'd say. "Look at the deer!"

Somehow '80 morphed into '93. Stories continued to flow, like the beer tap in the press room that kept the ballpark alive deep into the night. Video Dan collected more than when he was a bartender at Downey's on South Street. Video Dan—Stephenson, by the way, the Phils' video technician, duh—tells when manager Lee Elia ordered the video room off limits to players. The video room has always provided a haven for players, particularly for closers during the game. Steve Bedrosian would eat a sandwich and spend innings one through six with Video Dan. So when on this night Bedrosian knocked on the door Video Dan didn't open, citing manager's orders. "But it's me," Bedrosian said. "Open up."

"Sorry."

"Okay, I'll be back." And Bedrosian came back. With a fire axe. And he chopped a hole in the door, peeked through and said, "Here's Bedrock."

Then there was John Kruk, who lived in Delaware County at the time but slept on Video Dan's couch in his office on Saturday nights before Sunday games. Video Dan's dog slept on that couch. It smelled and springs jabbed outward. This one Sunday Video Dan arrived at his office, expecting the worst, seeing how the Phils were facing a tough lefty and Kruk had the day off. Sure enough, the video room was trashed, empty beer bottles strewn, cigarette butts on the carpet, but no Kruk. Ten minutes later he appears in long johns and socks, and he looks terrible, ashen and bloated. "I'm in a lot of trouble," he says. "I can't lift my arm above my head. I pitched 97 innings of Wiffle ball to the clubhouse kid. We played until six-thirty this morning. And Ricky Jordan got sick and I have to play." Kruk got three hits that game.

Harry Kalas smiles at all the stories. He has been here since it opened in '71. He made this place sound so enchanting. Just how he said the name. "I put the E in there—Vet-er-rans Stadium," he says with a familiar melody, then takes a long drag on a cigarette and peers out the yawning window of the broadcast booth, sizing up the building. The Liberty Bell used to be out there. So too were Phil and Phyllis, the Colonial brother and sister who played fungo in the outfield. Their cannon would boom after a home run. Richie Ashburn stood next to him then, right here in this booth, and spoke wistfully. I swear I can feel his presence. Harry Kalas misses Richie Ashburn.

From inside the shaggy green togs, he saw everything and blamed it on the funny-looking monster with the protruding snout and ample bulge. He was so good at it, in fact, people forgot Dave Raymond lived inside, an honest to goodness person. Born unto a time of the Great Wallendas and Kite Man, the idea came on the heels of the San Diego Chicken, the first mascot other than a boisterous hot dog man, like "Doggie Ho!", and Dave Raymond was flattered. He was an intern in 1978, along with current Phillies GM Ed Wade, and managing partner Bill Giles asked if he would be the creature created by a New York City group that worked with muppet master Jim Henson. Giles, wary of the press, gave him two rules for the Phillie Phanatic: Have fun and, whatever you do, be G-rated—which meant no pulling down tube tops.

That happened once, however, after a playoff game in '80, only the woman yanked down her own tube top and said, "Hi! You're the Phillie Phanatic! Would you sign these?"

"A mascot groupie," shrugs Raymond, who has since relinquished Phanatic duties to start his own company—one that designs sports and business mascots and consults on existing ones. "I'll tell ya, there was more sex going on in that place than anywhere in the city, especially in the 700 Level. I'd get the call. Section 724. I'd get on my bike, fly up there and interrupt them. They'd usually be under blanket. Sometimes you'd see them pull their pants up. I'd get out the Super Soaker and cool 'em off."

Most of Raymond's memorable moments occurred on the field during interplay with opposing teams. Dave Parker of the Pirates would slap the Phanatic across the head, then stalk off into the dugout, where he would yell to Raymond: "How'd we do? Are they booing me? Do they hate me?"

But they all didn't embrace the idea. Tommy Lasorda grew agitated with the Phanatic's continual barbs, particularly of the extra-pudgy dummy made to resemble the Dodger manager. It got to the point where Lasorda ordered the attendant in the visitor's clubhouse not to give Raymond a jersey. In fact, Lasorda refused to pack an extra jersey on his trips to Philadelphia. So Raymond made precautions. Either Steve Sax would bring him one or he would spend his own hundred and fifty dollars to purchase a replica. Lasorda would chew out the clubby. The clubby, a Japanese kid, would say to the Phanatic, "I don't like you. You very bad." And all the while the Phanatic laughed harder until one day Lasorda went completely berserk. "You cocksucker, Dave! I'm going to fucking kill you!" he skirled. He lunged for the crude effigy, grabbed the Phanatic and kept thrashing. He then grabbed hold of the monster head and tried to pry it off. Raymond had never been out of costume in front of the fans. "One more minute and I'm sitting there like a smacked ass," smiles Raymond.

Lasorda relinquished the dummy. But soon a Dodger player had it and hurled the dummy on top of the dugout for Raymond. So a fuming Phanatic retreats to the Phillies dugout so he can be in full view of Lasorda, finds an empty pizza box and has the Tommy dummy dive over and over into it. "After that he goes on talk shows and says how I'm teaching kids violence," Raymond says. "He beats me up and I'm promoting violence? But I heard he apparently has forgiven me."

It was so cold that day you couldn't get warm under an afghan, and he remembers how the frozen turf felt, like a slab of moonrock, more unforgiving than a scorned woman. It was so cold that he sealed chemical heat packs to his body, and then on the first play from scrimmage he got railed hard in the chest by Randy White on a play action pass and one of the heat packs ruptured. Chemicals blistered the skin on his belly. He kept patting that irritated spot in the huddle, and even on the next play after he handed the ball to Wilbert Montgomery and watched Wilbert run and run. Ron Jaworski knew Wilbert would score on that play because Dallas had lined up in a nickel defense and Dick Vermeil had told them that previous Wednesday that Wilbert could run for a mile against the Cowboys' nickel defense.

"Yes," agrees Bill Bergey, "cold as the dickens that day was." And, yes, agrees Bergey the Eagles had gameplanned the Cowboys forever. Their goal that season of '80 was not to play the Raiders in the Super Bowl. Vermeil established their goal on the night before training camp opened in July. "Men," he deadpanned, "we have to find a way to beat the Cowboys."

Both men swear separately that they knew—knew like they know the day is 24 hours long knew—the Eagles would win that day. Every once in a while in sport, a feeling is so strong that premonition seems fused with reality. Hugh Douglas says it was like that in the Eagles' playoff victory over Tampa on New Year's Eve 2000. Though Douglas wouldn't agree, you get the feeling it was like that in reverse the following week against the Giants.

"We didn't upset the Cowboys," recalls Jaworski. "We set them up. We were lying in the grass for America's Team. We ambushed them."

"Coming down the tunnel, we were so focused," adds Bergey. "There was no doubt we were going to the Super Bowl. We pulverized Danny White. We annihilated them in every phase of the game. It was 20-7 and they were so lucky to get off that easy."

Then on the ride from the stadium to a dinner party, after all the whooping in the locker room and owner Leonard Tose told them to drink the Dom Perignon, don't spray it, because it's the real thing, Bergey remembers the girl driving in front of him. Every time the cars pulled even she took off another piece of clothing. When she stripped to her bra, Bergey figured to hell with dinner, follow the car.

It Always Goes Back to '80, and it's fascinating to hear Jaworski describe the milieu: Sage trainer Otho Davis cooking chili. Players eating foot-long hoagies sent over from Vince's Deli every Wednesday on the house. Players huddled in mood rooms. Players fighting for the new Jacuzzi. Meanwhile, the weight room was a converted storage area. Vermeil called the DiMatteo brothers from South Jersey to do the job at cost. It had the shiny paneling of the '70s. The budget was so tight most of the equipment was donated. The Phillies' locker room was next door. They'd share shower and bathroom facilities. They'd always chat with those guys. "I think Pete Rose spent more time in the Eagles' locker room than the Phillies'," Jaworski grins. "I think he was looking for a tip which way to go on the game."

Then there's Bergey, whose nostalgia turns to nausea because the remembrance invariably becomes the Vet, and its knee-shredding turf. And wasn't it only two months ago, before the knee replacement surgery, that it seemed forever to climb the stairs. One step, left leg, right leg, rest. Then repeat. He can still see the wince on Jake's face. Jake's eyes said, "Whoa, Dad, you look old."

An orthopedic doctor told him it was the second worst knee he had seen. The worst one stemmed from a motorcycle injury. But the doctor said that turf made it close. That the insides his knee had turned into mashed potatoes. "For the first time I can remember I'm not in pain,"he says. "I don't have a limp. I still have a hobble—because my brain taught me to walk this way for so long. Vermeil hated the turf so bad he didn't let us practice on it. He didn't even like us to go there for the Saturday light warmup. It wasn't the injury factor. It was just so hard it took too much out of your legs. It was like laying a thin carpet on I-95. So let's just say I don't think I'll cry when they close the place. I could see it deteriorate year by year. I remember lifting weights in 1977 and I see this big ol' river rat run across the floor and into a hole. Then another. I remember thinking: Here I am in the NFL?"

The Biggest Toilet Bowl in America.

So herein lies football's legacy at Veterans Stadium? Turf by Thanatos? Critters and leaky pipes and paint chips? Peeping players and exploding tendons? Leather-lunged locos in the 700 Level who revel in a fallen man's agony? I mean, it doesn't have to be the sheer aesthetics of Flotsam Field, not with Buddy Ryan, the swaggering Svengali who ordered Randall Cunningham to fake-knee the Cowboys to run up the score for misdeeds done by Dallas scab players during the strike of '87, who held a press conference in the coach's office to announce the signing of Keith Jackson without informing management and who gave the tight end a game ball the following week for a two-catch game "just to shove it up The Guy in France's ass," who had his punter *throw* a simulated punt to force an interference penalty, who knowing he'd be penalized sent 14 guys to cover a punt to take seconds off the clock, who gave us the Bounty Bowl, the Pork Chop Bowl, the Fog Bowl, in fact, everything but a Super Bowl.

Not with Randall Cunningham, perhaps the adjective's greatest booster. So many words from which to choose, contradicting and contrasting words, like inspiring and infuriating. In the end, Randall was loping velvet on the outside, mystifying on the inside. Not with Seth Joyner and Reggie White and Wes Hopkins and Andre Waters, cinder block men, heavy snorters who embodied flesh on flesh football. Not with Donovan McNabb in the latter days, the current highlight who possesses all of Cunningham's physical ability, plus the football acumen to win in the playoffs. Not with Rich Kotite and his drippy chart on one side and Andy Reid and his Holy Writ of Offense directly opposite, and Ray Rhodes lost again in the middle, spouting bluster and curse words.

Merrill Reese, the man with the winged tonsils, remembers the night at Engine 46 for Rhodes's radio show after a tough loss against the Cowboys. It was Rhodes's birthday and during the third break every waitress in the place emerged around a perfect cake and began to sing. Rhodes leaned in toward Reese and groused, "I don't want no motherfuckin' cake."

"Just shut up and eat the motherfuckin' cake," Reese said.

I think, what will they remember? The lawsuit of two former Eagles cheerleaders who contend visiting football players spied on them while they changed in the adjacent locker room or the night the league cancelled a pre-season game because of the new turf?

Throughout the league, the word was that peephole was the only perk the Vet had to offer. The women could hear them giggling through the wafer-thin walls, like gradeschoolers, and some would be extra bold with lewd remarks and requests for dates. "They acted like idiots," one of the cheerleaders said. "They were grown men acting like boys. All the girls knew by the end so most of us covered up. But it's embarrassing."

Embarrassing, like when the new turf mimicked the old turf, spitting up at the seams of the bases for baseball. It began when Baltimore Ravens coach Brian Billick stumbled during his ritual of inspecting the field in the pregame. Soon he was mimicking a DUI test, walking one foot in front of the other around the second base cutout, all the while dodging the paint compressor. Soon stadium workers were frantically trying to fix the dents and divots but the soggy earth underneath wouldn't take to the carpet and heads nodded and faces frowned. The teams waited for a call from the league office in New York to okay postponement and eventual cancellation. All the while, the cameras from HBO kept rolling. The show was called Hard Knocks, a behind the scenes look at the Super Bowl champions in training camp, and boy did they have good fodder. For those familiar with the Vet, however, it was familiar fodder. The only fresh news was that a game was finally called because of the harrowing field conditions. A source tells me that three times in the past five seasons officials from an opposing team threatened not to play regular season games, the most serious coming in December 1998 from Arizona Cardinals owner Bill Bidwill, who was finally pacified by a last-minute touch-up to the infected areas.

In other words . . . been there, done that. Sometimes there's a wedge so big when the pitcher's mound is removed you can fit three fingers in the crevice. Seams bulge and pop like buttons on the suit of a man who swears he hasn't gained a pound in ten years. Whether it's former Bears wide receiver Wendell Davis shredding both knees on the same play or visiting players toeing each hashmark in the pre-game as one would a minefield, the story of the Vet turf, old or NeXturf, shaggy or coarse, has become an infinite sequel. It sells, especially to the rest of the nation. It's formula now, like toilet humor, like the story of the Philadelphia Fans. For example, crack reporting by the *Baltimore Sun* after the cancellation of the Ravens game uncovered the time Those Rocky Ruffians Pelted St. Nick With Snowballs.

The better story, in fact, was the neglect that has left this place in decay, that led to the near tragedy in the stands during the Army-Navy game, that led to the temporary field stands for football games left unbolted during that same Ravens game in August. Stadium operators are given skeleton crews to work with, and it's not uncommon to see a city worker asleep or drunk on the clock.

"The place wasn't that bad," Reese says. "It held the noise. It held the sound. Then it became smelly and broken down and depressing to be in the halls. I don't think that was necessary."

"I love the Vet," former Eagle Hugh Douglas once told me, swearing sincerity. "I'm serious—the roaches and the rats. That place is real, man. That's ghetto. And ghetto is good in football."

Ghetto is the coating of gunk on the turf, the cat droppings and seagull droppings, the shoal of worms that slither from the dirtbottom through the concrete porous for drainage, summoned by the peanut shells and dried tobacco juice. "Sometimes the field looks like it's moving," says one stadium worker. Ghetto is the stench of the place's belly and ghetto is dust so heavy it tickles your throat when you breathe and ghetto is the stray cats. God only knows how many inhabit the place. The Eagles' Troy Vincent describes the eerie sight of hundreds crawling over the seats during one of the team's Saturday walkthrough practice in an otherwise empty stadium. "Look," he told another player in his best Twilight Zone tone, "they're watching us." One starved feline fell from a drop ceiling into the office of Eagles offensive line coach Juan Castillo and spent a week locked in there while he was at training camp. The office left in shambles, it was still better than the rat that fell through the ceiling of another Eagles employee, the rodent clinging to the sides of panel directly above the worker as he talked on the phone.

"If a sports stadium is the lengthened shadow of lowbrow, regional culture, the Vet has been the Louvre of Loss, an upholstered sewer of Sorrow," harrumphs Bill Conlin, award-winning *Daily News* columnist. "Every winning season—22 out of a possible 58 by the Phillies and Eagles—sparkled like the Hope Diamond in a pig's ass."

I can't tell Bill Conlin that he is wrong. Three Rivers housed a Steeler dynasty and Riverfront the Big Red Machine. The Vet's truly memorable moments are as sparse as a happy ending season. But I can't help but look around me and reflect. Joey is a father, a business owner and has whispers of gray in his black hair. Boo made it through Temple Law, and now has three kids and lives in a big house in Media. Bobby, God bless him, must be strong now that he lost his childhood sweetheart. The kids depend on him. Andy lives in Bucks County, John in Sonoma County, a Silicon Valley software exec. Vinny is vice president for an airline, stationed in Appleton, Wis., where his secretary who embodies Middle America thinks he was a hoodlum growing up when I tell her how he punched people out at the Vet. My grandmother who used to love to watch Mike Schmidt "shake his gi-gi" is gone and the foul ball that my mother caught off the bat of the Cubs' Steve Ontiveros has turned yellow.

I still visit the Vet often, though now I sit in the press box, already on my second career. I look down and time is falling through my fingers like Wildwood sand. Soon we will park on the place, and no one will care to remember what once stood there.

THIRTY

RICHIE WE HARDLY KNEW YE

You could debate whether Richie Allen was a rebel ahead of his time or a self-destructive malcontent. Maybe a little of both.

Regardless, it's tough to argue that had "Crash" come into our lives 25 years later, we all probably would have appreciated his on-field brilliance enough to cope with his off-field peccadilloes. Instead, Phillies management issued ultimatums. Sports writers lectured in print. And as for the fans, we heckled him. Well, at least our fathers did.

He was like another Allen (Iverson) before The Answer existed—a breath-taking talent who had no use for practice, ignored his bosses and partied late and hard, even for a guy in the business. Replace Iverson's affection for Bentleys with Allen's love of the trotters, and you've pretty much got the same guy.

But while Iverson survived, even thrived in Philadelphia, Richie Allen could not. By his third season, the Phils' antebellum-era management was drawing lines in the sand. Ultimately, Allen responded by toeing messages into the dirt around first base.

"BOO," he wrote.

And so we did.

It's a shame, really. Allen's frank opinions, unexcused absences and overindulgent partying made him a whipping boy for local media, and thus the fans. But the monster home runs that exploded off his caveman-sized 42-ounce bat have never been duplicated in this town. Not by Mike Schmidt, not by Greg Luzinski, not by Jim Thome. Every fan from the era remembers the rocket shots that flew over the Coca-Cola sign on Connie Mack Stadium's left-field roof and deep into the North Philadelphia night. Kids in the neighborhood used to sit by the kitchen radio, glove in hand, listening to By Saam and Bill Campbell, just waiting for Allen to come to bat so they could run outside and maybe shag one.

Ah, what might have been. The promise of glory and pennants and a Hall of Fame career. It didn't work out that way. And it wasn't entirely Allen's fault.

The black kid from Wampum, Pa. joined the Phillies at a time when the organization was about as enlightened as your average plantation. They sent him to segregated Little Rock, Ark. in 1963, where the windshield of his car was painted with "Nigger, go home." He faced racist heckling and occasional death threats, but the Phils didn't even intercede when he was barred from joining his Arkansas Travelers teammates in restaurants.

So when he arrived in the majors late in 1963—the first high-profile African-American player in Phils history—he already had a chip on his shoulder. If Allen was guilty of anything, it was not having the patience of Jackie Robinson. He heard the slurs (including those coming from the bleachers at Lehigh and 21st), he seethed at the paternalistic attitudes of owner Bob Carpenter.

"The Carpenters thought of themselves as enlightened slave owners," says *Daily News* columnist Bill Conlin, who covered Allen's career. "The world was changing at the time, and Allen was part of the change. But Phillies ownership was still living in a previous century."

Still, Allen thrived. He won Rookie of the Year in 1964, hitting .318 with 29 homers. He wasn't just the team's first-ever black star; he was the first young star the Phils had developed in more than a decade. What everyone remembers is that the team collapsed down the stretch that season. In truth, without Allen, they would have been out of the race by July 4.

The real fireworks came a year later. During batting practice on July 3, 1965, teammate Frank Thomas—an inveterate racist—dug the needle a bit too deep into Allen's hide. Allen threw the first punch and then challenged the six-foot-three first baseman to take his best swing. Thomas did—driving his Louisville Slugger into Allen's right shoulder.

Thomas hit a game-winner homer that night. The next day he was placed on waivers without a public explanation. Allen was hurt (physically and emotionally), but management threatened him with a $2,000 fine if he discussed the fight with reporters. As the story came out in bits and pieces, fans came to blame Allen for Thomas's release and booed him every day for the rest of the season.

"The Phillies were the catalyst for the fate that befell Allen," says Conlin, "because they refused to come out and say that Thomas was released over a racial incident that he started. It's part of a rich tradition the franchise has of not being forthcoming with information that might clear up a messy issue."

Things were never the same after that. Certainly, there was enough blame to go around. Allen had a way of creating his own trouble and everyone else had a way of taking it too seriously. At least the adults.

The split of opinion on Mr. Allen was largely generational. Baseball writer Jayson Stark grew up in the Northeast idolizing the guy and says, "Whatever his flaws, he was our hero. We couldn't figure out why all the grown-ups heckled him."

That sentiment is reflected in songwriter Chuck Brodsky's ode to Allen called "Letters in the Dirt":

> Me and you, we never booed Richie Allen,
>
> Never understood why people did,
>
> He hit a homer every time he stepped up to the plate,
>
> That's what I remember as a kid.

But our parents remembered other incidents. In 1969, for example, he left the race track a bit late for a doubleheader at Shea Stadium and got stuck in pre-game traffic. When he heard on the radio that he was suspended, he turned his car around and disappeared for three weeks.

And remember the time in 1967 when he severed the ulna nerve in his right wrist? Allen insisted he shoved his hand through a taillight while pushing a friend's car uphill in a rainstorm. Then the story got out that he was slashed in a bar fight. To most people, the second story seemed far more plausible than the first.

In truth, Allen had a drinking problem. Or, as Manager Gene Mauch once cracked, "His problem is less with the high fastball than the fast highball." Had he come along later, Allen might have been placed in baseball's substance abuse program. In those days, however, he was merely a man's man or a bum, depending on how people chose to look at it.

Philadelphia was not an enlightened town back then. Allen's occasionally strange conduct only reinforced the stereotype that the fans and media had painted upon him in the first place. The city was not ready for a rebellious young athlete in the 1960s, let alone a rebellious young black athlete.

So Allen's hate mail piled up. Coins and bottles flew from the stands, so much that he took to wearing his batting helmet while playing the field. In a 1967 interview with Sandy Padwe of the *Inquirer*, Allen insisted that a cross had been burned on his lawn and that his children had been hassled at school. Police doubted the claim of the burning cross but, there was no arguing that many fans were more than eager to toss on spite by the shovelful.

"At the time, I thought of myself as a victim of racism," he wrote in his 1989 book, *Crash: The Life and Times of Dick Allen*. "But there were others who had to deal with racism, and handled it better than I did."

In those pre-free agency days, Allen begged to be traded. The team declined, so he started scrawling messages in the infield dirt, like so many mysterious crop circles: "Mom," "Why?" and "Oct. 2," the last one marking the end of the season.

He told anyone who would listen that he wanted to be traded to the Mets (putting him closer to some of his favorite racetracks), and put an exclamation point on the demand by hitting three homers at Shea Stadium the final day of the 1969 season. "The last one," recalls Conlin, "didn't just clear the park. It flew over the Phillies bus parked out beyond right field."

Ultimately, the team gave up and sent him to St. Louis. Even in leaving, he was part of a controversy. One of the players obtained for him, Curt Flood, refused to report to the Phils and initiated the court case that forever changed baseball.

Allen stayed with the Cardinals one season before moving to the Dodgers and then the White Sox. In 1972, he was the American League's Most Valuable Player, hitting 37 homers for Chicago. By contrast, the last-place Phils' first baseman that season, Tommy Hutton, hit four.

Along the way, he changed his first name from Richie to Rich and then to Dick. "Richie," he explained, "is a boy's name. Dick is a man."

And then, in 1975, he came back. The White Sox sold Allen to the Braves, but—independent as always—he retired rather than report to Atlanta. The Phils obtained his rights and broadcaster Richie Ashburn, an old friend, helped coax him back.

And so there he was—a little older, a little heavier—receiving a standing ovation on Opening Day at the Vet. He even wore the mod facial hair of the era. That no one had palpitations over it showed how attitudes had changed in those brief few years.

"Dick" still became "Richie" on occasion. Grousing about the Vet turf, he said, "If a horse can't eat it, I don't want to play on it." But, given a second chance with Mr. Allen, we didn't seem to mind his intermittent crabbiness. Sure, he wasn't close to being the jaw-dropping slugger we watched during the first go-around, but he was a contributor to an emerging Phils squad and—believe it or not—served as a mentor to the young stars who won the team's first division championship in 1976.

And then he was gone again, retiring in 1977 after playing out the string with Oakland. In recent years, Allen came back to the Phils' organization, making speeches to school kids and serving as a minor league instructor.

The Wampum Walloper.

Even today, when you catch a rare glimpse of him on-field, in uniform, the script "Phillies" written across his chest, you can't help but wonder: In a different time, would it have worked out? Had he entered our life a decade or two later, would we have more tolerance for his rebel stands? Would he have received help for his drinking problems?

Richie Allen still wouldn't be a role model in this new millennium, but he might have been a folk hero.

THIRTY-ONE

VOICES WE'VE LOVED

In looking back, it's not odd how they traveled with me from porch to porch, block to block, their voices wandering like the summer wind, soft and soothing. I can still hear them—together—on one of those Sundays in August, and I am immediately overcome with peace. Just the memory of them—together—led me there in a flash, and it's amazing the power of context. They suggest another time, a happy time certainly in my life, when baseball really counted and any form of it—halfball, fastball, ledge—kept us in fun for hours. There was no school and I couldn't wait to open a pack of baseball cards—God, I wish I could get that anticipation back, that rush of wow, just once. They suggest childhood, and how the game was bigger than life, even it merely sounded bigger than life to me. Just their voices did it, and really, they could be chatting about anything, about Maggie Arthur's cupcakes or John McBride turning a fabulous eighty one, or how good the Dodger dogs were. Their banter, I think, was most comforting.

They'd follow me from porch to porch, block to block, circa late '70s and early '80s, crooning from the old radios of smiling neighborhood men who forever called the Phillies bums but wouldn't say a cross thing about Harry and Whitey, especially Whitey. Oh, yes, they were a summer staple on the step in every Philadelphia neighborhood, along with a can of Schmidt's and one of those flimsy beach chairs with the green-and-white criss-cross middle that always sagged.

Harry Kalas and Richie Ashburn were more than the duet of Philly baseball. They were our friends. It may sound sappy to some, but they were a constant in our little sliver of a city. For whatever reason, they just worked.

Whitey was the adopted husk from Nebraska whom the oldheads knew as a centerfielder for the Whiz Kids, small but super fast, a darling leadoff man born from a poof of dust. For the rest of us, he was the kindly oldhead who offered wisdom from beneath a cool hat and a cooler demeanor. Meanwhile, Harry was the broadcast pro with the velvet voice and affable personality. But unlike many blessed with the pipes, Kalas offered substance. What made them work, I swear, is because you knew they were pals. They were a buddy movie with baseball the backdrop, inviting us along for the journey.

Invariably something distressful would happen in the game, and Whitey would say, "Hard to believe, Harry," and Harry would commiserate. They would talk food and birthdays and babes, commenting on every happening in a ballpark.

During his Hall of Fame speech, Kalas told a story of his departed partner and friend of how on nights the games dragged, Ashburn would wonder aloud on the air if the "people from Celebre's Pizza are listening." "Sure enough," Kalas said, "Fifteen minutes later, we'd have pizzas being delivered up to the booth."

The team later admonished Ashburn for offering free plugs for pizza because Celebre's wasn't a sponsor. It was all right to send out birthday and anniversary wishes, but payola was strictly prohibited. A few days later, another game droned into the night, and Ashburn said, "I'd like to send out very special birthday wishes tonight—to the Celebre's twins—Plain and Pepperoni."

After breaking into the majors with the Astros in 1965, Kalas came to the Philadelphia for the '71 campaign—the first season of Veterans Stadium. Kalas was supposed to be the fourth member of the Phillies' broadcast team joining Hall of Famer Byrum Saam, Bill Campbell and Ashburn. But the club decided to replace Campbell with Kalas, much to the dismay of the fans. The ill will disappeared quickly with the help of Ashburn's support and acceptance. Ashburn and Kalas became fast friends, and soon the two were inseparable. They dined together and played tennis together and golfed together. Until Ashburn died suddenly of a heart attack in a New York hotel room on Sept. 9, 1997, the two paired for 26 seasons, the longest stint of any broadcast team in baseball history.

To this day, Kalas will still grow misty when asked about Ashburn. He smiles a wistful smile, that kind of cracked smile that lifts one's cheek and quickly turns into pursed lips. "I think of Whitey every day I'm doing a game," Kalas says. "Something will happen in the booth or on the field that will remind me of him. I can still see him. He was always smiling or chuckling about something."

Ashburn's son, Richard, once told the *Daily News*, "I think they could've been brothers. They fought, they argued, but they had such a connection. They flowed together—they flowed beautifully. They were meant to be together. I tell you, I never met a better pair."

You don't need to get cosmic to understand what Kalas and Ashburn shared. Simply, they were friends who just happened broadcast baseball games together. "We just clicked right away," Kalas says. "So we had that kind of chemistry on the air. It was just so natural."

Perhaps because both were good men, with the ways of happy go lucky. It wasn't that deep with either of them. I'll never forget the first time I spoke with Harry. It was at Wrigley Field, and I thought him the ultimate gentleman. I had relocated to Chicago a few weeks earlier, and I was feeling quite homesick. I was thrilled because the Phillies were in town, and I would be covering the series. I saw Harry in the cafeteria before the game. I was 22, and in awe. Nervous, I approached him. I stammered and stumbled, rambled on until I bled his ears. He listened and smiled the whole time, and spoke about me during the broadcast, wishing me well on my career path and telling my family I was doing fine. My cousin Joey called me later. He had heard Harry.

From time to time, I saw Harry over the years. I wound up covering the Mets in New York, and then I moved home, and each time I ran into him in a press box he said hello and asked what I was doing. That meant a lot. It's funny, though, I used to get so nervous around him, even later in life. I thought about it. When it comes to the Phillies, Harry's all I've ever known. He's spanned my entire life.

As a child, I listened to him on my father's transistor radio that he got from his father, and used to put it under my pillow for West Coast games. I listened to him on the beach in Wildwood. When I lived in Chicago, I used to drive around at night and dial in the game. The Phillies station for so long—WCAU 1210—used to come in rather clear, and it comforted me because it was a taste of home.

Harry Kalas, from Naperville, Ill., has broadcast more than 5,000 Phillies games, as well as Notre Dame

Harry Kalas & Richie Ashburn

football and college hoops and NFL games and pieces for NFL Films. He has been honored some 17 times as the Philadelphia Sportscaster of the Year. He is officially legend. Still, today, we imitate him. So much to imitate with Harry Kalas. So many great calls. Obviously, the greatest of all came on Mike Schmidt's 500th home run on April 18, 1987—"The 3-0 pitch . . . Swing and a long drive. There it is! No. 500!"

They played the clip on the big-screen TV next to the stage at Cooperstown during Kalas' Hall of Fame ceremony, and Harry turned to glance at Schmidt—or as he called him—Michael Jack Schmidt—sitting behind him. "I looked back and he looked back at me," Kalas said. "He was just a special player, and it was a privilege to call his whole career. And I'm thrilled that we've been able to keep our friendship all these years."

Jayson Stark, the brilliant baseball writer for the *Inquirer* for many years, tells of the day Schmidt hit that home run and his teammates sat around the locker room afterward and actually chanted, "We want Harry." Someone whipped out a tape recorder, Stark wrote, "and they all sat and listened to the now-classic call of a classic moment. Once. Twice. Three times. Four times. Almost as if they wouldn't believe it had really happened until they'd heard Harry Kalas describe it."

So many great calls . . . .

My friends and I sit around over beers, and try to recite as many as we can. It's almost like a game. From the obscure —"Home run, Kim Ba-tiste! Put another one in the win column for the Fightin' Phils of '93!"—to the famous, occurring in the ninth inning of the Phils' pennant-winning Game 5 against Houston in 1980—"The pitch to Tri-llo . . . Line drive, fair ball, down the left field line . . . Aviles scores, here's Del Unser being waved around, he's gonna score! Manny Trillo at third, a triple, and the Phillies lead it, 7-5! What a comeback by this young bunch of Phils!"

Harry has that perfect lilt, that perfect elocution. The words just stand by themselves, hanging there in neon.

"This ballgame's over . . ."

"Watch that baby . . ."

"Struck heeeeeem out . . ."

Of course, "Outta here" has always been the best, his patented home run call. Too many home run calls are forced, SportsCenter scripted where they don't sound natural. Harry's has always been classic, and so the legend goes he stole it from Larry Bowa in the early '70s. Greg Luzinski was putting on a display of wondrous home runs in batting practice, when Bowa said after one impressive blast, "That ball is well outta here." Standing by the batting cage, Harry overheard Bowa and so it was done—for good.

"I had no idea it would stick," Kalas says. "I just like the way it rolled. It was one of those things you hear and you try."

Truthfully, it has rarely been much fun to be a Phillies fan. We are because we are, and we will always be. It's our calling. We've had our brief moments, the late '70s, going into the World Series of '80. There were near misses in '83 and again in '93. Mostly it's been desultory, a foray of mishaps and miscues. Harry's seen them all—he's broadcast almost 20 below .500 seasons to date—and the thing I always respected was that he never lost interest. Every pitch sounded like the first pitch. He always had hope thus we always had hope.

It's been that way in Philadelphia. For all of our passion, we've had to endure so much misery, indeed. But we've never had to go it alone. Our broadcasters have been brilliant: Saam and Campbell with the Phillies and the Flyers' Gene Hart and the Eagles' Merrill Reese, whose passion for football I truly admire. Reese treats each game like a mini Super Bowl and I can hear him always, falling hoarse with hooray, "The backs are split . . . Touchdown Iggles!" Someday, too, it seems the Sixers' Tom McGinnis will reach those lofty heights. Sport in this town hasn't been all that fun to watch over the years, but it's been a pleasure to listen to.

Gene Hart

We played the game he taught us after school in the street on feet, with plastic pucks and pads and orange balls and sticks with holes in the blade, dubbed "air flow," and we moved the net, or the two cinderblocks that constituted a net, when cars appeared, usually honking. While we played, we imitated him, a wailing, horrific impersonation that would have split glass quicker than a Reggie Leach slapshot. "He shoots, he scoooooooooooores!" we'd say, and the "ores" would travel to a squeak, just like his, though his was song.

We'd say all of his sayings. We'd all score for a case of Tastykake and we'd fasten our seat-belts late in a close game, and when there was a "rugby scrum" in front of the net, we'd scream in unison, "Oooh, they poke at it." We'd all drag our vowels like they were our schoolbags loaded with books. When the dinner bell finally tolled up and down the street, in the form of admonishing moms, we'd convene in front of the net, tap our sticks on each other's shins and repeat his valediction, "Good night, good hockey."

We imitated Gene Hart as much as Bobby Clarke, somehow morphing them into one, which they were in a sense. If Clarke provided the face of Philadelphia hockey, Hart provided the lungs. He breathed life into a foreign sport. He made hockey three-dimensional. He made it bigger than life. He made the Flyers part of the family because he brought the Flyers into our homes, the great conduit with the blessed pipes.

Every successful entity needs a messenger, particularly sport, which needs to do more than simply entertain the masses. Sport needs to captivate and stimulate and force the children of masses to emulate. It needs a buzz, and someone to facilitate that buzz, and the Flyers were lucky to have Gene Hart.

Truthfully, when Gene Hart died at the age of 68 in the summer of '99, some of my love for listening to Flyers games did, too. Hart broadcast Flyers games from their inception in 1967 over the next 28 years, calling more than 2,000 games and six Stanley Cup Finals. He was the undisputable voice of hockey in Philadelphia, working with five broadcast partners during his Flyers career: Stu Nahan, Larry Zeidel, Don Earle, Bobby Taylor and Gary Dornhoefer.

Steve Coates, current voice of the Flyers, described Hart's role with the Flyers the best. "He was the educator," Coates said. "The messenger. Someone has to educate the people and he became the liaison between the club and the fans."

Now I knew Gene Hart merely a little bit, if that, and if I'd never met Gene Hart at all, I still would have thought him jolly Gene, the sweet hockey Santa who always left the present of memory. For Gene Hart was an old-time storyteller, and because of the viewing nature of hockey it truly didn't matter if I was in my father's car or watching on Prism, I enjoyed just the same. I visualized the grace of Pelle Lindbergh and the brute of Tim Kerr, because Gene Hart painted the vision. He used such vibrant words and described the action in such comprehensive detail that as a child I swore I saw game through the blackness of my bedcovers and the gray squeaking of my transistor radio. I felt like I was either at center ice or the center of a campfire, hanging on Hart's every syllable.

It's fascinating how we view a broadcaster on television or radio, particularly those in the local market we see with great frequency. Like or dislike them, we conjure an image of them. Mostly, it's incorrect, usually by leaps and bounds, but I still swear Gene Hart was one of the few whose true being radiated through along with those radio waves. I still see him as the hockey Mr. French, the great teacher who knew a little of everything and lot about life; I see that he would be kind on a greet and meet and that he'd hold the door open for the women.

Gene Hart was truly a renaissance man, an oddity in athletics. He was a lover of the arts, particularly in opera and classical music, a lover of fine food and traveling and language. He loved the word, and that love came through during every broadcast. He was a lover of life who, along with his wife, Sarah, tried to instill that in his three children, Lauren, Sharon, and Brian. And every time Lauren sings at the First Union Center and smiles her radiant smile, I image

Gene nodding with satisfaction.

Gene Hart was one of the lucky ones. He got called at a young age, that Saturday night when he played with the radio dial and stumbled onto a broadcast of "Hockey Night in Canada." From then on—and he wrote it so, right there in an old autograph book—he wanted to someday be a hockey announcer. While it seems normal, consider for a moment how odd for a boy in those days of the NHL's original six from South Jersey to bond with hockey.

That was his biggest battle early on, as the Canadian writers and broadcasters didn't think an American could do the game justice. Eventually, Hart earned their respect, and the respect of the entire sport. In 1997, he was inducted into hockey's Hall of Fame—where there are fewer than two dozen announcers—and sported that blazer with the patch on it with great pride.

The beloved voice of the Flyers, Gene Hart.

That pride was about the sport. Certainly there was no question of his loyalty when it came to the Flyers, but his passion for the game overshadowed everything. He took his role seriously as hockey educator/ambassador.

At an afternoon luncheon the day before the Flyers defeated the Soviet Red Army team in 1976, Hart, who spoke excellent Russian, prepared a speech for Flyers owner Ed Snider in Russian.

"Gene not only understood the language but was one of the few people who could pronounce every name correctly," Snider recalled. "He prepared this speech and went over it with me. When I got up to speak, the Russians were all sitting there smirking, and that bothered me. I never gave the speech. Only Gene and I knew we had written it in Russian."

Hart wrote a book in 1990 appropriately entitled *Score!* It's an amazing collection of his stories and memories, and here are a couple of his thoughts on dramatic happenings in Flyer history.

Regarding Kate Smith's initial appearance at the Spectrum: "It was the culmination of the most bizarre, the most unexplainable, and the most wonderful and memorable partnership imaginable . . . A 66-year-old pop singer of thirty years before with a rough and crazy bunch of mostly Canadians called the Broad Street Bullies."

Regarding Pelle Lindbergh's death in 1985: "I can remember very clearly sitting there, in tears, hoping that a miracle might happen and that Pelle would pop up again, smiling."

Regarding his famous call after the Flyers won their first Stanley Cup in 1974: "I was no longer the professional who was saying those words. I was a fan who had tears in his eyes and goose bumps all over, as I realized what an extraordinary thing that team had done."

Like any other longtime Flyer fan, I can still hear that call and see the seconds ticking away in the Flyers' 1-0 win over Boston at the Spectrum. In fact, I owned the album as a child. It was deep orange emblazoned with a shimmering silver Stanley Cup on the cover. I played it often on my record player.

"The Flyers are going to win the Stanley Cup! The Flyers win the Stanley Cup! The Flyers win the Stanley Cup! The Flyers win the Stanley Cup! The Flyers have won the Stanley Cup!"

Said Snider of the call, "His voice kept getting stronger and louder, and to this day, I think it remains one of the greatest calls in sports I've ever heard."

I think of Gene Hart often during hockey season, especially as the broadcast concludes. I have such fond memories of orange pucks and peanut butter Tandykakes. Just once, I'd like to hear again:

Good night, good hockey.

THIRTY-TWO

GREAT MOMENTS 6:
SALUTING THE PRESIDENT

There is an old cliché in sports: The worst circumstances often bring out the best in someone.

On September 20, 2001, that aphorism came true in Philadelphia. At the worst time, and with the whole world watching, we did our best. Our fans, so often lambasted by outsiders, got it exactly right.

The setting was a pre-season contest between the Flyers and New York Rangers. Typically, there is nothing more insignificant than exhibition hockey, but this night was different. The game came just nine days after the terrorist attacks on the United States and, clearly, the nation was still in shock. For most of the 14,000 fans that night, it was their first time out since the attacks. It was not a return to normalcy so much as a chance to gather as a community, to commiserate, to share a bond as Americans.

Each fan was handed an American flag upon arriving at the First Union Center. Many carried patriotic banners. But the building was eerily hushed as people went to their seats.

The Flyers staged a touching pre-game ceremony. Lauren Hart sang "God Bless America," in front of the U.S. Marines color guard. Players from both teams skated in "NYPD" and "FDNY" jerseys during warm-ups, and then presented the jerseys to a contingent of local cops and firefighters.

Fans certainly appreciated the gestures. An occasional chant of "USA, USA" broke out. But, mostly, everyone was silent.

For two periods, the Rangers and Flyers skated in a robust game that featured four major fights. The score was tied, 2-2, although no one really seemed to care about that.

And then, after the Zamboni had circled the ice before the third period, President George W. Bush began a scheduled address to a nation still emotionally devastated and girding for war. Arena officials flashed the beginning of the President's speech on the Jumbotron screen. Folks in the crowd who had been out at the concession stands rushed back to hear the President lay out his plan for the war on terrorism.

With Bush a few minutes into his speech, players skated back onto the ice. And suddenly, the President's image was replaced by a message saying that the game would resume and his address would be shown on screens in the Broad Street Atrium.

And with that, Philadelphians let loose with a message of their own: "Boooooo!"

"Leave it on! Leave it on!" they chanted. Hockey, on this night, no longer mattered.

"It was an amazing moment," says Flyers chairman Ed Snider. "The fans were really letting us know what was important. And they were right."

Within seconds, the President's image reappeared. Players skated to their benches to watch, and the building filled with a stream of patriotic energy. Fans rose from their seats with repeated ovations as Bush vowed to rid the world of terrorism. Players took off their gloves and applauded. Some, in the time-honored hockey tradition, banged their sticks against the boards in a show of support. Fourteen thousand people watched together, cheered together, bonded together.

"It was one of my proudest moments as an American, and as a resident of this area," says Lou Nolan, the Flyers long-time public address announcer. "Watching the President on TV in my home would have been one thing. But sharing the power of the event with thousands and thousands of others—seeing that many people come together as patriots—was inspirational. It was one of those rare times when sports serves as a means to the greater good. I'll never forget it."

For nearly 40 minutes, fans and players united, sharing a dramatic and historic moment. When the President finished, people rose to their feet, cheering and chanting. The big screen showed a waving flag. Some started singing the National Anthem.

And then, for a few moments, no one knew what to do next. The two teams—who had combined for 23 penalties in the first two periods—looked at each other. How could they go back out and scrap now?

Flyers officials conferred with the coaches, Bill Barber for the Flyers and Ron Low for the Rangers. The coaches looked to the players. Said Flyers winger Mark Recchi, "That was a no-brainer there. We all knew what was the right thing to do."

And that was to meet at center ice and shake hands. Flyers and Rangers, Americans and Canadians, Russians and Swedes, all embraced.

Nolan told the crowd that the game was being suspended as a tie "in respect for the United States and in support of the President's speech."

And nobody in Philadelphia booed.

Quietly, everyone filed from the First Union Center. No one demanded his money back. No one heckled the visiting team.

"It was great to be a hockey player and sit on the bench and watch, with your opposition and with the fans, watching the President speak," Flyers winger Rick Tocchet said afterward. "The fans were totally silent when listening, then they would cheer together. It was an amazing thing."

That night, the event was shown on ESPN's SportsCenter and the other sports wrap-up shows. The next day it was replayed on the CBS Evening News. Anchorman Dan Rather called the Philadelphia crowd "extraordinary."

The whole nation saw our response. This time, we weren't shooting off flare guns or cheering an opponent's injury. This time, we were showing that, when things really matter, Philadelphians know how to respond.

Bill Lyon of the *Inquirer,* summed it up best: "Philadelphia sports fans, so often the object of sneering derision, had their finest hour."

THIRTY-THREE

DONOVAN MCNABB: THE GOOD SON

The sentiment of babes haunts me. Here I am, the Good Son before me, his smile aglow, beaming light to a subjugated sports city, and I can't get some kid's expression out of my mind. I told him I would be meeting who I thought was a hero of his, and he made this dismissive gesture. Worse, he made this face, an awful, contorted face. Clean forehead suddenly wrinkled by the world. Eyebrows snaked downward, finding a flared left nostril. Lips pursed. Flat eyes. "He's lame," the kid snorted. "He's always smiling."

I guess he saw my hurt because the kid retreated into tact, albeit teenager tact. "I mean, I like him OK on the field," he continued. "It's just, he's not that cool. Why does he always have to smile?"

I wanted to shake him. Scream that it's good to be the good son. That the alternative is a mindset created by the hollow and the short-sighted because stupidity and moral bankruptcy, as well as misery, loves company. That it's even cool. Because it takes balls to smile when everyone around you wears a thug's grimace while grabbing their balls. Because it takes bigger balls not to follow, or to follow a tired path of the gangster's paradise when, in fact, a gangster's paradise would be your portfolio without the threat of genocide or the joint. I mean, is there anything more ridiculous than an athlete with a $100 million contract who still wants to grow up to be a gangster?

I said nothing. It is a realization this kid, who is, otherwise, bright, and bred from stout fabric, must embrace himself, perhaps with help from the Good Son in the end. But now? What could I say to subvert pop culture? It's geeky to be good and the flipside is tantalizing, buoyed by hedonism and sneaker commercials, and presented as the pinnacle of cool by too many sources. It grapples with maturity for the driving force of every libidinous young male. I don't know why I should be hurt by the kid's response, seeing how I rooted for Tony Montana—the anti-hero in *Scarface*—back in the day. But has it gotten so backwards that an honest smile is such a turnoff these days? Or, as the kid described it, "a little too dorky"?

In truth, my biggest regret was that of a selfish nature. That I didn't see from him the pie eyes and goose pimples of youth, the genuine tingles that arise with the chance meeting of a sports luminary, especially the quarterback of the Eagles. The expiration date on innocence early in the third millennium might as well be that of a gallon of milk, unless of course, I might introduce him to Allen Iverson. Then, he said, he would gush. But the Good Son . . . .

So, yes, I oblige happily Donovan McNabb's appeal for me not to laugh when he orders his beverage before dinner. I almost don't want to say what it is because I can see the kid's eyes rolling like a tumbleweed through the ghost town of virtue.

A Shirley Temple.

There is a gentle moment of incomprehension from Pietro, the co-owner and chef of Mezza Luna, which serves the best of God's nectars—particularly a postmeal limoncello—under a crescent moon on Catharine Street. His face, however polite, begs, "Wouldn't you prefer to see my wine list?" And McNabb's face begs back, "I know my request might seem a tad anomalous but I can go for a little ginger ale and three parts grenadine over ice about now." Our host returns shortly with a pelican-shaped glass, the content the color of a prom dress, and hands it to the football player, who doesn't give a damn that Dick Butkus, I presume, wouldn't drink a Shirley Temple if it was mixed at the Fountain of Youth and tasted like Jack Daniels.

Indeed it takes boffo balls for a football player to order a Shirley Temple.

But everything about Donovan McNabb seems a tad anomalous, as he nears the peak of his profession, a billion dollar industry built on the two primal instincts of man: the physical domination of another man and the rooting for the physical domination of another man. Narcissism might as well have laces and NFL commissioner Paul Tagliabue's signature on it; everything about football and what it takes to become a great football player is antisocial in the real world. And when success as rare McNabb's comes along, the real world becomes morphed into an orgy of freedom and fanfare and pleasure and pastel colors and pleas from the parishioners. Boundaries dissolve, barriers melt, with such success, which is the common thread in all of our dreams—a twitch of the nose and anything earthly is in reach, without the burden of refinancing or rational thinking. It's all so intoxicating. So much so that you never see the crack form under your feet, the crack that all too often swells to a sinkhole and leads to an unkind abyss.

Donovan McNabb, despite the debilitating condition of youth, checks the ground more than he does his hair. He checks himself—constantly, sometimes to a fault, according to a hypocritical media, which begs for celebrity warts to glorify and ultimately to use as fodder in the palace coup. Off the field, he couldn't contradict more than on it, where he plays with a graceful flare and an edge of unpredictability, a fact that he has yet to fully harness his powers. This might make him less alluring to the fickle MTV market when compared with, say, Iverson.

Look at Ron Artest, McNabb says, referring to the young NBA player of middling talent: "he has his own barber, his own tailor, his own chef, his financial guy, his marketing guy. He has a lot of people on his team he has to pay. You know who's on my team? My mother, my father, my brother, my dog, and now my fiancée. I do have a barber. I've known him eight years. I like him a lot and he comes to the games, but he's not on my payroll.

"I know a lot of guys, they go buy big houses. They go buy cars. They change their wardrobe. Next thing you know, they have $100,000 left. Then they have to sell everything off for dirt-cheap."

Money is always an issue. "I treat it like a whore," an athlete once told me, "because then I won't miss it when it goes away." This is typical of the relationship between an athlete and his money, especially those from impoverished upbringings. It's one of resentment and bitterness, as though there has been this war waged since childhood and the only way to win is to disrespect it now. How else can you explain the local player who once left behind two KFC bags in the trainer's room, one filled with chicken bones, the other with $19,000? Conversely, McNabb—who spent a summer in high school working in Chicago's Mercantile Exchange and Stock Exchange—has the reputation of being rather frugal, even cheap, which somehow doesn't seem as sinful as drunken spending. "Anytime you look at something," he grins, "and say, 'I can buy that so I'll just buy it,' you don't really need it. It's a waste. A lot of people waste a lot of money. I'm very protective of my money."

I swear, he is your father's quarterback, consumed by the electric bill and leaving the bathroom light on, mindful of every acorn. I met him after his rookie season at the TGI Friday's just off South Street and nodded toward his car, a burgundy Chrysler, a dealer's car, and he sprang to defend it, "What did you expect? A Benz? I like this car. It's a nice car." I shrugged. I had also thought it to be a nice car.

That day we hung at a back table, along with former Eagles tight end Luther Broughton and a female friend, and had a bar food feast—buffalo wings, chicken fingers, potato skins, mozzarella sticks. He wildly dipped everything in Ranch dressing, and anointed it "the bomb, especially when you run out of mayonnaise." It was so college, so twenty-something, and here on this day in a fine restaurant, he leans over after we order a cold appetizer of fresh prosciutto and buffalo cheese drizzled with olive oil and asks, "They have mozzarella sticks?" I swear he hasn't changed a lick from the first time I met him four years ago, right there in his parents' family room of their split-level in the southern burbs of Chicago, the smell of Wilma McNabb's hotcakes wafting in the summer morning.

I found him to be unsullied then and attributed it to upbringing and playing his college ball at Syracuse, way up north, imprisoned by the murky Finger Lakes and a dreary, endless winter, but close enough to swill Canadian perspective. Truthfully, I figured fame would deflower him, if only because I've seen it countless times—apple-cheeked, aw-shucks sort takes one bite of the big-time and forever loses his soul under the thick, fatted layers of ego. But here he is, two Pro Bowls and a Chunky Soup campaign later, a season of Super Bowl aspirations looming, and he remains as together as mashed potatoes, as grounded as the curb.

Maybe it's all about wearing your older brother Sean's hand-me-downs, being raised with just enough, no more, under the watchful eye of two sturdy parents, in a simple home on a simple street, located in a leafy suburban sprawl like Dolton, forty-five minutes south of Chicago's Loop.

Maybe it's the fact that he grew up so ordinary, starkly different than, say, his best friend in football, former Eagle linebacker Barry Gardner, who hails from neighboring Harvey, Ill., but once held the hand of his dying friend riddled by stray gangland bullets, or, say, his coach, Andy Reid, who grew up a gringo in downtown Los Angeles.

Maybe it's the fact that Samuel and Wilma McNabb have been married twenty-five years now, and Sean paved a nice way for him and that Donovan can say now, "Ever get to the point where you're ready to hang up on (your parents)? It's like that after every game. My dad's saying, 'What were you thinking on this one?' I'm like, 'Dad, can we talk about something else, please?' My dad was just talking about that. It's great. My household was so much fun. We're pretty much comedians, cracking jokes all the time. My mom'll be there talking about something in the game, like, 'Your pants were too tight,' and that propels everything."

Maybe it's all of those factors and going to an all-boys Catholic, sports-crazed school of about 800 kids like Mount Carmel and living on a street like Diekman Court, the archetype of middle class, proof that ordinary ol' America works.

It is a most uncomfortable position, because who wants to be the standard for another? In the end, he has his own problems because he's not perfect and he doesn't want to be perfect, at least not in that way. He knows it's a matter of taste between him and the basketball player, and, yes, there are racial undercurrents and social implications, though they are the same race and nearly the same age. And, yes, he will be painted as the Good Son, if only because practice won't ever become an issue with him, and because he just has a different way about him. He likes to quote lines from Julius Erving's *The Fish That Saved Pittsburgh* with his brother and scare his parents with a fictitious tattoo of a "big ol' cross on my back, outlined with dreads" or bust his brother's balls by quoting his mother saying—"What's wrong with you? You don't know your damn name?"—after he got his name tattooed on his leg. He worries that someday he'll do something bad and somebody will say something like, "Yeah, he walked funny. And he hit that girl with the Pac Man lunchbox in the sixth grade." He knows his way is tame, and more palatable to the masses, but it's just who he is and he can't help it if the basketball player likes after-hour clubs and Corona and creates a stir. Who cares? He is a fan of the basketball player, by the way. So why does it always have to be that deep? Can't he just do his thing? And the basketball player do his?

But Donovan McNabb knows that he is linked with Allen Iverson in this weird way, because this city is so damn small for its size, so parochial, because they are just two now and they are as different as the seasons.

"People are always saying Allen Iverson is not a good person," McNabb shrugs. "That you can't sit down and talk to him. That he always has eight or nine guys around him. That he has all these tattoos. Stuff like that. If you get a chance to sit down with the guy and get to know him, you'll realize he's not a bad person. I mean, if you want to compare me to Allen Iverson, go ahead. I have no problem with being compared with a guy who wants to win."

There, he said it.

The comparison, however, continues, because he is so the anti-Allen. Never mind that he is unlike any sports luminary this town has seen; he isn't as bizarre as Randall or as tragic as Lindros or as biting as Barkley or as aloof as any of the Phillies. "Look," McNabb says, "everyone has their own flavor. Everybody has their own look. Me? I have to look professional. After a game, I have to wear a suit. Or if I'm not wearing a suit, it has to be nice. It's for the occasion. Now if I'm going to practice, I wear a sweatsuit. Wearing a headband? I wouldn't get into that too much. I may wear it playing basketball. That's about it. Doo rags, that's just not me—unless, maybe, I had a bad hair day."

Please, he begs, let's not invoke pop culture, since it's so freaking subjective, and when we categorize we always put people in the wrong category. For example, he says, "I think people have a different definition of hip hop. Hip hop pretty much is music. It's an expression through music. When you listen to hip hop it maybe someone's life story or what someone may have been faced with. Hip hop isn't what you're wearing. Hip hop isn't the way you walk. Or the way you act. People say hip hop in the sense of Allen because maybe he wears some baggy clothes or the doo rags or the head bands. But Allen is pretty much being himself. You walk around Philly and see a lot of people now wearing what Allen is wearing. Does that mean they are hip hop? No, they are looking for new trends."

McNabb is a Michael Jordan disciple, a proud one. It makes sense, of course, seeing how he was so enamored with Jordan growing in the shadow of the Magnificent Mile, and he banged pots and pans together when the Bulls won all of their titles. He met Jordan recently, and he's not ashamed that he gushed. In fact, he wore Jordan's shoes last season and Jordan told him that his feet looked real good. So he does what he figures Jordan would do off the field. "The way he carries himself," McNabb gushes. "The way he treats others. What he does for the community. How he conducts himself. Like I might be a little hip hop—say, 'What's crackin'?' Something like that. But that's normal. I'm not going to be in an interview talking like this . . . ."

He begins to wiggle his hands and tilt his head and gesture and gyrate, and then offers a lilted patois: "You know what I'm sayin'…you know, I got to be me . . . you know what I'm sayin' . . . I'm feelin' dat . . . see, what I'm talkin' 'bout . . . it's like dis . . . OK . . . you know . . . you know what I'm sayin'."

There is belly laughter.

"Oh, yeah," he says, turning serious, "I definitely care about image. Image reflects on who you are. How you portray yourself. How you dress. How you act. How you talk. That's a reflection on who you are." He refers to Jordan's representing McDonald's, and how he himself has a become a staple with Campbell's Soup with their Chunky Soup campaign, along now with Wilma, who didn't like it a little bit that they hired some actress to play his mom in the first set of commercials (she will appear in the new ads this season and was the inspiration to use all of the real moms). He perks up again. "I'm definitely into it," he beams. "It's a part of image. Campbell's Soup wouldn't go get a guy that doesn't comb his hair, that walks a little bit differently. They want a guy with a good reputation, who knows how to handle himself. They went with good guys—Brian Urlacher, Michael Strahan, Jerome Bettis."

A plate of spinach gnocchi is in front of him. He forks one, swirls it around his dish, lathering it with the light cream sauce and plays for a nonexistent camera and the table, which includes Eagles publicist Rich Burg and security director Anthony Buchanico.

"Mmmmm . . . good," he announces. "Very light. Oh, yeah, smooth. Mmmmm . . . good." There is belly laughter.

"You won't see me cussing folks out or giving the finger or kicking cars," he promises. "See? I'd rather be the good son. My mother always told me to be the good son."

Donovan McNabb is getting married, and he doesn't understand why it's news. He huffs and mutters something about Palestine and holds up his palms, as if to say, "Now that's news." He can't fathom why the *Daily News* plastered his fiancee, Raquel Nurse, on the cover of the paper that Saturday in May, or that anyone really cares about his personal life. In his mind, it's not complicated or cosmic. It's just life. Now this makes him fidget. He's not angry as much as he's troubled. This is the one aspect of this world that he has yet to comprehend, perhaps because he is so grounded, so well adjusted, so you-and-me.

I tell him what Al Pacino said in a recent interview with *Esquire:* "Until you are famous, you can never understand the haven of anonymity."

Someday Donovan McNabb will adjust. Now he's fighting it. For as engaging as he can be a lot of the time, he will also clam up, suddenly sealing tight his thoughts, and his life in Cherry Hill and in Arizona, where he keeps an offseason home. It's as though he is booby-trapped and the wrong question will unleash some protective spinning blade out of Indiana Jones and lop off my head.

We talk of his engagement to Roxie, whom he has dated for seven years, the usual love story of the college sweetheart, and I ask what I perceive an innocent question: How did you ask her to marry you? Did you get down on one knee? Dress up as a knight? Put your jersey over a puddle. How?

"Let's just say it happened," he says coldly, and I feel like some sleazy reporter on the Hollywood beat. (For the record, he proposed on a cruise.)

Are you romantic?

"No."

Was she surprised?

"Yes."

Okie-dokie.

"I don't get too deep into it. Let's just say it was done."

Thank God for the entrée. The whitefish eases a budding tension.

"I know that being a figure in the city of Philadelphia, people wanted to know. Obviously, when people get engaged it's a wonderful thing for the two parties. When you do something like that, you want to make it special and not have everybody in America know what's going on. My thing is how it all went down. It's not for my sake. I'm looking out for her. No one knows who she is. Now that all came down, she can't go get a loaf of bread.

"When people heard it, the first thing that came to mind is 'Not Donovan. Who is she?' I think it hurt people. They have to realize I have a personal life, that I'm normal. On this side, it's like when they heard I got engaged the first thing they were looking for [was] is she a star? Is she a model? Is she an actress? They're looking for an athlete to be with somebody that you see on TV and when they found out she wasn't they weren't interested anymore. Everyone gets so caught up in it. If she's not a star, it's like we'll talk about it, but it's not good news."

I beg to differ, I told him. The fact that Roxie was a college sweetheart, who played basketball at Syracuse, who now advises student-athletes at Villanova University, makes the whole story that much more endearing. That people care, but they really don't. That because he is in their family room every Sunday makes him a pseudo member of the family and their curiosity, while intrusive, was born of good intention.

So, I ask, was there a girl before Roxie who broke your heart? And he says, "No, I broke their hearts. I gave them the business. I said, 'I'm going to have to let you go. Turn in your playbook.'" And we laugh, and he would prefer I don't speak with Roxie, just the same. Can he talk about his dog? Of course, what kind is he?

"A killer," he says of Sinbad, and he perks up again.

It is perpetually on his face, as indelible as a beauty mark. Wide and round and you just know it creases, too, on the inside. It fills a room and tells his story. In the end, there's nothing not to smile about for Donovan McNabb.

Why does it bother some people? I can almost understand the kid's sentiment, as much as it's ass-backwards. But I've heard it several times on my radio show: *What's with that smile? It's annoying.*

It's McNabb being a tad anomalous. The smile is his thing the way the tongue was Jordan's, and the opponent knows. I first saw it when I first saw him play in person, back upstate, on one of those iced-over Saturday nights in November along the Finger Lakes. He had just scrambled thirty-nine yards on fourth down late in a game against Virginia Tech, an apparition in the night, and stumbled over to the sidelines for a timeout and threw up.

Right there.

Then he smiled.

Then he actually made a miracle, rolling out to his right on the final play of the game, buying time like cheap stock, and heaved a skin-tight spiral across his body to a plodding Polish tight end with ham hands by the name of Steve Brominski to win the game and send the 'Cuse to a big bowl.

Then he smiled again, and it was just like the first drive of the Tampa game. Of course, the smile dissipated so quickly, the ending not the ending he expected. Hard to figure last season. It started out so wonderfully, with the Eagles scoring all sorts of points. Then the Cardinals game came, and the ankle cracked, hell, he wasn't coming out of the game, no way, no how. He threw four touchdowns, and would have been named the NFL's player of the week if the league wasn't so hypocritical and didn't want to draw attention to an injured player playing, a warrior winging it.

McNabb worked hard to get back for the Falcons playoff game. The Eagles didn't really need him to win. They needed him against the Buccaneers, and he just couldn't find himself. Certainly rust had something to do with it, along with the Bucs defense, but the worm balls? Fans worry about everything, and those turf-hugging passes are their latest fret. They ask, will Donovan be okay with his accuracy?

McNabb shouldn't read much into this. Fans worried about Jaws and Randall, too, and McNabb may be the best quarterback in franchise history. The relationship should be interesting.

Later on the night we dined, someone spots McNabb walking to his car along Catharine Street. Word of his presence spread quickly through this Bella Vista neighborhood. Screen doors creaked open to create a rowhome symphony. People emerged with footballs of all hues, mostly scuffed from play. Some of the people are barefoot, some in socks. Some wear nightclothes. One boy, maybe 7 or 8, seems extra giddy, and he jumps up and down, his pie eyes growing even wider. A man in his thirties has that same expression. The world seems honest. And there is Donovan McNabb in the middle of this throng of humanity, a heavy crease of a smile beaming under a faint streetlamp.

THIRTY-FOUR

THE UNIFORMS THEY WORE

More than 2,500 players have put on the jerseys of Philadelphia's four major league teams since 1960.

Only one, Wilt Chamberlain, deserves to be remembered as No. 13.

Uniform numbers are like birthdays—everyone has one, and the people who share them often seem to have nothing else in common. Consider, for example, the No. 9, worn over the years by the Eagles Sonny Jurgensen, the Flyers Bob "Hound" Kelly, the Sixers George Lynch and the Phillies Manny Trillo. A more disparate group would be tough to gather.

Or the No. 11, donned by the Sixers Manute Bol and the Flyers Don Saleski—two gawky, clumsy non-scorers. Hmm, maybe they do have something in common.

Certainly, every Philadelphia kid had his favorite number growing up. If you wore No. 31, you were Wilbert Montgomery playing football, Garry Maddox playing baseball and Pelle Lindberg playing hockey. And certain numbers adopt different personalities among the different teams. The No. 21 has always been worn by graceful defensive backs (Eric Allen, Bobby Taylor) for the Eagles or nasty fighters (Frank Bathe, Dave Brown, Mike Busniak, Sandy McCarthy) for the Flyers.

For fun, we tried to come up with the most memorable Philadelphia athlete to wear each jersey number since 1960 (apologies to old-timers who remember Al Wistert's No. 70). In some cases it was easy—who else but Dr. J could be remembered as No. 6?

In some cases, it was impossible. We're not choosing between Bernie Parent and Richie Ashburn for No. 1. Or between Billy Cunningham and Steve Carlton for No. 32.

Or consider the No. 10. The Sixers retired it to honor Mo Cheeks, so we'll award it to him on this list. That still ignores guys like Mel Bridgman, John Leclair, Larry Bowa and Darren Daulton.

On the other hand, find us a good No. 64. We ended up handing it by default to Eagles tackle Ed George, who spend most of his three years in town accumulating holding penalties.

One number between 0 and 99 was never worn by a pro athlete in town since 1960. Can you figure it out? We've already tossed you a clue.

0 – Orlando Woolridge, Sixers.

00 – Eric Montross, Sixers.

1 – Bernie Parent, Flyers. (The is one of three uniform numbers retired by two local teams. The Phils retired it in honor of Richie Ashburn, whose playing career here ended in 1959.

There appear to be no plans for the Eagles to retire it for Tony Franklin.)

2 – Moses Malone, Sixers; Mark Howe, Flyers.

3 – Allen Iverson, Sixers.

4 – Barry Ashby, Flyers (retired); Lenny Dykstra, Phillies.

5 – Donovan McNabb, Eagles; Pat Burrell, Phillies.

6 – Julius Erving, Sixers (retired). Apologies to Johnny Callison, Phillies.

7 – Bill Barber, Flyers (retired); Ron Jaworski, Eagles.

8 – Dave Schultz, Flyers (Mark Recchi was certainly a better player who wore the same number, but Schultz is the guy whom Flyers fans associate with the uniform).

9 – Sonny Jurgensen, Eagles; Manny Trillo, Phillies.

10 – Mo Cheeks, Sixers (retired); John Leclair, Flyers; Larry Bowa, Phillies.

11 – Jimmy Rollins, Phillies.

12 – Randall Cunningham, Eagles; Tim Kerr, Flyers.

13 – Wilt Chamberlain, Sixers (retired).

14 – Jim Bunning, Phillies (retired); Pete Rose, Phillies.

15 – Hal Greer, Sixers (retired), Steve Van Buren, Eagles (retired), Richie Allen, Phillies.

16 – Bob Clarke, Flyers (retired).

17 – Harold Carmichael, Eagles; Rod Brind'Amour, Flyers.

18 – Ben Hawkins, Eagles.

19 – Greg Luzinski, Phillies; Rick MacLeish, Flyers.

20 – Mike Schmidt, Phillies (retired); Doug Collins, Sixers; Brian Dawkins, Eagles.

21 – Eric Allen, Eagles; Bake McBride, Phillies.

22 – Andrew Toney, Sixers.

23 – Troy Vincent, Eagles.

24 – Bobby Jones, Sixers (retired).

25 – Tommy McDonald, Eagles.

26 – Brian Propp, Flyers.

27 – Ron Hextall, Flyers.

28 – Bill Bradley, Eagles.

29 – Harold Jackson, Eagles; John Kruk, Phillies.

30 – George McGinnis, Sixers.

31 – Pelle Lindberg, Flyers; Wilbert Montgomery, Eagles; Garry Maddox, Phillies.

32 – Steve Carlton, Phillies (retired); Billy Cunningham, Sixers (retired).

33 – Hersey Hawkins, Sixers.

34 – Charles Barkley, Sixers (retired).

35 – Bob Froese, Flyers; Clarence Weatherspoon, Sixers.

36 – Robin Roberts, Phillies (retired).

37 – Eric Desjardins, Flyers; Tom Woodeshick, Eagles.

38 – Curt Schilling, Phillies.

39 – Jim Kaat, Phillies.

40 – Tom Brookshier, Eagles (retired).

41 – Keith Byars, Eagles; Chris Short, Phillies.

42 – Jerry Stackhouse, Sixers.

43 – Roynell Young, Eagles.

44 – Pete Retzlaff, Eagles (retired).

45 – Tug McGraw, Phillies.

46 – Herm Edwards, Eagles; Dallas Green, Phillies manager.

47 – Larry Andersen, Phillies.

48 – Wes Hopkins, Eagles.

49 – Jose Mesa, Phillies.

50 – Steve Mix, Sixers.

51 – William Thomas, Eagles.

52 – Barry Gardner, Eagles.

53 – Bobby Abreu, Phillies; Hugh Douglas, Eagles.

54 – Jeremiah Trotter, Eagles.

55 – Dikembe Mutombo, Sixers.

56 – Byron Evans, Eagles.

57 – Mark Woodard, Eagles.

58 – Ike Reese, Eagles.

59 – Seth Joyner, Eagles.

60 – Chuck Bednarik, Eagles (retired).

61 – Steve Everitt, Eagles.

62 – Guy Morris, Eagles.

63 – Hank Fraley, Eagles.

64 – Ed George, Eagles.

65 – Charlie Johnson, Eagles.

66 – Bill Bergey, Eagles.

67 – Gerry Feehery, Eagles.

68 – Dennis Harrison, Eagles.

69 – Jon Runyan, Eagles.

70 – Worn by no one in any sport. Retired by the Eagles in 1955 to honor Al Wistert.

71 – Ken Clarke, Eagles.

72 – Tra Thomas, Eagles.

73 – Ron Heller, Eagles.

74 – Mike Pitts, Eagles.

75 – Stan Walters, Eagles.

76 – Bob Brown, Eagles (you were expecting Shawn Bradley?).

77 – Paul Coffey, Flyers.

78 – Hollis Thomas, Eagles.

79 – Manny Sistrunk, Eagles.

80 – Irving Fryar, Eagles.

81 – Charles Johnson, Eagles.

82 – Mike Quick, Eagles.

83 – Don Hultz, Eagles.

84 – Keith Krepfle, Eagles.

85 – Gary Ballman, Eagles.

86 – Fred Barnett, Eagles.

87 – Claude Humphrey, Eagles.

88 – Eric Lindros, Flyers.

89 – Chad Lewis, Eagles.

90 – Corey Simon, Eagles.

91 – Andy Harmon, Eagles.

92 – Reggie White, Eagles.

93 – Greg Townsend, Eagles.

94 – N.D. Kalu, Eagles.

95 – John Bunting, Eagles.

96 – Clyde Simmons, Eagles.

97 – Jeremy Roenick, Flyers.

98 – Greg Bunting, Eagles.

99 – Jerome Brown, Eagles (retired).

THIRTY-FIVE

THE QUINTESSENTIAL SPORTS FAN: RENDELL

He's all worked up now. Sitting in the back of a limousine, putting down his budget papers to shout into the cell phone, Ed on a Mobile is steaming over the recent moves of his beloved Eagles.

"How could they just let Hugh Douglas leave?" barks Ed Rendell, Governor of Pennsylvania. "Even if you think [replacement Derrick] Burgess will be good, he's not Hugh Douglas. Hugh is a special player. Don't they want to get to the Super Bowl now? This is just wrong."

It is mid-March 2003. The Governor is mired in a frustrating budget war with the Republican-controlled Legislature. He is currently stuck in a two-hour drive from East Stroudsburg, where that city's leaders groused to him about rate hikes on the Delaware River tolls. When he returns to Harrisburg, he will go to work on a property tax reform plan for the state's senior citizens.

"Glamorous life, eh?" cracks Rendell.

Like the rest of us, he needs an escape from the drudgery. Like most of us, he finds it in sports.

So, sitting in the back of the limo, Governor Edward G. Rendell morphs into Eddie from East Falls.

"See, I would have hocked the ranch to get to the Super Bowl this year," he's shouting. "The Eagles are so close, they've got to take that extra step, even if it means spending more than they want to right now. But [Eagles management] is looking very long term. They believe as long as they've got Donovan McNabb they'll be a contender. I'm not sure that's true."

At this moment, he's not the Governor. He's a long-time season-ticket holder, aggravated by owner Jeff Lurie's business policies as the club moves from the Vet into Lincoln Financial Field.

"They haven't been a bad management, but they do pissy little things. They become their own worst enemy through little PR mistakes. Like, why not let fans use a credit card to buy their season tickets? See, that's pissy. It just makes the fans angry. The bottom line, though, is that no matter how angry the fans get, they still love the Eagles."

He pauses for a moment and says what you already knew.

"Well, I certainly love the Eagles."

Oh, he loves his Eagles. And his Phillies, recalling 35 years later every detail of a home run he saw Richie Allen hit out of Connie Mack Stadium. And his Sixers. And his Flyers although, truth be told, hockey isn't really his sport. Perhaps most especially, Ed Rendell loves his Penn Quakers, who lost all but one Ivy League football game during his four years as a student there.

What does it say that his favorite player from his college days was a punter?

"We beat Harvard, score of 7-2, in 1963," he recalls. "Bruce Molloy dropped seven kicks inside their 12-yard line. Greatest game I ever saw a punter have."

He's laughing into the phone now, as the conversation rambles from how he would have guarded Princeton's Bill Bradley back in the day to his bullish critique of the Phillies farm system. Those partisan battles with the state's mossback Legislature are now the last thing on his mind.

"You know, there's nothing I enjoy more than talking sports," he says. "If we could grab a beer and a place to sit down, I could do this all day."

How do you choose the quintessential Philadelphia sports fan? How do you profile one person to represent the obsession of millions?

The players are famous. The fans are anonymous. Their strength is in the collective. It's not one fan, but rather 20,000 who pack the First Union Center several times a week to cheer on the 76ers and Flyers. It wasn't one person, but 1.5 million who lined Broad Street in June 1983 to watch the Sixers parade with the NBA championship trophy. That famous "twelfth man" is actually 68,000 strong at every Eagles game.

A few fans have become somewhat known over the years. John Rodio, aka "Sign Man," got a name by painting the thoughts of thousands of us onto broadsheets that he hung at Eagles games. Shaun Young, in painted face and full Jeremiah Trotter uniform, was a magnet for every television camera, the "Where's Waldo" of Philadelphia sports. Vince Mola, an aspiring filmmaker, created the hilarious character of "Superfan," all angst and id on caffeine, a desperate fan just searching for a little love and a winning streak.

But they were largely acts and sideshows. The parsley on the plate.

Before that, there was Yo-Yo, which is how everyone knew Harry Schifren, a homeless man who became the unofficial mascot of the Big Five and the old Philadelphia Warriors. Yo-Yo's hilarious routine included a goofy dance and pantomime foul shot. When Yo-Yo started working the crowds at Phillies games, owner Bill Giles liked him so much he gave him a free lifetime pass. Legend has it that Yo-Yo was actually Giles's inspiration for The Phanatic.

Going back, you've got the Kessler Brothers of North Philadelphia, profiled earlier in this book. And in the 1940s and 50s, the archetype of 700 Level denizens was a fleshy, fog-horned heckler named Pete Adelis. He was at every A's and Phillies game, taking up two seats in the front row to spit invective into the virgin ears of visiting players. Adelis's act was good enough that *The Sporting News* once paid him to write his "Seven Rules for Scientific Heckling."

My favorite Phillies fan was the anonymous old coot who wandered the bleachers for decades, repeatedly screaming out, "Everybody hits, woo-hoo!" like some unfortunate Tourette's sufferer. He disappeared a few years back, but in 2003, the mantra was heard again. A group of young men, who remembered the "Woo-Hoo Man" as fondly as I did, took up the chant. You can sometimes hear Harry Kalas chuckle as they shout in unison over his radio broadcast.

But fandom here is not about being a show. It's about trotting outside in robe and slippers before starting up the morning coffeepot to fetch the newspaper for the West Coast box scores. It's about sitting in the rain through a 3-13 Eagles season, dying a slow death every Sunday, but clinging to hope that the latest tyro quarterback may, indeed, be the real deal.

Enter Ed Rendell.

Sure, being Governor and, before that, Mayor of Philadelphia, has its perquisites. No doubt, to Hizzoner Ed, the best part of the job was getting a primo luxury box to all Eagles games. Remember when he was feuding with owner Norman Braman in the early 1990s? The two men had adjacent suites at the Vet. The priggish Braman, annoyed by Rendell's over exuberant gestures, had privacy shades put between them. The next week, Rendell ordered city workers to tear the shades down (city property, after all) just to further jab the joyless owner.

Governor Rendell meets the Dude.

Truth be told, Rendell always preferred his longtime seat in Section 639 of the Vet. He was there every Sunday, kibitzing with section mates who knew him as just plain Ed. For years he shared high-fives and an occasional bag of peanuts with the guy sitting right behind him, a retired African-American longshoreman he knew only as "Smitty."

"He didn't have much money," recalls Rendell, "so as ticket prices went up, he dropped from two tickets a game to one. But he never missed a game. In the snow, in bad seasons, he was always sitting right behind me. We cheered, booed and argued about every player and coach who came through town for years."

One balmy Sunday, Smitty didn't show up. No way he'd miss a game, Rendell knew. It took Rendell a few days to track down the man's family and, when he did, he learned that Smitty had died and the funeral had already taken place. He was distraught at losing a friend whose full name he never knew, whose family he had never met.

But this is the beauty of sports per Ed Rendell. Their shared passion for the Eagles brought him together with a guy he otherwise would have never met. It led a future mayor and a former longshoreman to take turns buying beers.

Cities have a heart and a soul, and our teams are perhaps the best way we come together as a community. They are the unifying force that cuts across racial, economic and educational lines. They are the entity that brings together the city and the suburbs. Philadelphia certainly has terrific universities, cultural treasures and medical institutions, but who goes out to wave pompons for the Hospital of the University of Pennsylvania?

"Remember the great Sixers run in 2001?" he asks. "Remember what a special time it was for the city when everyone hung flags on their cars, everyone rallied together? We were one city. The problems that sometimes divide people by race or economics disappeared, at least for a while. We became one city, all over a basketball team.

"See, sports is the thing that the shoeshine guy and the corporate executive have in common. They can talk about it, debate it, and no one's opinion is better than the other."

He learned this first as a student at Penn in 1964, a New York City transplant watching this community go through agony as the Phillies blew a 6-½ game lead down the stretch. Rendell, like his dad, had been a New York Giants fan. He stayed loyal to that team even after it moved to San Francisco. But watching Gene Mauch's Phils choke and shrivel made him a real Philadelphian.

"It was stunning," he recalls, "to see the town die a little more every day. I saw the construction crews and the cleaning ladies in the dorm, the professors and dining hall workers. I never saw such collective grief, such a universal involvement in a team's fate. It convinced me that Philadelphia's relationship with sports is far beyond other cities', including New York."

He's seen it again and again. He recalls when he was mayor in 1992 and the Eagles surged into the playoffs and beat New Orleans. The fervor was so high the following week as the town girded to face Dallas that Rendell jokes that he could have raised the wage tax and no one would have noticed.

And when things go bad, he's found himself in the position of defending our passion. As mayor, he was regularly asked by peers from other cities: "What's with those nasty Philadelphia fans?" Rendell doesn't need a teleprompter to recite his stock answer on this one.

"The same passion that helps us lift a defense into a great goal line stand, to boo Burt Hooton from the mound, that same passion produces a negative side. That same passion sets the table for our fans to be viewed differently."

He's on the campaign stump now, defending our honor.

"For all the raucous things our fans do—snowballs at the Vet, throwing stuff at J. D. Drew—other cities' fans did worse. The flare gun? You would have thought 17 people were massacred. The McNabb thing? New York fans boo their draft pick every year—they had demonstrations when the Jets picked Kyle Brady—but it's not considered a civic crisis there."

So why is it a civic crisis here? Rendell blames the local media for blowing incidents out of proportion and creating the aura of us as barbarians. In New York, he suggests, the more urbane media doesn't go through the hand-wringing and self-flagellation. But here, we beat ourselves up and then invite the rest of the nation to gleefully join in.

If he's a bit defensive, it's because he's one of us. Ed Rendell is not a dilettante politician who shows up at games to be seen. He's a two-sport season-ticket holder (Eagles and Phils) who, when he had more time on his hands, attended more than 50 games a year. He's a passionate fan who heckles (he admits to booing Derrick Coleman) and sometimes gets carried away, as when he got busted challenging a fellow Eagles fan to toss a snowball back in 1989.

But we love the politician for his impolitic approach. Remember when he publicly challenged Braman to re-sign Reggie White? No way his successor, John Street, sticks his neck out like that. Remember when he presented Ricky Williams with an Eagles jersey to lobby the club to draft the Maxwell Club Trophy winner? Team management was furious, but Rendell was only speaking for most of the rest of us.

Remember back in 1993 when he told reporters that the Phils would never be swept by the Blue Jays? "Sooner or later they've got to start Todd Stottlemyre," he cracked. The Jays, of course, won the World Series in six and, at the rally in Toronto, Stottlemyre said, "The mayor of Philadelphia can kiss my ass."

Okay, point taken. Still, Rendell takes glee in reminding you of Stottlemyre's stats in the only game he started: 2 innings, 3 hits, 4 walks, 6 runs, a whopping 27.00 earned run average.

He truly knows stats and numbers and down-the-road phenoms. Sometimes he's painfully wrong—such as when he predicted in 1997 that Phils' young pitcher Scott Ruffcorn would become a star. Eighteen games later and holding a 7.71 ERA, Ruffcorn was gone. But that's part of the joy of being a fan—sticking your neck out and sometimes being wrong.

Twice, he's been tempted to forsake politics for a career in sports. In 1983, when he was preparing his first (and unsuccessful) run for governor, Rendell was asked to consider taking another high-profile job by Sixers owner Harold Katz, a friend and campaign contributor. Larry O'Brien was retiring as commissioner of the National Basketball Association, and the NBA owners were looking for a successor. Katz wanted to put Rendell's name up for consideration, but Rendell declined. Seven years later Katz asked Rendell to become the Sixers general manager for business operations. Once again, Rendell said no thanks.

More recently his name was tossed out as a potential candidate for baseball commissioner. "Maybe, when I'm done with this job," he says. "I'd love it." Without prompting he launches into his plan for the National Pastime—aggressively marketing the game, developing interest in inner cities, putting franchises in Puerto Rico and even Havana, Cuba.

Maybe he'll do that some day. The hunch here is that he ends up back in Philadelphia, brushing the peanut husks off his lap so he can keep score at a Phils game. What he wants more than anything is for younger fans in this city—his son, Jesse, included—to experience the joy of winning a title.

What would a sports championship mean to Philadelphia?

"In terms of economics, not much," he says. "In terms of emotion, it would mean fulfillment. It's interesting how much people my age remember the Eagles title game in 1960. It wasn't a Super Bowl, they didn't even play the Super Bowl back then. Unfortunately, a whole generation of Eagles fans 50 and under have no recollection of that.

"For all the people who sat there in the rain during losing seasons, for all the guys like Smitty who had to squeeze their payroll to get to the game, it would mean a lifetime of fulfillment. People would be so happy they wouldn't be able to talk."

You get the sense that Ed Rendell would be one of those losing his voice.

I wrote this story for the *Inquirer* in the late summer of 1999, and I thought it apropos for this book. It's a look into our future and our past through the eyes of the men on The Step. Those men represent the lifeblood of our history as Philly sports fans. They are a dying breed in our society, and indeed both the men in this story have since passed. They were two good men, and God bless their souls.

Enjoy.

Harry Kalas wails, "Outtttttta heeeere," and it bites through the neighborhood like news of another defector to Jersey. The Phillies have surrendered another home run in this September swoon, and Uncle Lou pounds a meaty fist on the hot cement. "Bums," he har-rumphs, speaking to the faded transistor radio that only gets AM.

Uncle Lou Troilo, 73, a stocky man with a fighter's face, sits on the step of his McKean Street rowhouse, turning a deep Phillies red because, after all these years, the Phils haven't changed all that much.

"They still can't pitch," says his lanky neighbor Frank Pugliese, 74, in a classic South Philadelphia patois. "Connie Mack said it years ago: Baseball is 90 percent pitching. If these guys don't start spending some money on pitchers, I think there's going to be a revolution in South Philly. Pitchers are hard to come by in this day, I guess."

"How come these other teams get them?" Uncle Lou snipes.

"I don't know, maybe it's Philadelphia luck," Frank says.

This is a familiar conversation on The Step, a place bypassed by time, where men gather to spend their golden hours listening to a ball game and debating it deep into a starry city night. It is a place where Eagles are "Iggles" and Phillies are "bums," and where history is pre-served, encased in the memory of those who for so long balanced this town on chafed shoulders and life-weary bones.

There is a lifetime of simmering passion on The Step, and let's gets one thing straight: It is The Step, not The Stoop. "Stoop is New York," Uncle Lou says. "We hang on The Step in Philadelphia." The beauty of The Step is that it can be anywhere in this City of Neighborhoods: West Philly and North Philly and the Great Northeast and Kensington. On this day, it is in South Philly, right outside the screen door that allows through it the tempt-ing smell of Uncle Lou's tomato sauce made with veal bones. It is for the love of the game—any game—that Uncle Lou and Frank are here.

"Look here," says Frank, briefly forgetting the Phils to recall a fonder moment, when Steve Van Buren and the Eagles won the NFL championship in 1948. "There was a terrible snowstorm that day at Shibe Park. They had a big black canvas to cover part of the field, but there was so much snow on it, the grounds crew couldn't move it. So people came storming out of the stands to help roll it up and get it off the field, and I was one of the guys that did it, right before the championship game."

Uncle Lou : "Remember what happened? Tommy Thompson calls a pass on the first play of the game and Jack Ferrante runs it in for a touchdown. But the linesman calls offsides. How could he make that call? You couldn't see a foot in front of you and Ferrante was lined up at the opposite end."

Frank: "We won the game, finally, 7-0; Van Buren on a short plunge, one or two feet from the goal line."

Uncle Lou : "We haven't had an offensive line since."

School has let out, so in the distance there are children playing football on McKean Street. They run their patterns in between the silver Taurus and the white Caddy, an old trick of the street.

"Touchdown, Duce Staley!" one yells and does a shimmy.

The Step is the perfect theater seat. Surely, there are those who would opt for a grassy knoll under a leafy elm over concrete with green weeds sprouting from its cracks. But for Uncle Lou and Frank, this is quality time, sipping a water ice and being thoroughly entertained by the past as the sun bathes them.

Frank: "I was a Phillies rooter, but we were split up in my family. My father and my one brother liked the A's."

Uncle Lou : "We used to call the A's the Chicken Neckers—because Connie Mack had a long, scrawny neck. They had a white home uniform. They looked like bakers. I was always a Phillies rooter, back when they played at the Baker Bowl on Broad and Lehigh. I started out as a Knothole Kid."

Frank: "It stemmed from kids who used to look through the knothole to watch the games. They could never get in. This guy was a philanthropist in the city and he started it for the downtrodden. You used to show them your report card and they gave you tickets to the Phillies game."

Uncle Lou : "They used to come right to the school yard at St. Rita's on a horse and buggy. I remember the Phillies had a guy called 'Boom Boom' Beck, because every ball he pitched got hit off the right-field wall."

Frank: "The A's had a shortstop, 'Hit It to Me' Jack Wallacea. He was a rangy guy and he had this great form, but the ball would go right through his legs. Supposedly, Connie Mack paid his rent and gave him a few bucks a week."

Uncle Lou : "How 'bout the catcher who they said used to take the subway to the park and sell peanuts before the game? But you know, before the war, the A's had a better team than the Yankees. They had a hundred-thousand-dollar infield. Hundred thousand, back then. They had to sell all the players off because they weren't drawing flies."

"But I'll never forget I went down to Memorial Stadium in Baltimore in 1958 to see the All-Star Game, and Turk Farrell, a relief pitcher for the Phillies, struck out four guys in a row—Ted Williams and the all the best hitters in baseball. The fans were like, 'Who's this guy?' A Phillies player. I was so proud!"

Uncle Lou was a ballplayer. You can tell by his legs. His left ankle looks permanently swollen, and there is a jagged scar down the back of it, where he once ruptured his Achilles tendon. His right knee is scarred and puffy. Both calves are discolored, black and blue, from all the times he was spiked covering second base on the double play.

His nickname was "Weasel" because he could run so fast. He also loved to play football, but he got thrown off the team all four years at Southeast Catholic, which is now St. John Neumann. One time, the coach punched him and Uncle Lou punched him back. The coach didn't like Italians, Uncle Lou says.

Frank: "The Phillies are the worst. Are they going to sign that kid Abreu? They better."

Uncle Lou: "I don't like Gant. The way he stands there. To me, he's a showboat."

Uncle Lou: "Sosa hit one today. Fifty-nine."

Frank: "I'm rooting for him. He deserves it. He's a gentleman."

Uncle Lou: "He's an ordinary guy. Looks like a big, happy kid who loves to play ball."

Frank: "I never thought I'd see the record broken—61."

Uncle Lou: "How many guys took a run at DiMaggio's record and they ran into a stone wall? I don't think that'll ever be broken." (He was referring to Joe DiMaggio's record of hitting in 56 consecutive games.)

Frank: "If it's true what I heard about the baseball, that they put in 20-some more stitches, they're playing with a golf ball."

Uncle Lou: "Ohhh! You see the way the ball bounces on these fields? It bounces three, four stories in the air. That ball is lively and the bat is like a whip. We used one of Babe Ruth's bats. It had no knob and the end was perfectly round. We had nails in the handle, covered with tape. Guys would choke up big time. You couldn't swing that bat. It was 48 ounces.

"When he played, they used the ball for the whole game. Us, when our ball wore out, we taped it. What they did, they used a spitball, a mudball, and the ball was black at the end of the game. It was dead and the wood was a piece of lumber. That's just what the hell it was.

"It had no bounce to it. These bats are like whips. There's a little bend and they break like toothpicks. They took the mound away from the pitcher. You see the guys hitting home runs today? It's ridiculous."

Frank: "I swear to God, Kalas the other day called one a pop fly and it went right over the fence!"

Frank's daughter lives in Richmond, Va., but she is the reason he will enter his fifth decade with season tickets for the Eagles. He says she's crazy to drive up for each game, but deep down he doesn't think so. She is just like him.

Frank used to stand on the landing for Eagles games at Shibe Park, because that was where the high school coaches were and he wanted to learn all he could about the Single Wing and the Classic T. He broke his nose six times. They didn't wear face masks back then.

Frank still has a picture of himself in shoulder pads. In it, he is 16, a boy with fire in his wide eyes. Though his head is now snow-capped and his walk slow and sometimes painful, that fire still rages.

Uncle Lou: "Know who used to kill us? Eddie LeBaron, the quarterback for the Redskins. He was 5-6, shortest quarterback ever. It got so bad that the officials were blowing whistles when they thought the play was stopped at the line and LeBaron was running down the field with the ball. He was a magician with the ball. They used to tell the officials before the play who would end up with the ball so they wouldn't blow the whistle.

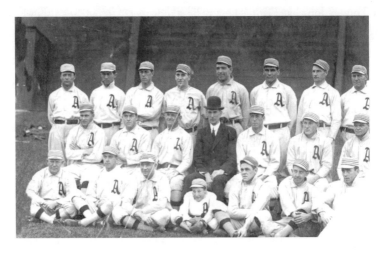

Cornelius McGillicutty, better known as Connie Mack, with his Athletics.

"They talk about Sammy Baugh as one of the greats. They never mentioned he was one of the greatest defensive backs in history. Weighed 165 pounds. In those days, you played two-way football. Today, they talk about these 300-pounders, but they're specialists. Those guys played 60 minutes . . . . The placekickers played. Lou Groza for the Browns? He was a tackle and a kicker.

"I never thought the games were fixed, but I remember this one: The Steelers were playing the Eagles. [They] blocked three extra points in that game, which was unheard of. Anyway, I was 26 and I bet the Eagles. It was late and Pittsburgh went for it on fourth and 1 at the Eagles' 10-yard line. They brought out the chains to measure. They were stopped. Then all of a sudden they call for a remeasure and they make it on the second try. Unbelievable.

"I remember the Warriors . . . . They were leading by 18 points with two minutes to play. . . . This friend of mine . . . he's in the back, screaming behind us. I turned and said, 'Joe, what's going on?' He said, 'We got $5,000 we pooled on the game. We got it on the Warriors.' I said, 'What's the line?' He said six points. They won by six points.

"Joe said he never bet a game after that."

Uncle Lou was born in this country. His grandfather had come to the United States in 1875, after being run out of Italy by the Black Hand, the original term for the Mafia. His grandfather showed him letters that ordered expulsion from the homeland, all stamped ominously with a black hand.

Before working for the Social Security branch of the government, Uncle Lou served in the Navy toward the end of World War II and was stationed near Okinawa. A kamikaze hit the ship next to his, the Pennsylvania. He never learned how to swim.

Frank, meanwhile, joined the Army. He was in Europe during the war. He would rather not talk about what happened.

When they came back from the war, there was baseball once more.

Frank: "My man was Larry Doby. I saw him hit the transformer at Shibe Park. They had a fence 42 feet high. On top of that was a light standard, and then there was the transformer, and Doby hit it."

Uncle Lou: "I saw King Kong Keller do that in right-center field. I was up there the day Joe DiMaggio made a double error. He dropped a fly ball and then threw it into the third-base stands. My father's whole gang was out there. They had hoagies and gallons of homemade wine. Well, this guy stood up and started calling DiMaggio all kinds of names. My father broke the seat off and chased the guy all around the park with it. He would've killed him if he caught him."

Frank: "DiMaggio was like a god to us growing up. I used to love when he made the last out in center field. He'd come running in, take about five or six steps and throw the ball. That ball would roll over second base, go up, hit the mound and end up right where the pitcher used to dig out for the hole."

Uncle Lou: "All of South Philly was there when Joe came to town."

Uncle Lou and Frank didn't miss much in all these years. There are more tales to tell on another day. Maybe Harry Kalas will offer better news next time. Either way, The Step, thankfully, will be there.

THIRTY-SEVEN

THE FUTURE CAN ONLY GET BETTER...RIGHT?

The losses mount like debris on the hillside of a dump, stained legal papers that were no doubt the core of something unholy and the rotting peels of oranges and bananas and other once suc-culent and healthy fruits and the assorted toxic goop of man's everyday life. The losses coat, too, like blackness on a smoker's lungs. The losses weigh tons now, and they are not biodegrad-able, scraps of pain and time spent, a lifetime of time. Some are hardened by that time, healed by scab that will never be fully callous, and some are soft and mushy and gaping and burn to the touch.

Losses blur into losses blur into more losses, until they all become somehow linked, the chain fence of Sports Philadelphia that houses our tortured fansoul. It goes something like this: Joe Carter begets Bobby Nystrom who begets Rhonde Barber who begets Tayshaun Prince who begets the fog off Lake Michigan which begets the Rain in '78 which begets Don Koharski who begets Shaq's elbows which beget Bonnie and Carl Lindros who beget Vermeil's Burnout which begets Small Market Baseball which begets Doug Moe who begets Randall's broken leg and Donovan's broken leg which beget Jeff Ruland's bone on bone and Andrew's feet which beget Bernie's eye and Pelle's Porsche which beget Tyler Green's arm and Darren Daulton's knee and Lenny Dykstra's abused body which beget Lance Parrish who begets Ron Solt who begets Shawn Bradley who begets Chris Gratton who begets Kotite's Chart which begets Fregosi's Foul-up which begets the Flyers' Power Play which begets Paul Pierce and Mo Pete who beget Forsberg who begets J.D. Drew who begets Jon Harris who begets Combine Gorilla which begets Mamula who begets Billy Tibbetts who begets Andy Ashby who begets Derrick Coleman (the first) and Keith Van Horn who beget Rolen who begets Five For One which begets We Owe You One which begets For Who, For What which begets the Barkley Trade which begets the Schilling Trade which begets the Lindros Trade which begets Goodbye, Reggie White which begets Johnny Davis and Brad Greenberg and John Lucas who beget Pat Corrales and Terry Francona who beget Swamp Fox who begets Poor Billy Barber and Poor Roger Neilson who beget hopelessness and disappointment, feelings as Philly familiar as a city wage tax frown.

Roman Cechmanek has just wigged out in the playoffs and he won't be back, though the Flyers fell to Ottawa again because they couldn't score again. It's the spring of 2003 and four out of six years out in the first round, though the coaching wheel has finally stopped for good on Ken Hitchcock, which is good, but John LeClair's health and/or game is not and the Flyers have a better chance of moving back into the Spectrum than they do of moving LeClair and his $9 million salary or any of the other big ticket boys who are too old now. And by the way, we still need a goalie to split time with a guy named Robert Eshe, who's no relation to Jean Marc Pelletier or Maxime Quellette or Brian Boucher or any other Bob Froese of the future, and why do I fear the second coming of the Beezer? It can't be the Beeze, of course, but the Flyers do have more sequels than Sly Stallone and more encores than *A Few Good Men* on TBS.

Meanwhile, we tried to give Keith Van Horn a Code Red and KVH scored two points in 45 minutes in the dust-off Game 6 of the Pistons series, and before that, he got his dunk blocked by no defense-playin', check-stealin', AARP-joinin' Cliff Robinson. Aaron McKie is still guarding Tayshaun Prince and Allen Iverson missed two free throws and shot 5 for 25 and showed up 40 minutes before tip because, dawg, there's traffic on 76 East during rush hour on Fridays, and thank God for AI because he was the only one to show up, sans maybe D.C. II and E Snow. This just in: Larry Brown won't be back, either, and he's not going to Carolina, though I heard Coach would have a tough time turning down Coach more times than "if we only had Monty (Williams)." And Mo Cheeks can't come here and Tubby Smith and Jeff Van Gundy won't come here and it's gonna take big cash and lots of prizes to land someone because Larry Brown dug us a hole in the future and parachuted out and over to a town with more talent, and we get no compensation. So the future is falling down fitful, with traded first-round picks and nobody young who can play and too many old tightening the salary cap tighter than a Barkley bear hug. Speaking of Barkley, why do we fear Andrew Lang, Tim Perry and Jeff Hornacek all over again because of the out in AI's contract, though is that as scary a prospect as signing him to the max salary for six seasons after this next one, taking him to the year 2010?

Meanwhile, it's spring of 2003 right now and the Phillies' bullpen is microwave popcorn and the Phightins' bats have taken a vow of silence, and dammit, I swore Thome and Burrell would hit 90 bombs, and just so you know, the stinkin' Braves are still winning.

I apologize for the tone, but I can't take it no mo'. I forget Fo-Fo-Fo. I swore Moses told us we were going to "'peat, man," and the only repeat since then has been that day where the players clean out their lockers with long faces and maudlin speeches. As of the writing of this book, there are now two high school graduation classes that weren't alive the last time this city held a parade other than the Mummers'. There have been two titles since the Sixers won in '83: Villanova and the naming of Philadelphia as the fattest city in the country. Which means, if you're scoring at home, 0 for 80 seasons and counting. Even Steve Jeltz had a higher batting average.

The town is tortured, and starting to lament not being a grotesque city in the grayness of Ohio, because at least Cleveland has LeBron James. It's to the point where we are going mad, married to malevolence. We are the pied pauper, with gloom and letdown and all of the sports lepers following dutifully behind. It's uncanny, really, when you look at what's transpired in Sports Philadelphia.

Even our heyday was merely OK, certainly not a gusher. We spoke longingly of 1980 earlier in the book, but 1 for 4 doesn't get you in the Hall of Fame. Truth is, somebody other than the Phillies should have won their championship series, especially with Magic being only a rookie and the Flyers going unbeaten in 35 games and the Eagles being the favorite over the Raiders.

For a clue to our soul, our breathing boos and potty mouths, digest the Sixers franchise for a moment, from a modern-day perspective. They lead Portland in the Finals 2-0 in '77, and lose four straight to a team with less talent. Then they lose the conference finals to the champion Bullets and the conference semis to the champion Spurs. Then comes '80, and there was Kareem Abdul-Jabbar out for Game 6 on that Friday night and Magic romps for 42. Then comes the next year, when the stars appear to align "finally" as the Sixers take a 3-1 lead on the Celtics in the Eastern Conference Finals, and it might as well have been the Finals, because Houston won the West and all the Rockets had was the splendor of Moses Malone and some red glare. So the city is about to finally cash on We Owe You One and the Celtics win Game 5 in Boston. No problem, right? Game 6 comes on a Friday in Philly, and the Sixers were span-dex tight with sweaty palms and lost, and, of course, there was no chance in Game 7 at the Boston Garden, the ghosts up there cackling and making choke sounds. What happens? Of course, the Celtics take out the Rockets with ease. I still contend that was our title.

So the following year, the Sixers squander another 3-1 series lead to our mortal enemy and face another Sunday Game 7 in Boston Garden and fans foreshadow Tom McGinnis with a flaccid, life-ain't-fair, "Are you kiddin' me?" Nobody gives them a shot in the game because the whole thing is getting ridiculous for even Philadelphia, so, yeah, they win, actually thump-ing Bird's boys on their parquet. Boston fans still outstage us in our moment of triumph, how-ever, because with the Sixers up big in the fourth quarter, they chant the sweet and throaty "Beat LA! Beat LA! Beat LA!" Way cool, right? Yes, yes, sure, sure. Alas, isn't it easier to pass a starving man a turkey leg when you've already eaten? Anyway, just when we think karma is our friend, when everything fits like a tailored suit, we split the seat of our pants and don't beat LA, our other mortal enemy.

Now the Sixers sign Moses Malone that summer to ensure 1983, but he should have meant multiple titles. Forget greed is good, justice and equity after losing three times in the Finals and all those deep playoff runs in six years should have etched a 'peat in stone, particu-larly with that dominant a team. Bobby Jones, years later, called it the best team he's ever seen, and Jones displays the ultimate modesty. "Not because I played on the team," he begins, try-ing to couch his statement. The Sixers spent the next season inventing challenges, because, in reality, they were still the best team in basketball by a universe. They built massive deficits and would suddenly turn it on in the fourth quarter to win the game. They made it a game with-in a game, right up to losing the first two games at home in a five-game, first-round series with the Nets. They won the next two in Jersey with stunning awe, and then Doc said it. "Mail in the stats," he proclaimed, which was out of character for Julius Erving, which meant decisive Game 5 at the Spectrum was a no-doubt, stone-cold mortal lock, right?

"Yeah, I still can't believe we lost," Jones laments with a half-smile. "I still don't know what happened. We just weren't hungry. We had problems all year staying focused. But I can tell you, nobody on our team believed we were going to lose that final game to the Nets. Nobody."

I remember being in the skinny third level of the Spectrum and silence blared like sirens, a building left bewildered, sort of like the Vet in the NFC Championship Game of 2003. Obviously, the day wasn't as devastating as the Eagles' loss to Tampa, but that reaction felt the same. That I Don't Comprehend What I'm Watching reaction, where you think, "Everything will be normal when I wake up." You see, repeat resounded all season, and here they were, the mighty Sixers, booted in the first round by a nobody Nets team, without the slightest notion of Jayson Kidd.

Let us also tell you that this team was set up for dominance for decades, thanks to former GM Pat Williams, who operated like a Las Vegas scuffler lining the future for fool's gold, with Cleveland usually playing the fool. Think about it: A team with Moses, Doc, Andrew, Mo Cheeks and Bobby, not to mention some decent role players, owned three first-round picks in 1984, including the No. 5 and No. 10. What transpired from there is a hoops tragedy, a crash of epic hoops proportions, akin to squandering a fortune. Suddenly, the Sixers' side of the Spectrum became Silicon Valley during the Dot Com fall.

While Charles Barkley proved a great pick, Leon Wood dropped the point guard baton toss from Cheeks, and the Sixers lost again to the Celtics in the Eastern Conference Finals. The following year, Doc had an open free throw line extended jumper to win Game 7 of the conference semis at Milwaukee's Mecca and front-rimmed it. Everything went downhill quicker than Alberto Tomba thereafter, as Harold Katz clunked the franchise-saving first pick in the '86 draft, trading it to Cleveland for Theo Ratliff-clone Roy Hinson and then dealing Moses for a cartilage-free Jeff Ruland. Philly learned all about God's great creation called the knee, as Bone on Bone became the epitaph.

See why we're bitter? We had the raffle wired and all those raffle tickets resulted in one measly title, and ultimately, Barkley for Andrew Lang, Tim Perry and Jeff Hornacek, and Shawn Bradley and Jerry Stackhouse and the Dana Barros Dark Ages.

The Sixers alone would drive you to subtitled films, but what about the Flyers? Arguably, the Flyers had more raffle tickets than the Sixers over the last 25 years, and we still must glory back to the pre-Prism days of mutton-chop sideburns and bench-clearing hockey fights. Ever since Hat Trick in '76 hit the post and the Flyers got swept by the Canadiens in the Stanley Cup Finals, we've had to endure Misery on Ice.

Let's recap: The Flyers were so dominant in '80 they played 35 games without losing, raising our hopes higher than God's loft. Alas, Leon Stickle blew the offsides call on Bobby Nystrom and the Flyers lost the Cup to what would be the start of an Islander dynasty. The Flyers played enjoyable hockey in the '80s, but in the end, they were regular season wonders in long pants. Consider, they registered 106 points in '82-83, won the Patrick Division title and what happened? The Rangers, a small, speedy team nicknamed the Smurfs, swept the Flyers in three games in the first round, taking the first two at the Spectrum.

Bobby Clarke called it a career the following season amid the unfairness of going out in three straight again in the first round, this time at the hands of the Capitals. In '84-85, the Flyers were able to regroup behind a dazzling Swede goalie, and the chants reverberated throughout the Spectrum: "Pelle! Pelle! Pelle!" So the Flyers had us again, racking up a whopping 116 points during the regular season, and blew through the playoffs, sweeping the Rangers, and thumping the Isles and Nordiques, winning their fifth conference title in 11 years. Lindbergh proved impenetrable against dangerous Edmonton in Game 1 of the Cup Finals, as the Flyers won 4-1. But just as we removed the pots and pans from the cupboard, Wayne Gretzky and his Oilers won the next four, scoring 17 goals in the final three games.

Tragedy struck that November, when Pelle's high-octane sports car couldn't negotiate a turn at dramatic speed one early Sunday morning after leaving a popular South Jersey nightclub. Pelle perished, and a city mourned. See, the demise of a sports figure, particularly that of a beloved one, stings in an odd way. Perhaps it's because of their youth and strength, and because we feel an entitlement toward them because we root for them. I remember receiving a phone call from my cousin and commiserating, much like we did after I called him to inform of Jerome Brown's untimely death, as if death is ever timely. I remember distinctly the weeping fans that attended the Flyers' first game back—against Edmonton—later that week. Lindbergh's fault or not, we wept for the senseless tragedy of it all, and truthfully, for ourselves because we were cheated as fans. I know the latter sounds selfish and morbid, but man by nature makes himself the center of all happenstance, good or bad, even though we are merely bystanders.

In '87, the Flyers won a Cup rematch against this Cowtown dynasty, and the series will go down as perhaps the best ever in this town. Of course, this being Philadelphia, it ended in heartbreak. The Flyers had battled back from a 3 goal deficit to tie the series after an epic Game 6 on a Friday night at the Spectrum, capped by J. J. Daigneault's goal with just over five minutes left. It brought the hope of anything can happen in Game 7, like anything but the Sixers against Boston. But despite the heroics of Ron Hextall, who was named the series MVP, that day ended empty after a close, tough game.

Soon darkness would descend upon the organization. The Flyers missed the playoffs five straight years in '89-94, and when the rubble cleared and the chants of "Jay Must Go" (as in team president Jay Snider) finally subsided, a false messiah appeared. Eric Lindros was the Next One . . . to break our hearts, indeed. Despite the deep pockets of owner Ed Snider, and later partner, Comcast Corporation, and a plush new building, the storyline stayed the same.

And a sports nation wonders why we're embittered? The Lindros Era and the subsequent years following symbolized our plight. We were promised Stanley Cups, the emphasis on the plural, and who were we to disagree? Lindros's talent certainly resembled that of Wayne and Super Mario. He had all the physical tools to become a needy league's poster child and a needy city's savior, and the rugged good looks to play the role and make the girls swoon, perhaps even more than Rick Tocchet did. He said and did all the right things, down to the fact that he was a Bob Clarke fan growing up in hockey-wired Toronto. Once again, the cosmic configuration seemed to be aligned pefectly. But, as usual, the flight plan took a horrible U-turn.

So the Flyers forge through the '97 playoffs with an air of invincibility, busting Pittsburgh in five and Buffalo in five and the Rangers in five. The looming Red Wings surely could fly and they played that lethal tic-tac-toe hockey, with all those skillful skating former Soviets, but the Flyers had home ice and maybe it was only right that the Flyers break the town's title drought because they broke it the last time, ay?

What is written shall never transpire, according to some obviously biblical edict. For the Flyers, following a dramatic pep rally at City Hall, lost the first two games of the series at home and got swept in Detroit like salt on the kitchen floor. The series was over before we could boo or take that stinkin' jersey off Billy Penn.

Then we assumed the position, and braced for a revolving door of coaches and flying barbs between 88, his overbearing parents and the organization. It's truly a drag for a fan because a fan doesn't like to choose between coach and star player and general manager and star player and general manager and next coach and everybody and star player. A fan's motive is the purest in sport because the fan in sport is the only entity without agenda, resembling the innocent child of divorce. When the relationship between the Flyers and Lindros turned unbearable for both parties, their unmentionables hung out to dry on the Philadelphia skyline. Very messy and public did they part the ways, with Lindros, now woozy from a series of concussions, forced to sit out a year in limbo. But that wasn't all of it. The popular Roger Neilsen fell stricken by cancer and Bob Clarke fell to his poor public relations, and there was that time ESPN showed the captain's "C" being unstitched from Lindros' sweater. Even after the club finally traded Lindros to the Rangers, our favorite hockey family felt stained. Four out of five years of being ousted in the first round soured enough, but then came a player mutiny against coach Bill Barber and a near fan mutiny against Clarke.

A sports nation asks why we are what we are, and shouldn't the above give them a clue? Throughout it all, we remained loyal to the colors, while we were shaken through one controversy after another. And where could we take solace? The Eagles helped. But then again, we have yet to tell you about our tiresome love affair with football. To understand our makeup, know that we love football because football is raw and football is, yes, primal, and we are primal people, forced to battle the unkind elements of the northeast and the second-city insecurity that's been in the water since Washington, D.C., took over as country's capital and New York City as center of the universe. We live vicariously through our athletes, and football is the most fun, particularly defensive football with lots of big hits. It's how we jettison frustration of living here, an aesthetically beautiful historic city but if we could choose our birthplace, seriously, why not Honolulu? Football just jibes with Philadelphia, yet while the Eagles currently reside in an exhilarating upswing, we do not know what Green Bay or now Tampa Bay knows. "Just once before I die, I want to see the Birds win the Super Bowl," the Eagles fans say in quiet moments, after the spell chant (E-A-G-L-E-S, EAGLES) has long extinguished.

After all, what does it say about our fandom that our consensus favorite years took place during a time when the Team didn't win a single playoff game? Because that one Super Bowl appearance in New Orleans against the Raiders is so long ago now, the memory yellowed by many, many Roman numerals, the glory days are Randall and Reggie and Buddy because the glory days cannot be the present. In truth, the present is all we've got as Eagles fans. God bless Jaws and Bergey and Carmichael and Quick and Montgomery, but most of our football lives have been spent worrying that a dear but troubled owner, now departed, would sell the team to pay off his casino marker or that the Cowboys would win yet another Super Bowl before we took one. We saw Buddy blunder in big games, his charming bravado blurring the reality that he couldn't gameplan, and Kotite crash and burn amid a boil of folly and Ray Rhodes curse and swear and M-F, and show that his best work in this league was as a coordinator, and Randall imitate his wacko Jacko buddy, his grace and brilliance lost amid his escapades as wacko quarterbacko. I mean, did we really deserve to see one of our most exciting athletes ever wear his jacket inside out and a hat that said, "I'll be back, scrambling," while his teammates stood as far away as they could from him, rolling their eyes? Did we really deserve Norman Braman's tightwad ways and Ricky Waters' alligator arming and Mike Mamula's seditious silence? Let's be real here, I don't care how hard he got it from the press for his combine skills, who did Mike Mamula think he was?

All those games, all those endings, we remember each like they were tattooed on our calf. We lived each one, without payment or gratitude, and I guess we deserve for someone to ridicule, "Get a friggin' life." I mock those who fled the flock, but perhaps football fandom doesn't have to be self-mutilation and the Cowboy and Raider traitors among us have a point that we'll never get. What do we get? Scolded by the masses, branded medieval because of a few drunken ghoul fools in green who misbehave and couldn't tell the Forty-Six from a forty.

Which brings us to Phillies in a perfect segue, the team that should officially reach 10,000 losses in the second season of the new ballpark, assuming they continue their resurgence. Our oldest franchise is our losingest, and maybe that's the way it ought to be. Let the record show the Phillies were never bums to me, but they were bums to my father and his father and his father's father, a lesson learned quickly upon departing that boat and finding the enclave in South Philadelphia. We study history to unlock the mystery of self, or at the very least learn about self, and thus even those who weren't born in '64 can understand that this team in red pinstripes with the skinny "P" define our sports soul. One grand season in '80, buoyed by a flawed sort who's really a Red, can't change that truth or the subsequent seasons of phutility that gave us so little that we cling to a year that was really Joe Carter's and the Blue Jays'.

An optimist, my memory gravitates toward the good, so I must travel to my wee youth to gobble my baseball beignet. Recently, I played a game with a friend and former colleague of mine. We were to draft Phillies over the last 30 years and see who could come up with the best team. Under the guidelines, we could select two starting pitchers apiece for our team. I chose Steve Carlton. He picked Curt Schilling. Because Kevin Millwood was here less than 10 starts at the time of our little exercise and deemed unavailable, I chose John Denny. I figured at least he won a Cy Young. Meanwhile, he maimed his brain, wincing over two full rounds at the bar, and finally chose Larry Christenson over Terry Mulholland. The point of the story is that there have been two Phillie no-brainer starters in 30 years, and we wondered if another franchise could be that pathetic.

Truly, I love the Phillies with all my heart, solely because they have been a constant in my life. I also love the Jersey Shore, though I've been to beaches around the world that fell off Elysium. Since the retirement of Carlton and Schmidt and the passing of Whitey, sans 1993 and the Dude, the best things about the ballclub entering a hopeful 2003 have been Bowa the manager and Harry the K, and maybe the Phanatic.

Seriously, we have to be pine nuts to be a Phillies fan. We have to be coconuts to be a Philadelphia sports fan. Close your eyes, pick a city, and anywhere on the map that dart strikes will make you a winner in something sooner or later, except, of course, if it lands here in the Triangle of No Triumph. Sport is cyclical everyplace but Philadelphia, a fact to keep in mind during Judgment Day, whenever the next one is.

Alas, I paint a brooding portrait, but it's not scary because we've been to the bottom of the abyss and bobbed back. There's no place to bob but up, and while it's OK to mourn another season of next year, it's never OK to adjourn for good. While the losses mount and the losses coat and the losses weigh down, we know the losses can't kill because we still care. We're lifers, forever four for fourers, a unique breed where loyalty still lives. Someday, in this life or the next, we'll get our parade and it'll be a doozy.

PHOTO CREDITS

INDEX